STUDIA TRADITIONIS
THEOLOGIAE

Explorations in Early and Medieval Theology

Theology continually engages with its past: the people, experience, Scriptures, liturgy, learning and customs of Christians. The past is preserved, rejected, modified; but the legacy steadily evolves as Christians are never indifferent to history. Even when engaging the future, theology looks backwards: the next generation's training includes inheriting a canon of Scripture, doctrine, and controversy; while adapting the past is central in every confrontation with a modernity.

This is the dynamic realm of tradition, and this series' focus. Whether examining people, texts, or periods, its volumes are concerned with how the past evolved in the past, and the interplay of theology, culture, and tradition.

STUDIA TRADITIONIS THEOLOGIAE

Explorations in Early and Medieval Theology

9

DEFENDING CHRIST:
THE LATIN APOLOGISTS
BEFORE AUGUSTINE

Nicholas L. Thomas

BREPOLS

Cover illustration: *Tabula Peutingeriana* © ÖNB Vienna: Cod. 324, Segm. VIII + IX

© 2011, Brepols Publishers n.v., Turnhout, Belgium

D/2011/0095/86
ISBN 978-2-503-53669-9

For my parents

CONTENTS

ABBREVIATIONS

ACW	Ancient Christian Writers
AJPh	*The American Journal of Philology*
ANCL	Ante-Nicene Christian Library
ANRW	*Aufstieg und Niedergang der Römischen Welt*
BICS	*Bulletin of the Institute of Classical Studies*
CCSL	Corpus Christianorum Series Latina
CJ	*The Classical Journal*
CPh	*Classical Philology*
CQ	*Classical Quarterly*
CR	*Classical Review*
CSEL	Corpus Scriptorum Ecclesiasticorum Latinorum
FC	Fathers of the Church
HSPh	*Harvard Studies in Classical Philology*
HTR	*Harvard Theological Review*
JECS	*Journal of Early Christian Studies*
JEH	*Journal of Ecclesiastical History*
JHI	*Journal of the History of Ideas*
JRH	*Journal of Religious History*
JRS	*Journal of Roman Studies*
JTS	*Journal of Theological Studies*
LCL	The Loeb Classical Library
P&P	*Past and Present*
PL	*Patrologia Latina*
REAug	*Revue des Études Augustiniennes*
RMeta	*Review of Metaphysics*
SC	Sources Chrétiennes
SP	*Studia Patristica*

TAPhA	*Transactions and Proceedings of the American Philological Association*
TU	Texte und Untersuchungen
VC	*Vigiliae Christianae*
VT	*Vetus Testamentum*

INTRODUCTION

1. Preparatory outline

This study is an analysis of the apologetic writings of the early African Latin fathers of the Christian Church, culminating with the work of Lactantius. Conventionally, the apologists in this period of the African tradition are Minucius Felix, Tertullian, Cyprian, Arnobius of Sicca, and Lactantius. Although Minucius Felix places himself at Rome, his general identification within the African tradition, based largely upon his connections with Tertullian, ensures that the two apologists are often considered together. The purpose of this study is to contribute to the discussion of a potential tradition of African Latin apologetics, through an examination of these apologists in this period of early Christian literature. Common themes, shared arguments, and probable lines of influence all support a highly workable generic connection of African Latin apologetics, provided that the nuances of each text are taken into account. It will be argued that although formal classification into a genre of Latin apologetics may be a step too far, clear threads of a developing apologetic tradition can be noted from lines of influence stretching through the texts in question. In this study, each apologist is considered individually, in a chronological progression beginning with Minucius Felix.[1] The texts under consideration are Minucius' *Octauius*, Tertullian's *Apologeticum*, *De testimonio animae*, *Ad nationes* and *Ad Scapulam*, Cyprian's *Ad Demetrianum* after a brief discussion

---

[1] Although the exact dating situation between Minucius Felix and Tertullian is controversial, the priority of Minucius is adhered to throughout this work, but with the necessary proviso that the dating evidence currently precludes a definitive conclusion on the date of the *Octauius*.

I

of the place of the *Quod idola dii non sint*, Arnobius of Sicca's *Aduersus nationes*, and Lactantius' *Diuinae institutiones*. Each work is contextualised as far as can be achieved, before being discussed and interpreted as individual pieces of Christian apologetic in differing settings with differing concerns, yet all still articulated through the versatile medium of the Christian apology. The early African location provides a focused window of engagement into what would otherwise be a much wider-reaching category, detracting from the depth of engagement as a result. For this reason above all, the terminus date follows Lactantius in order to cut the subject off before the *De ciuitate dei* of Augustine of Hippo. This study can thus remain concerned with Augustine's forbears in Latin apologetics, by being restricted to the earlier period. The ambition of this work is essentially to formulate a picture of African Latin apologetics before the production of the towering *De ciuitate dei*. These earlier apologists, albeit with the technical exception of Lactantius, represent the Latin literary defence of Christianity before Constantine's imperial toleration. They are the voices of Latin Christianity when the Church is still threatened by the Roman state. The era within which they lived and operated extends into just over a century and a half; the period from the end of the second century into the opening of the fourth, and is one of the most formative time-frames in the development of the doctrine and practice of early Christianity. Apologetics plays its role within the evolution of early Christian doctrine as a major literary component in the work of the Church fathers, and a vital feature in the life of pre-Constantinian Christianity.

Methodologically, each apologist is considered in chronological succession, with an immediate focus on contextualisation. Problems and concerns of dating are examined where appropriate, as an awareness of the background is always essential in understanding any ancient work. One of the central arguments underlying Robert M. Grant's *Greek Apologists of the Second Century* is this prerequisite of considering each separate apologetic piece within its individual setting, and it must be continually re-emphasised that each text remains a product of its own particular culture. Grant argued:

> While there is a certain timeless character to the Christian apologists of the second century, they are deeply involved in the political and social struggles of their time and cannot be understood apart from the precise circumstances in which they are writing.[2]

[2] *Greek Apologists of the Second Century*, p. 10.

Notwithstanding the distinction between the cultures of Greek and Latin, Grant's words are highly relevant to the Latin apologists addressed in this work. Their texts are principally created as responses to significant contemporary events, regardless of a general lack of explicit background details within the works themselves. Furthermore, of all literary forms, apologetic is an inescapably relevant one. The leading arguments are often highly context-specific, and therefore possess great value of insight into the actual situation of the time. An understanding of the contributing factors behind each separate work underlines the contemporary relevance of the early apologists, and demonstrates the significance of their individual locations. In short, the background is absolutely key to introducing each text in its own circumstances. Different aspects of each text can then be discussed, in order to bring out the varying apologetic, doctrinal, and theological features that occur as a result of their differing motives and subject-matter. Strong attention is also paid in each chapter to locating each apologist within the influence of his own African Latin predecessors. As a rule, the main critical editions of the texts used are cited at first use, and in footnotes at the opening of each chapter. Any variant readings are noted as required. All translations are original, and are included in order to facilitate a greater ease of immediate engagement with the cited original sources. Where the New Testament is directly cited, unless the extract in question has been given in Latin by the original apologist, for the purposes of this work it has been left in Greek. This is to move away from the anachronism of unavoidably citing a much later Latin translation of the Scriptures, and in respect of the issues surrounding the *Vetus Latina*. The early Latin apologists' understanding of Greek is accepted, but the development of the New Testament in Latin during the period c. 200–c. 325 is more difficult to ascertain. It is in the interest of evading such pitfalls in this work, that the New Testament is engaged with in Greek.

Commodian

The absence of Commodian (often qualified further as 'of Gaza'[3]) from this study of the early African Latin apologists is calculated, due to

---

[3] Primarily from an attempt at understanding the enigmatic subtitle *Nomen Gasei* heading the final acrostic of the *Instructiones*, revealing *Commodianus mendicus Christi* if read upwards from the end of the text. See *Instructiones*, 39: 1–26. Against this, compare J. E. B. Mayor arguing for *gaseus* as *gazaeus*, thus referring to Commodian as *arcarius gazae*; the 'keeper of treasure', rather than 'Man of Gaza'. 'Commodian's *Instructiones*. Days of the Week', p. 240.

the fundamental difficulties inherent in any investigation of the work of this obscure Latin poet. Although the basis for further research is set following the publication of critical editions of both the *Carmen apologeticum* and the *Instructiones* that are attributed to him,[4] serious contextual difficulties preclude his inclusion alongside the early African apologists. The traditional position of placing Commodian somewhere in Roman Africa at the middle of the third century now seems to be more unlikely than formerly considered, and finds no modern defenders. Instead, his location in fifth century Gaul looks to be the more probable situation, and is here maintained.[5] It is to be hoped that a critical study of Commodian himself, coupled with modern translations of the *Carmen apologeticum* and the *Instructiones*, could fire new scholarly development on the subject. But for the current moment at least, it seems likely that Commodian's fifth century placement would be further justified on the back of greater research. With relation to this current work, Commodian cannot be discussed alongside the conventional Latin African apologists due to such insurmountable difficulties of contextualisation.

Christian anti-Jewish literature

Early Christian anti-Jewish works of this period are sometimes classified with apologetics without much other explanation,[6] but establishing a wider positive connection is not entirely as straightforward. Some general characteristics of apologetic work do tend to be there, and the texts often include the commonly apologetic combination of a defence of Christian belief coupled with an attack on the positions of the opponent. Whenever Christian standpoints are grounded in the principal texts of the opposition in question, the beginnings of an apologetic methodology can be noted. But anti-

---

[4] By Joseph Martin in the CCSL, Vol. 128 (1960), Bernhard Dombart in the CSEL, Vol. 15 (1887), and Ernst Ludwig in the Teubner series (1877).

[5] And also with the testimony of Gennadius, the earliest extant commentator on Commodian. In his update of Jerome's *De uiris illustribus*, Gennadius locates Commodian after Prudentius and Audentius, and before Rufinus; therefore potentially equating an approximate date of the early fifth century. See Gennadius, *De uiris illustribus*, 15. Following Gennadius on the fifth century dating, see also Edgar J. Goodspeed, 'The Date of Commodian', pp. 46–7, and C. Brakman, 'Commodianea', pp. 136–40, able to place Commodian only as *paulo post Prudentium* on the basis of what little evidence there is. Over eighty years later, Brakman's conclusion is still valid.

[6] For example, Quasten identifies Tertullian's *Aduersus Iudaeos* as one of his apologetic works. *Patrology*, Vol. 2, pp. 268–9.

Jewish literature also holds a purpose, revealed by an analysis of its method, that is of necessity different from traditional Christian apologetics aimed at Rome. Writings such as Tertullian's *Aduersus Iudaeos*, or the first book of Cyprian's *Ad Quirinium*, are not as concerned with responding to current issues in the contemporary dialogue as more conventional pieces of apologetic. These works are primarily works of exegesis, rather than responses to dialogue. The most prominent thread that connects them all is an engagement with the Old Testament, employed to validate the coming of Jesus while simultaneously convicting the Jews of forsaking the salvation ordained in their own Scriptures. Justin's *Dialogus cum Tryphone* is perhaps more relevant, but still ultimately based upon the same lines of Old Testament interpretation. The extent to which such writings actually impact upon contemporary Judaism has to be questioned, and then followed by the postulation of whether they are not much more than works of engagement with Scriptural citations used to represent principles of Jewish belief. The versatility of conventional Christian apologetics, taking all its numerous forms, is notably absent, and instead replaced by an unchanging and probably unrealistic characterisation of Judaism. The citations from the Old Testament provide the key interpreted evidence in the debate, which is often unchanging, and Christianity is throughout represented as the true fulfilment of Judaism, away from any association as merely a wayward sect. A clear divide between Christians and Jews is drawn, and an underlying theme of the Christians' grappling with the label of apostasy can be felt.[7] Indeed, for Tertullian the major part of his understanding of Christianity originates with the Gentiles, rather than with the Jews. God has demoted the Jews in favour following the admission of the Gentiles to divine grace.[8] As with Christian apologetics aimed at Rome, Christianity is defined as the one true form of religion; but the sense of perspective in the argument is markedly different. Although it cannot always be strictly isolated, the defensive tone of conventional Christian apologetic literature is not as prevalent in anti-Jewish writings. It is instead subsumed by an aggressive Scriptural exegesis, and an interpretation of history that can end up as

---

[7] See Justin, *Dialogus cum Tryphone*, 10; Trypho's accusation of the Christians' abandonment of the law of God, followed by Justin's lengthy response in the succeeding chapters.

[8] *Aduersus Iudaeos*, 1.

not far short of being directly threatening.[9] Although anti-Jewish literature can share common themes with apologetics, the texts merit their own consideration as a separate genre. They are therefore not addressed in this work.

The field of study

The African Latin apologists themselves, outside of the broader genre of Christian apologetics, have enjoyed something of a surge in popularity on the back of the comparatively recent publication of several works in the field. First and foremost, there are the chapters of Simon Price, 'Latin Christian Apologetics: Minucius Felix, Tertullian, and Cyprian', and Mark Edwards, 'The Flowering of Latin Apologetic: Lactantius and Arnobius', in *Apologetics in the Roman Empire*.[10] Separately, there are the multiple contributions to the area of Late Antique Latin Christianity by Jean-Claude Fredouille, G. W. Clarke, and the article of the late W. H. C. Frend, 'Some North African Turning Points in Christian Apologetics'. These studies have laid the immediate grounding for further development in the area of African Latin apologetics.

When beginning any study of the early Church, the best places to start are often general introductions to early Christianity and Late Antiquity, providing the wider foundation necessary for anyone embarking on an exploration into ancient Christianity. Modern students in English are very fortunate to possess Mark Humphries' *Early Christianity* (2006), and Josef Lössl's *The Early Church* (2010). Humphries and Lössl have also both outlined the subject of religious vested-interest inherent in the examination of certain aspects of the early Church, and noted how the personal issues that each researcher carries can impact any such study. Even under the growing secularism of the twenty-first century world, the interpretation of religious history remains a controversial topic. The landmark works of Henry Chadwick and W. H. C. Frend still stand as highly important pieces of scholarship on the subject, and particularly Chadwick's *Early Christian Thought and the Classical Tradition* (1966), *The Early Church* (1967, rev. 1993), and *The Church in Ancient Society* (2001), and Frend's *Martyrdom and Persecution in the Early Church* (1965), and *The Rise of Christianity* (1984). Other works of note include David Rankin's *From Clement to Origen: The Social and Historical Context of the*

---

[9] Tertullian, *Aduersus Iudaeos*, 13.

[10] Mark Edwards, Martin Goodman, and Simon Price eds.

Church Fathers (2006), Robin Lane Fox's *Pagans and Christians* (1986), and Peter Brown's *The World of Late Antiquity* (1971, repr. 2004). The *Oxford Dictionary of the Christian Church* (2005), the *Oxford Classical Dictionary* (2003), and the *Cambridge Ancient History* (1970–2000) are indispensable places of reference for a wide range of subject areas in the ancient world. For a good overall introduction to the numerous literary sources for the period, the two sourcebooks by J. Stevenson, revised by W. H. C. Frend, *A New Eusebius* (1987), and *Creeds, Councils and Controversies* (1989), along with their companion volume *Doctrine and Practice in the Early Church* by Stuart George Hall (2005), are a readily obtainable mine of information in the form of translated and contextualised snippets from the primary sources. If they can be used to point the way towards a further reading of the primary texts themselves, then they have provided an even greater service. Robert L. Wilken's *The Christians as the Romans Saw Them* (1984) is of particular use in the preparation of apologetic research, for its thematic overview of some of the key episodes in the clash of Christianity with Roman religion and philosophy. Pieces of critical academic biography, including Timothy D. Barnes' *Tertullian*, Michael M. Sage's *Cyprian*, and Michael Bland Simmons' *Arnobius of Sicca*, tend to be the next step regarding the location of the work of particular Christian writers in their own individual circumstances. New translations and editions also often include valuable introductions to their particular author, with the most notable examples in Latin apologetics being the modern English edition of Lactantius' *Diuinae institutiones* by Anthony Bowen and Peter Garnsey, and G. W. Clarke's version of the *Octauius* in the Ancient Christian Writers series. By presenting an accurate and readable English translation along with a detailed introduction, indices, and footnotes throughout, Bowen and Garnsey have substantially aided modern students of Lactantius, and Clarke's *Octauius* is the unsurpassed English edition both for quality of translation and depth of notation. English readers are also fortunate to possess translations of multiple treatises of Tertullian, Cyprian's *Epistulae, De lapsis, and De catholicae ecclesiae unitate*, and Arnobius' *Aduersus nationes* in the readily accessible Ancient Christian Writers volumes. The overall quality and length of detail in the notes to the translations of this series is to be highly commended. Cyprian's *Ad Demetrianum*, and most of Lactantius' *Diuinae institutiones*, added to his other works, can be found in Latin and French in the equally useful volumes of the Sources Chrétiennes. Such modern renderings can be preferred to the now outdated, if often still helpful translations in the Ante-Nicene Christian Library and Ante-Nicene Fathers collections. The critical textual editions generally exist in the Corpus Christianorum Series Latina, the Bibliotheca Teubneriana, and the Corpus Scriptorum Ecclesiasticorum Latinorum. The online *Library of Latin Texts* (LLT), produced and maintained by Brepols, has also created an internet home for the critical editions of the Corpus Christianorum Series Latina and the Corpus Scriptorum Ecclesiasticorum Latinorum. However, Jacques-Paul Migne's *Patrologia Latina* still continues to be consulted even over a century and a half after first publication. The ease of access of the volumes in Migne's series, due to their free online availability in the public domain, is a highly convenient service to scholars engaged in Patristic research. Provided Migne's texts are read with the sensible cautionary awareness of many other scholarly works of such great age, the *Patrologia Latina* can still provide a useful contribution. The critical advances of scholarship made in more modern editions must be followed, but Migne's online *Patrologia Latina* ensures that the texts of the Latin fathers can be made available to a wide audience, and is at least a starting-point for exploring the textual sources of early Christianity in their original languages. With such resources made instantly at hand, the modern student of early Christianity enjoys a previously unprecedented degree of access to the historic literary sources.

2. An introduction to apologetic writing

Throughout the history of Christianity, the seedlings of thought presented in the Scriptural texts, interpreted using the methods of philosophy and tradition, have developed into expansive and wide-ranging theologies. In its turn, apologetic expression is an important literary factor in this growth. The example of martyrdom for the cause of religion emphasises the strength of belief that can be formed in a setting of opposition leading to direct confrontation, and in a nutshell, apologetic writing is often the literary output of such circumstances. In his description in the *Historia ecclesiastica* of the martyrdom of Polycarp, Bishop of Smyrna, Eusebius of Caesarea provides an embodied illustration of the nature of Christian apologetics:

Ὁ Πολύκαρπος εἰ κενοδοξεῖς, φησίν, ἵνα ὀμόσω τὴν Καίσαρος τύχην, ὡς λέγεις προσποιούμενος ἀγνοεῖν ὅστις εἰμί, μετὰ παρρησίας ἄκουε· Χριστιανός εἰμι. εἰ δὲ θέλεις τὸν τοῦ Χριστιανισμοῦ μαθεῖν λόγον, δὸς ἡμέραν καὶ ἄκουσον. ἔφη ὁ ἀνθύπατος πεῖσον τὸν δῆμον. Πολύκαρπος ἔφη, σὲ μὲν καὶ λόγου ἠξίωκα, δεδιδάγμεθα...ἐκείνους δὲ οὐκ ἀξίους ἡγοῦμαι τοῦ ἀπολογεῖσθαι αὐτοῖς.[11]

Polycarp's direct appeal to the officiating proconsul at the trial is emblematic of the apologetic propensity for a work to be directed at a highly-placed figure of secular authority. The desired aim is to solicit the influence of a truly powerful advocate; usually one with the power of life and death over the persecuted Christians. This is shown in Polycarp's readiness to relate the doctrines of the Church to the proconsul, if not to the assembled crowd themselves. The apologetic schema of a Christian defence within the framework of explaining the real truth behind the activities of the embattled religion, is also evident in Polycarp's final argument before the proconsul. This incident of Polycarp's trial represents, in effect, apologetics in action. It is also a suitable case in point for beginning to recognise the importance of the apologetic work of the early Church. The following preliminary introduction aims to broach the subject of apologetic writing through a number of illustrative examples, in order to locate the work of the early African Latin apologists themselves.

The template of an *apologia* itself was in place as a literary concept from the textual accounts in the aftermath of the trial of Socrates (399 BC). Both Plato and Xenophon employed the format, articulating apologies recording the form of Socrates' speech in his defence. A literary apology, by this definition, expresses the defensive explanation of a personal position. This can then be further extended to include the more exoteric definition of a system of belief in opposition to the ideological opponent, if still grounded by the greater need for defensive explanation. That is to say, a standpoint can sometimes be best defended through the means of an aggressive deconstruction of the positions of the opponent. Stout denial may come first, but the more positive establishment of innocence follows. A crucial legal element remains in attendance throughout,

---

[11] 'And Polycarp said, "If you vainly suppose that I will swear by the genius of Caesar, as you say, pretending to be ignorant of who I am, then hear plainly: I am a Christian. But if you wish to learn the doctrine of Christianity, give a day and hear". The proconsul said, "Persuade the people". But Polycarp said, "As for you, I have thought you worthy of an explanation ... but as for these, I do not deem them the proper persons to whom to make my defence"'. *Historia ecclesiastica*, 4: 15. Greek text in Eusebius, *The Ecclesiastical History*, Kirsopp Lake ed., Vol. 1.

being inseparable from the etymology of the term *apologia*, in perpetual reference to the original courtroom defence later adapted into the literary representation of Socrates. The usage of apologetic is present as a viable Christian mode of expression from the writings eventually enshrined as books of the New Testament. Even granting the apologetic purpose underlying the Acts of the Apostles,[12] a more explicit definition of the place of apologetic within the understanding of the earliest Christians could scarcely be formulated than that given by the writer of 1 Peter:

Ἕτοιμοι ἀεὶ πρὸς ἀπολογίαν παντὶ τῷ αἰτοῦντι ὑμᾶς λόγον περὶ τῆς ἐν ὑμῖν ἐλπίδος, ἀλλὰ μετὰ πραΰτητος καὶ φόβου, συνείδησιν ἔχοντες ἀγαθήν, ἵνα ἐν ᾧ καταλαλεῖσθε καταισχυνθῶσιν οἱ ἐπηρεάζοντες ὑμῶν τὴν ἀγαθὴν ἐν Χριστῷ ἀναστροφήν. κρεῖττον γὰρ ἀγαθοποιοῦντας, εἰ θέλοι τὸ θέλημα τοῦ θεοῦ, πάσχειν ἢ κακοποιοῦντας.[13]

This is a purely Christian foundation of apologetic, and a good demonstration of its significance within the means of self-presentation of the early Church. Most importantly, the connection of harassment and persecution with the motivations for apologetic literature is present, and forms the basis of its explanation to the audience of the Petrine text. Apologetic is presented as a natural formula for the articulation of the Christian defence, redefining the primarily legal implications of the *apologia* term into the service of a religious cause. The precedent for employment of the strictly Christian *apologia* in vindication of the faith of its believers is thus outlined in the most recognisable terms in 1 Peter, and with a purpose that resounds throughout the later apologists of the Church.

But within each apologetic piece itself, there is also an accompanying prospect of elucidation to one's own prior compatriots. With particular reference to the Christian usage, this takes the form of a mode of teaching the finer points of faith that is distinct, if sometimes not completely far removed, from the sermons of the pulpit. This level of duality of audience poses the issue of the joint nature of apologetics.

---

[12] On this subject, see Loveday Alexander, 'The Acts of the Apostles as an Apologetic Text', in *Apologetics in the Roman Empire*.

[13] 'Always be prepared to make your defence to anyone who demands from you an explanation of the hope that is in you, but do it with gentleness and respect, having a good conscience, in order that when you are slandered, those who revile you for your good conduct in Christ may be put to shame. For it is better to suffer for doing good, if it is God's will, than to suffer for doing evil'. 1 Pet 3: 15–17. All Greek New Testament citations within this work are from Barbara Aland et al. eds., *The Greek New Testament*.

Such twin audiences have even been considered to point towards a completely diverging thread in apologetic literature, meriting its consideration as a genre comprising of two distinctly separate disciplines.[14] But although argument for the vindication of the cause at hand tends to be the explicit aim of apologetics, the deepening of understanding of some key controversial points in the defended faith to its prior adherents is a naturally attendant prospect. Brian Hebblethwaite's modern apologetic work *In Defence of Christianity* has identified the crux of this issue. Observing that many Christian believers are often born into their religion rather than converted, Hebblethwaite argues:

> Few people are actually reasoned into faith. The arguments which I intend to sketch here are more like buttresses than foundations, reasons that can be given, as I say, in support of faith.[15]

This would certainly be the case in the modern world, and does much to stress the issues involved with primary and secondary audiences of apologetic texts. But the circumstances of the ancient world where the early apologists found their motivation are profoundly different. As an example, far fewer people were born into Christianity in Tertullian's era unlike in later epochs of the Church. One of his most enduring phrases originates with this situation; the famous declaration *fiunt, non nascuntur Christiani.*[16] Other early apologists write following outbreaks of persecution for the Church, bringing together their defences of Christianity with anti-Christian punishment very fresh in mind.[17] Many were also themselves converts, and created their apologetic pieces in order to outline and rationalise to

---

[14] As with this definition of Alan Richardson, *Christian Apologetics*, p. 20: 'Apologetics is primarily a study undertaken by Christians for Christians; and in this respect it is to be distinguished from the task of apology, since an apology is addressed to non-Christians. Apologetics is thus a necessary preparation for the work of an apologist, or, more simply, it is a part of the essential training of Christian preachers, evangelists and teachers'. But this is an unnecessarily convoluted explanation – the twofold audience of apologetics does not have to carry two different motivations. The primary recipients are those with whom each author is concerned with directly addressing, while the Christian community takes its place as a secondary, though still intended, beneficiary of the work.

[15] *In Defence of Christianity*, p. 1.

[16] 'Christians are made, not born'. *Apologeticum*, 18: 4. The Latin text for all Tertullianic citations in this work can be found in E. Dekkers ed., *Quinti Septimi Florentis Tertulliani Opera*.

[17] As with Cyprian's *Ad Demetrianum*, following the Decian persecution, and Lactantius' *Diuinae institutiones*, likely originating from the general milieu of the Diocletianic persecution.

their opponents the validity of their religious transference.[18] Each piece of early Christian apologetics bears the imprint of its own personal background. They are, above all, insights into religious dialogue; and in addition, also often into religious conflict.

Apologetic literature exists in a perpetual state of adaptation and realignment; mainly towards changing opponents in different settings, but also representative of the divergent employers of apologetic self-explanation. Its interpretative value for the finer points of theological exposition can, however, be undermined due to the essential nature of each apologetic statement. As it is framed by its surrounding circumstances, so it is often unavoidably limited by them. Alfred Ernest Garvie's statement in *A Handbook of Christian Apologetics* that 'there must be selection, as it is clearly impossible that all the matters relating to Christian creed or conduct should be fully discussed',[19] highlights the often patchy expositions of certain theological subjects on the part of the apologists. It is primarily owing to this situation that the apologists' depth of theological awareness is intermittently questioned. The prominent example of this within Latin apologetics would be Philip Schaff's well-known criticism of the doctrinal shortcomings of Minucius Felix as a defender of Christianity,[20] even if a phrase placed into the mouth of the non-Christian Caecilius in the *Octauius* expressly attests to the constraints of formulating an apologetic argument.[21] These constraints are of a literary piece that has multiple topics to address within a relatively short textual space, and one that is throughout submitted to the precedence of an apologetic methodology. Minucius Felix is no systematic theologian in the *Octauius*. Apologetic reasoning must be concise and persuasive, solidly based on commonly-respected textual authorities, and in possession of studied rhetorical touches in order to be taken seriously by the intellectual demands of its audience. Very high standards in the relevance of argument, supplemented by the recourse to proper textual support, and put across throughout by a rhetorically-proficient mode of expression,

---

[18] As with Arnobius' *Aduersus nationes*.

[19] p. 12.

[20] In his brief illustration of Minucius Felix, Schaff wrote: 'the apologetic value of this work is considerable, but its doctrinal value is very insignificant ... It is an able and eloquent defence of monotheism against polytheism, and of Christian morality against heathen immorality. But this is about all. The exposition of the truth of Christianity is meagre, superficial, and defective'. *Ante-Nicene Christianity*, Vol. 2, p. 838.

[21] *Multa ad haec subpetunt, ni festinet oratio.* 'Much might be added to this, but the speech hurries [to its end]'. *Octauius*, 11: 5. The Latin text of the *Octauius* used in this work is the Teubner edition of B. Kytzler.

are all exhibited to a greater or lesser degree by the African Latin apologists. This emphasises the attention to detail that each work must provide, in order to form a cogent answer to the situation that it is intended to respond to. The appeal to philosophy and precedent, a marked characteristic of the African Latin apologists, underlies an attempt to justify Christian belief from a more universal perspective. Where the Scriptures are unknown, and even at times ridiculed, their apologies would work to ground Christian belief instead as an acceptable philosophic system, supporting a religion of deep and untainted moral purity.

Brief illustrative examples of ancient apologetics – Josephus

The apologetic writings between Christians, Jews, and 'Pagan'[22] adherents of traditional Roman religion exist in a number of different forms, and occupy the broad landscape of the religious conflicts of the first centuries AD. Although a genre of 'Jewish apologetic' is difficult to define due to a lack of material, one of the primary contenders would have to be Josephus' *Contra Apionem*.[23] As the central concern of the text is the vindication of the antiquity of the Jewish people in the minds of the conquering Romans, so a classification as apologetic is justifiable.[24] But the apologetic of the *Contra Apionem* should rather be defined as the 'apologetic of history', where the defence of the historicity of the Jewish people is Josephus' crucial purpose. He interprets the history of the Jews in order to celebrate a recognised foundation in antiquity,[25] but is expressly concerned with a recourse to non-Jewish sources throughout. Josephus writes of criticisms already faced for basing his historical arguments on strictly Jewish works rejected by his detractors, and must therefore validate the antiquity of his people by the concentrated citation of predominantly Greek historical texts.[26] If his opponents can be refuted using their own sources, then

---

[22] Due to its nature as a term loaded with pejorative negativity, 'pagan' is otherwise avoided within this work when referring to the followers of traditional Roman religious systems. It is in line with the note of Henry Chadwick, *The Early Church*, p. 152, n. 1.

[23] The so-called *Apology for the Jews* by Philo of Alexandria has been lost, and survives only in passing mentions by Eusebius at *Praeparatio euangelica*, 8: 2, and *Historia ecclesiastica*, 2: 6.

[24] In the mind of H. St. J. Thackeray, at *Josephus: The Man and The Historian*, p. 76, the *Contra Apionem* is Josephus' 'fine apology for Judaism'.

[25] With motives 'both apologetic and historical'. Mireille Hadas-Lebel, *Flavius Josephus*, p. 216.

[26] *Contra Apionem*, 1: 1–2.

a great ideological battle has been won. To disarm the accusers by making their literary weapons redundant, that is, by appropriating their own textual authorities for the cause of the opposition, is to radically readdress the nature of the quarrel in hand. This position is also characteristic of the early Latin apologists, due to their own problems with the usage of Scripture as a justifiable textual recourse. Josephus' *Contra Apionem* is an early testament to the methodological expedient of conclusively moving away from the partisan textual sources of only one side in the debate, and taking the dialogue onto a level where the authorities that provide the necessary foundations for argument are mutually respected by all participants. For the Latin apologists, themselves highly aware of the stylistic deficiencies inherent in the Christian Scriptures, this consideration would prompt the comprehensive refusal to expressly cite from the Scriptures that can be noted especially in Minucius Felix's *Octauius*, and Arnobius' *Aduersus nationes*.

Justin Martyr

The archetypal character of the early Christian apologist belongs to Justin. A brief discussion of his life and work is fitting to introduce the Christian apologists who followed him, for they did just so to a very large degree. His apologetic work focuses on a defence of Christian virtue under a plea for justice for those harassed under persecution, which is then substantiated by a critique of the vanity inherent in the materialism of contemporary Roman religion. This style, added to much of the imagery and terminology that Justin employs, goes on to become a familiar subject in the writings of successive generations of Christian apologists. Justin's apologetic writings, surviving in the format of the *Apologia Prima* and *Secunda*, are addressed to the emperor Antoninus Pius and the Roman Senate, and seemingly already stood within an established tradition of aiming Christian defences at the highest possible public authority. Eusebius has recorded the examples of Quadratus and Aristides, two early Christian apologists who favoured the emperor Hadrian (117–138) with the direct address of their works.[27] Quadratus and Aristides would be the earliest literary apologists of Christianity outside of the apostolic writings. If Eusebius' word is to be accepted, then the Christian tradition of addressing apologies to occupants of the imperial throne can thus be traced from a relatively early date. But a

---

[27] *Historia ecclesiastica*, 4: 3.

significant level of doubt has recently been cast on the accuracy of Euse-bius in dating Quadratus and Aristides to the reign of Hadrian; prepar-ing the way for the greater influence of Justin. Sara Parvis has argued for the probability that Eusebius has fallen victim to a mix-up in separating two historical persons named Quadratus, and is then further lumping Aristides alongside his original mistake.[28] Parvis' aim is to re-introduce Justin's *Apologia* as the first of its kind in two major ways – the first public apologetic work of Christianity, and also the first that carries an imperial address as an opener.[29] Although the situation remains unre-solved at present, Sara Parvis' work has raised several critical points. Justin's status as an apologetic archetype has always been accepted, but he could now potentially be understood as even more pioneering than previously believed.

Justin's apologetic is constructed in a style that is instantly recognis-able in later Christian apologies, and across both the Greek and Latin forms. He appeals for justice for the believers, punished as criminals although innocent of all charges. His apologetic work is an outpouring of the truth behind the allegations of atheism, immorality and sedi-tion, compiling a direct plea to the authorities to consider all evidence before continuing with the anti-Christian punitive measures.[30] Justin builds his case on the Christians' purity and innocence, before pro-ceeding to attack the rites and customs of Roman religion as a coun-terpointed example to the perceived immoralities of Christianity.[31] It is the Christians who are the most moral, and it is Roman religion that breeds the impure.[32] Christian monotheism is starkly contrasted with the irrationalities of Roman image-worship and deification; indeed, the Christians often speak of nothing too disparate from the poets and philosophers, so are not so far removed from all aspects of Roman religion. Christianity articulates monotheism similar to Plato, and criticise image-worship along the lines of Menander.[33] When Justin does move on to defend the Christian rituals, he writes in explicitly

[28] Sara Parvis, 'Justin Martyr and the Apologetic Tradition', in Sara Parvis and Paul Foster eds., *Justin Martyr and His Worlds*, pp. 120–122.

[29] 'It was he who had the brilliant idea of attempting to bring before the emperor himself the legal anomaly under which Christians were suffering, for nothing more than the name of Christian … It was he who first risked his life, lifted his head above the parapet, to try to do so'. Ibid. p. 127.

[30] *Apologia prima*, 2.

[31] *Apologia prima*, 24–29.

[32] *Apologia prima*, 25.

[33] *Apologia prima*, 20.

transparent language, and makes a point of explaining each facet of Christian ceremony in progression.[34] The style of Justin's apologetic becomes heavily influential in the creation of numerous later Christian apologies, and can specifically be recognised in Latin apologetics with Tertullian's *Apologeticum.* But one key difference of Justin's apologetic work when generally compared with the Latin apologists is his methodological usage of the textual support behind the surface argument. For Justin, the most part of his evidence for the truth of Christianity comes from the prophecies of the Old Testament, cited as proofs that the Christian religion has an ancient heritage in the divinely-inspired utterances of generations of Hebrew prophets.[35] The Christian understanding of Jesus is grounded by the prophecies traced by Justin to their first manifestation five thousand years before his bodily birth.[36] Whereas the Latin apologists would work to ground Christian belief in the arguments of philosophy, Justin is concerned with validating the character of Jesus, and the subsequent beliefs of his followers by extension, in the interpretation of the ancient prophecies of Scripture.

Throughout his life, death, and writings, Justin is very much the paragon Christian apologist. Accusations against the Christian religion are met, countered and riposted, as if Christianity itself was standing in the dock, and with ample reason. For Justin, the illegality of the Church was a prime concern, and one which would eventually cost him his life. His execution at Rome in 165, bestowing martyrdom upon himself and five of his followers,[37] testifies to the penalty that all apologists could pay for their work. It stood as stern warning against public exponents of Christianity, and one of which the later apologists would have been severely aware. As with all Christian apologetic of this period, this consideration is of the utmost importance in interpreting the context; the genuine danger of mortal punishment hanging over the production of each apologetic piece. Every single Latin apology analysed in this work bears witness to the persecution of Christians to varying degrees. Tertullian passionately attempted to

---

[34] *Apologia prima,* 61–67. As part of this express lucidity in detailing Christian practice, Justin translates the otherwise obscure usage of the Hebrew 'Amen' by the assembled believers. *Apologia prima,* 65.

[35] *Apologia prima,* 30–53.

[36] *Apologia prima,* 31.

[37] The legends surrounding the events of his trial and martyrdom at Rome under the prefect Q. Iunius Rusticus exist in three recensions. For an introduction to the texts, and a brief discussion on the relationships between the recensions, see Herbert Musurillo ed., *The Acts of the Christian Martyrs,* pp. xvii–xx.

clear the Church of all charges of illegality, Cyprian paid for the criminality of his religion with his life, and Lactantius watched the opening
events of the Diocletianic persecution unfold at the imperial city of
Nicomedia itself.

Origen

After Justin, and before Augustine of Hippo's *De ciuitate dei*, Origen's
Contra Celsum stands out as one of the most momentous Christian
apologies. The foremost theologian and exegete of his day, Origen
moved into the field of apologetics with the *Contra Celsum* in order
to counter the lengthy series of damning criticisms of Christianity
advanced by the philosopher Celsus in his Ἀληθὴς λόγος – the *True
Doctrine*. Origen left behind a vast amount of literature on a wide
array of Scriptural and theological issues, and although perhaps most
renowned as an exegete, his capabilities as a philosopher and theologian are of the very highest class. His *Contra Celsum* is a highly
nuanced piece of Christian literature, and the result of a task demand-
ing all the faculties of a great theologian at the very apex of his skill.
The original *True Doctrine* partially survives through the citations of
the *Contra Celsum*, but as an individual Celsus himself remains in
obscurity. He is the subject of confusion only around seventy years
later, and Origen is unable to give many details regarding the personality of his adversary.[38] But the fragments of the *True Doctrine* show
Celsus to have been a man highly aware of the history of Christianity,
the Scriptures,[39] and the theological and philosophical weak-spots of
Christian belief. Celsus is no mere peddler in common anti-Christian
assumptions, but a sophisticated and well-informed intellectual har-
bouring serious doubts with the truth of the Christian religion. His
text picks apart aspects of theology, doctrine and practice, and comprises a weighty corpus of argument against the religious and historical claims of the Church. The *True Doctrine* can itself also be located
within a running argument, as Celsus feels the need to defend the

[38] *Contra Celsum*, 1: 8. Origen is unable, for example, to conclusively define the
philosophical allegiance of Celsus. On the implications of his labelling of Celsus as an
Epicurean, see Robert L. Wilken, *The Christians as the Romans Saw Them*, p. 95. For a
more detailed discussion on the subject of Celsus' identification by Origen, see Silke-
Petra Bergjan, 'Celsus the Epicurean? The Interpretation of an Argument in Origen,
Contra Celsum', pp. 191–5.

[39] If perhaps not possessing direct knowledge of many Old Testament works himself. See Gary T. Burke, 'Celsus and the Old Testament', pp. 244–5.

issue of image-worship from its Christian detractors,[40] which could potentially even include Justin Martyr's *Apologia*.[41] In any case, Celsus' work is certainly not the prime mover in the debate, but is at least in part responsive to an ongoing religious dialogue. This is then continued at c. 245–8,[42] when Origen is persuaded, ostensibly by his patron Ambrose,[43] to take up his pen in opposition to Celsus' work.[44] The result is Origen's point-by-point refutation of the statements of the *True Doctrine*, continually studded with direct citations, through the eight books of the *Contra Celsum*. The debate is nothing less than a major theological contest between two intellectual heavyweights on severely opposing sides of a religious divide. In view of the gravity of Celsus' anti-Christian contentions, and sharpened by the context of the eve of the Decian persecution, Origen's *Contra Celsum* is Christian apologetics at its greatest consequence.

The nature of Origen's debate with Celsus is varied and far-reaching, involving issues including human morality, history, antiquity, theology and philosophy. Celsus pulls out lines of argument that penetrate into even the most sacred areas of the Christian world-view. He is aware of a range of detail in the gospel accounts, and relentless in drawing criticism at any multitude of problems or inconsistencies in the narratives. The character and personality of Jesus, as explained by the writings of his early followers, comes in for the greatest barrage of assault. He is painted by Celsus as being only a magician of Egyptian influence,[45] an ordinary human male born of a soldier yet professing to be born of God,[46] and so uninspiring as to be unable to command the total loyalties in life of even his most chosen and trusted few.[47] His divinity is rejected on philosophical grounds; the incorruptible God can never be made subject to the confines of a

---

[40] *Contra Celsum*, 7: 62.

[41] On the possibility of Celsus showing evidence of Justin based upon textual incidences in the *Contra Celsum*, see Eric Osborn, *Justin Martyr*, pp. 168–70.

[42] For a brief overview of the dating arguments, see Henry Chadwick, *Contra Celsum*, pp. xiv–xv. Robert M. Grant follows Chadwick in assigning the date of the *True Doctrine* to c. 178. 'The Chronology of the Greek Apologists', p. 29. Pierre Nautin affixes the date of the *Contra Celsum* to 248/9 in his *Origène: Sa Vie et Son Oeuvre*, p. 376.

[43] On the patronage of Ambrose, see Henri Crouzel, *Origen*, p. 13.

[44] *Contra Celsum*, Praef.: 1.

[45] *Contra Celsum*, 1: 68.

[46] The story of Mary and Panthera. *Contra Celsum*, 1: 32.

[47] *Contra Celsum*, 2: 12.

worldly body.[48] For Celsus, the theological implications of such a belief are intolerable. The Church itself is also accused of a multitude of crimes and moral shortcomings, including unfaithfulness to antiquity, treasonous secrecy and sedition, and its followers are painted as a rabble of incredulous yokels eager to believe all things without questioning.[49] Their leaders are actually keen to encourage gullibility amongst the believers, and can hardly tout a lineage from the apostles depicted by Celsus as the very worst of men.[50] He is also concerned with identifying the connections of Christianity with Judaism, as a means of establishing the Christians' unfaithfulness to the religious traditions of their heritage.[51] Theologically, he attacks such key positions as monotheism and the resurrection of the dead;[52] taking his assault on Christianity into multiple fronts.

Because of the diverse nature of Celsus' anti-Christian contentions, Origen adopts a multifaceted form of response, and the subsequent methodological versatility demonstrated in the *Contra Celsum* shows him to be a highly skilled defender of Christianity. The Scriptures are cited alongside the witnesses of philosophy as viable textual authorities, and Origen displays no reticence in engaging with the purely Christian writings because Celsus has been unafraid to employ them himself. Supporting the claims of Jesus from the gospels can then essentially become a matter of exegesis, where Origen is to be found most comfortable. He explains his usage of the philosophers as perfectly harmonious with Christian standpoints – where the parties concur, the common principles of argument can be cited as appropriated pieces of Christian evidence. Apparently, Origen would even agree with Celsus himself, should he ever defend a correct theological position.[53] On the subject of the connection with Judaism, Origen turns to the apologetic value held in the interpretation of history, and appeals to the destruction of Jerusalem as proof that

[48] *Contra Celsum*, 4: 14.

[49] *Contra Celsum*, 1: 9.

[50] *Contra Celsum*, 1: 62.

[51] *Contra Celsum*, 5: 25. On the employment of the Judaeo-Christian connection in anti-Christian discourse, see Louis H. Feldman, 'Origen's "Contra Celsum" and Josephus' "Contra Apionem": The Issue of Jewish Origins', pp. 107-8.

[52] On monotheism, see *Contra Celsum*, 1: 23. On the resurrection of the body, see *Contra Celsum*, 5: 14. Henry Chadwick comments: 'Perhaps no doctrine was so peculiarly nauseating to him as the Jewish-Christian doctrine of the resurrection of the body'. 'Origen, Celsus, and the Resurrection of the Body', p. 83.

[53] *Contra Celsum*, 8: 76.

God has definitively passed his favour from Israel onto the Church.[54] The *Contra Celsum* contains a unification of differing methodologies through its free recourse to Scripture, philosophy, and history, and all deployed as features of argument in the ultimate goal of the vindication of the practices of Christianity. It is an important representation of the apologies of the early Church, and a key example of the very highest calibre of intellectual Christian apologetic.

Symmachus

The document entitled *Relatio* 3 of Quintus Aurelius Symmachus stands out as a leading candidate of an apologetic expression of Roman religion under the Christian emperors. The intellectual and political defender of traditional Roman ceremony, the *praefectus urbi* of Rome in 384, Symmachus is not strictly an apologist as such, but a statesman with the necessary political influence needed to voice a protest against the Christian-driven abandonment of traditional aspects of Roman public ceremony. *Relatio* 3 is a directly focused petition pleading for a return to traditions gradually proscribed as a result of the growing dominance of Christianity. The incidence of Gratian's removal of the altar of Victory from the Senate-house in 382 is one of the crucial events upon which Symmachus' opposition takes its focus, added to the imperial withdrawal of the privileges traditionally enjoyed by the Vestal virgins. Symmachus categorically details his mission from the Senate,[55] perhaps betraying its own reactionary leanings in opposition to the progressively more Christian occupants of the imperial throne. His petition for the restoration of the altar, presented as the appeal of the embodied Roma herself, rings with apologetic terminology:

> *Utar caerimoniis auitis, neque enim paenitet! Uiuam meo more, quia libera sum! … Eadem spectamus astra, commune caelum est, idem nos mundus inuoluit: quid interest, qua quisque prudentia uerum requirat? Uno itinere non potest perueniri ad tam grande secretum.*[56]

---

[54] *Contra Celsum*, 4: 22.

[55] *Relationes*, 3: 1.

[56] 'Let me practice my ancestral ceremonies, for I do not regret them. Let me live in my own way, for I am free! … We look at the same stars, the sky is common to all, the same universe envelops us. What does it matter by which route we seek the truth? So great a secret cannot be arrived at by one road only'. *Relationes*, 3: 9–10. Latin text in R. H. Barrow ed., *Prefect and Emperor: The Relationes of Symmachus A.D. 384*. A key distinction with the Christian apologists is that their crucial monotheism would have prevented an assertion like *uno itinere non potest perueniri ad tam grande secretum*.

In its defensive plea for freedom of worship, an apologetic character is unmistakable. *Relatio* 3 voices a cry for the increased imperial sanction of Roman religious customs falling into neglect after their official supplanting by Christianity. The emperors themselves are not called to abandon their own Christian sympathies, but it would suffice to allow Roman religion to be practiced without religious or financial restraints.[57] Symmachus argues that if all men are free to worship their own respective deities in their own individual ways, then the empire can be granted divine support on all fronts;[58] a position in itself similar to that employed by Tertullian in the *Apologeticum* almost two centuries earlier, where he vouched for the Christians' fidelity in praying on behalf of the safety of the emperor.[59]

Symmachus' *Relatio* 3 can also be cited in introduction to another theme running throughout Latin apologetics, namely the controversial question of the breach with religious practices justified by established antiquity. He exemplifies the sense of outrage at the ever-widening separation of the Roman state from its ancient forms of ritual, which is pinpointed as being of the utmost importance to the future vitality of the empire: *non sunt haec uitia terrarum, nihil inputemus austris, nec rubigo segetibus obfuit, nec auena fruges necauit: sacrilegio annus exaruit. Necesse enim fuit perire omnibus, quod religionibus negabatur.*[60] The core of his complaint is the demise of imperial support for traditional Roman ceremony, accompanied by a fear of the consequences of the public rejection of its ancient modes of worship. Symmachus exclaims that Rome is not yet so friendly with the barbarians that an altar of Victory is not required.[61] It may read as satirical, but refers to a highly important subject. The extent of the prospective divine displeasure should Rome completely abandon her ancestral religion is always unknown,[62] but for the like-minded allies of Symmachus, is an unthinkable situation. Antiquity and tradition provides a refuge, and

---

[57] *Relationes*, 3: 7–8.

[58] *Relationes*, 3: 19.

[59] *Apologeticum*, 30–32.

[60] 'They were not the fault of the earth; we should not blame the winds. Blight did not spoil the grain, nor did weeds kill the crops. Sacrilege dried up the year's yield. It was inevitable that all would perish, because religion was being neglected'. *Relationes*, 3: 16.

[61] *Relationes*, 3: 3.

[62] Symmachus picks out the recent famine in Africa in 383 as an example of the punishment that the gods are capable of enacting, should Rome continue moving away from her traditional religious practices. See *Relationes*, 3: 15–17.

also a point of embarkation in opposition to the novelties of Christianity. At the heart of this understanding lies the conviction that Christianity and the ancient traditions that have guaranteed Rome's safety over the centuries are fundamentally incompatible. This position has a long history throughout the opponents of the Christian apologists, and can be particularly observed in Latin apologetics with the standpoint of Cyprian's rival Demetrianus in the *Ad Demetrianum*, and in Augustine of Hippo's motivation behind the *De ciuitate dei*.

Throughout his speech on the subject of the altar of Victory, Symmachus refrains from expressly disparaging his adversarial religion, in respect of his own position in the debate. He is arguing against an imperial action, and is therefore mindful of the advantages of restrained language in his argument. As a comparative example, some thirty years before Gratian's removal of the altar of Victory, the Latin Christian writer Firmicus Maternus had called for the imperial-sponsored annihilation of non-Christian practices. Embarking on a fiery exegesis of Dt 13: 6–10, Firmicus declared:

> *Sed et uobis, sacratissimi imperatores, ad uindicandum et puniendum hoc malum necessitas imperatur et hoc uobis dei summi lege praecipitur, ut seueritas uestra idololatriae facinus omnifariam persequatur... Nec filio iubet parci nec fratri et per amata coniugis membra gladium uindicem ducit. Amicum quoque sublimi seueritate persequitur et ad discerpenda sacrilegorum corpora omnis populus armatur. Integris etiam ciuitatibus, si in isto fuerint facinore deprehensae, decernuntur excidia.*[63]

The contrast with the far more civilised and unquestionably less bloodthirsty plea of Symmachus is sharply defined, and serves to illustrate a change in perspective after the change in religious fortunes. Symmachus' plea is an appeal for equality and religious freedom, which is emblematic of the change in status of the two religions in the period following the Constantinian toleration. Perhaps his speech can even be to some extent aligned with the standpoints of the early Latin apologists; themselves at times producing their work from marginalised

---

[63] 'But you, Most Holy Emperors, must order the punishment and retribution of this evil, and by this law of the Supreme God it is ordered that your severity should be set forth in every way on the crime of idolatry... He commands that neither son nor brother is spared, and orders the avenging sword against the limbs of a beloved wife. A friend too he persecutes with lofty severity, and all the populace is roused to rend the bodies of sacrilegious men. Even upon entire cities, if they are discovered in this crime, destruction is decreed'. *De errore profanarum religionem*, 29: 1–2. Latin text in Robert Turcan ed., Firmicus Maternus, *L'Erreur des Religions Païennes*.

positions on the receiving end of imperial legislation, facing calls from certain quarters for violent repercussions, and often wavering on the brink of active harassment.

Augustine

One of the few unsurpassed pillars of Christian theology, the figure of Augustine of Hippo has exerted continual influence since his lifetime by virtue of his extensive and wide-ranging corpus of theological work. Within this is the *De ciuitate dei*; Augustine's magnificent establishment of the Christian faith in response to negative criticisms of the Church. An apologetic character is immediately identifiable, although the work will go on to supersede any classification as solely apologetic in itself. Dated following the fall of the city of Rome to the armies of Alaric the Goth, Augustine cites his motivation as being responsive to allegations of Christian blame for the current misfortunes that assail the Roman world.[64] It appears that accusations of culpability for the sack of Rome are being aimed at the Christians, following from the apparent semblance of divine punishment that has ordained the terrible events. Augustine himself is comparatively controlled, but a real sense of mourning for the sack of Rome can be heard in the words of Jerome on the subject; *haeret uox et singultus intercipiunt uerba dictantis. Capitur Urbs, quae totum cepit orbem.*[65] In the aftermath, it is the search for meaning behind the public disaster that eventually leads to the production of Augustine's *De ciuitate dei*. It is argued by the opponents of Christianity that Rome suffers because she has abandoned her ancestral worship, and the fall of the great city can be firmly attributed to the change in religious practice. The *De ciuitate dei* opens with a direct statement of Augustine's form of response to this prevalent issue of religious culpability for human suffering, and tackles the subject head-on. The work thus begins as ostensibly apologetic, but will later transcend the primarily defensive qualities of the *apologia* format. The *De ciuitate dei* spans twenty-two books of focused argument, and engages with a wide range of subjects in its vindication of the true religion solely held in the Christian message. It becomes a handbook of a Christian understanding of purpose alongside the sinful world of

---

[64] Detailed by Augustine at *Retractiones*, 69.

[65] 'My voice breaks, and sobs interrupt my speech as I dictate. The city that took the whole world has been taken'. Jerome, *Epistula*, 127: 12. The Latin text of Jerome's letters used throughout this work is in Isidore Hilberg ed., *Sancti Euesbii Hieronymi epistulae.*

human society, illustrated through the dominant analogy of the two *ciuitates* of Augustine's world-view. On the back of the catastrophe of the sack of Rome, Augustine's comments carry intense gravity. The earthly city must fall, but the city of God will endure.

A century after the Constantinian toleration, followed by the favour of a succession of Christian emperors,[66] Augustine is still addressing his work at a generically non-Christian Roman populace.[67] He attacks the Roman cults, particularly responding to the religious framework advanced by Varro,[68] and the philosophical perspective of Porphyry of Tyre.[69] The interpretation of history is also a key element of the work, turning the argument of Christian blame for the sack of Rome back onto its advocates. For Augustine, Rome was only spared total destruction because of the Christianity of its occupiers.[70] The Church bears witness to the great number of refugees granted mercy by the invading armies under the shelter of the sanctuaries of Christianity.[71] But still the Christian believers are vilified. Augustine is confident that the Roman empire has suffered for centuries due to its neglect in recognising the true God,[72] and that the innocence of the Church can be justified by the clear arguments of history. But even after the advent of Christianity, Rome will continue to be punished while it houses the unbelievers.[73] The falsely-identified gods of Roman religion are impotent when it comes to the protection of their people.[74] Overall, everything can be ultimately traced by Augustine to the metaphorical image of the two

---

[66] *De ciuitate dei*, 5: 24–6. Augustine lauds the successes of Constantine and Theodosius, and interprets them as the just rewards of God upon sincere Christian emperors.

[67] As in the appeal for conversion at *De ciuitate dei*, 2: 29.

[68] First introduced at *De ciuitate dei*, 3: 4, and then more fully dealt with in books 6–7.

[69] At *De ciuitate dei*, 10: 9-11, 19: 22-3, and 22: 26-8. Augustine engages with Porphyry's Ἐκ λογίων φιλοσοφίας (*Philosophy from Oracles*), referring to him as *doctissimus philosophorum, quamuis Christianorum acerrimus inimicus*. 'The most learned of philosophers, although the bitterest enemy of Christians'. *De ciuitate dei*, 19: 22. Latin text in Bernhard Dombart ed., *Sancti Aurelii Augustini episcopi De ciuitate Dei libri XXII*, Vol. 2.

[70] *De ciuitate dei*, 1: 1.

[71] *De ciuitate dei*, 1: 1.

[72] *De ciuitate dei*, 3: 1.

[73] *De ciuitate dei*, 1: 9. On the issue of communal punishment elsewhere in Latin apologetics, see Tertullian, *Apologeticum*, 41: 3, and Cyprian, *Ad Demetrianum*, 19: 2.

[74] The overall object of the illustrative historical examples occupying *De ciuitate dei*, 3.

opposing cities. He is more than comfortable in the usage of Scripture throughout his work, and interprets Genesis to establish the ancestry of Abel behind the Church, while those of the earthly city belong to the line of the fratricidal Cain.[75] The Old Testament is interpreted allegorically to support the pre-ordination of Christianity as divinely foretold. Augustine defends the authority of both Old and New Testaments as the inspired words of God himself,[76] and therefore has no issue with holding them back as textual evidence on any level. In the methodology of the *De ciuitate dei*, Augustine can cite the prophecies of Scripture and the principles of the philosophers together, and interpret the events of both Roman and Biblical history for the same ends. Even the evidence posed by contemporary miracles is drawn in support of the constant validation of Christianity as the true religion.[77] At heart is Augustine's continually reinforced plea to his audience to fully enter into communion with the city of God,[78] and partake of its glorious future rewards.[79]

The *De ciuitate dei* is unquestionably the monumental work of later Latin apologetics, even if it represents a considerable level of divergence from the earlier apologists in the African tradition before him. Lactantius' *Diuinae institutiones* is its only real forerunner in the African Latin field, although perhaps also Cyprian's *Ad Demetrianum* to a certain extent for its common treatment of similar key concerns. Augustine is highly conscious of a need for the positive establishment of Christian standpoints; lifting his work out from the essentially responsive structure of defensive apologetics, and towards the format of a proactive manual of Christian belief. The *De ciuitate dei* opens with its refutation of those who would hold that Roman religion is necessary for the assured prosperity of the Roman world, but then widens into the service of its cardinal purpose. This is the exposition and vindication of the truth of Christianity, the most fitting religion of the earthly city due to its unique origin with God alone.

Modern apologetics

Christian apologetics is not a phenomenon peculiar to the religious tensions of the ancient world, but has developed, and continues to

---

[75] *De ciuitate dei*, 15: 17.

[76] On the Scriptures, see *De ciuitate dei*, 11: 3, and 18: 42–3.

[77] *De ciuitate dei*, 22: 8.

[78] *De ciuitate dei*, 2: 29.

[79] *De ciuitate dei*, 22: 30.

develop, out from its historic formation. Modern examples would be Richard Wurmbrand's *Tortured for Christ*, compiled in defiance of the prohibitions of Christianity under the Soviet Union, and the popular website CARM.org;[80] which collects and updates an online library of strongly evangelical definitions of Christian belief. Both examples represent evangelical sectors of the modern Christian Church that feel an increasing sense of isolation from current religious dialogue, and have chosen to vent an evangelical current of responses to prominent religious and moral questions. In essence, they are attempting to address the changing state of the modern secular world through the methods of apologetics. It is also a wider symptom of the secular culture of late twentieth and early twenty-first century Western society that ecclesiastical statements relating particular aspects of belief are often characterised by a defensive standpoint. Perhaps the roles have again been reversed, and Christianity is now showing signs of becoming demoted to the prominence of secularism. On this subject, regarding the scope of modern apologetics, the mission-statement of the website CARM.org is:

> To equip Christians with the truth, to expose the error of false religious systems, evolution, to teach apologetics, help Christians defend the faith, and to glorify the Lord Jesus.[81]

The dual purpose of apologetics in educating Christians as well as confronting the criticism of religious opponents is still present. But such modern forms of evangelical apologetic expression as CARM. org also arouse a certain level of condescension from more traditional Christian perspectives. Evangelical apologetic movements often face an attitude somewhere close to disdain from such quarters as the critical schools of Biblical interpretation, modern liberal theology, and the developing 'post-Christian' study of the history of Christianity. As the early Christian apologists launched their work into a hostile world, so too it seems do their modern successors. But if nothing else, the CARM.org website is a testament to the adaptation that is required in the developing world of Christian apologetics. The sphere of apologetics has been transformed, and secularism has now become the main

---

[80] Christian Apologetics and Research Ministry. Website address <http://www.carm.org/>. Date accessed: 30/11/2010.

[81] <http://www.carm.org/general-information-about-carm>. Date accessed: 30/11/2010.

concern for Christian apologies. Another twentieth-century Christian apologist has outlined his own explanation of the meaning of the modern apologetic genre, stressing the need for continual re-evaluation in compatibility with cutting-edge scientific enquiry:

> Apologetics deals with the relationship of the Christian faith to the wider sphere of man's "secular" knowledge – philosophy, science, history, sociology, and so on – with a view to showing that faith is not at variance with the truth that these enquiries have uncovered. *In every age it is necessary that this task should be undertaken*; in a period of rapid developments in scientific knowledge and of vast social change it becomes a matter of considerable urgency.[82]

Apologetics is an area of the Christian mission that is tied to ceaseless growth and development. There may not always be an obvious connection in the issues addressed by the ancient apologists with their modern counterparts, because the physical subject-matter of all apologies is necessarily a response to contemporary concerns. But there does remain a similarity of motive that unites Christian apologetic over the centuries. As an example, although the voices of Tertullian or Lactantius may not be heard in the statements of the modern CARM.org, their influence in contributing to an apologetic schema as a viable Christian outlet in its relationship with the world, can still be clearly felt.

[82] Alan Richardson, *Christian Apologetics*, p. 19. Italics mine.

MINUCIUS FELIX

1. Introduction

Although the dating range of every individual piece of literature is crucial for its contextualisation, it is not always easily achieved. Minucius Felix's *Octauius* is the premier example of this in Latin apologetics.[1] Acceptable estimates of the dating period for the text range from the late-second century to the mid-third, and although the evidence has remained the same since Lactantius and Jerome, the arguments continue to vary. Throughout this study, Minucius Felix is considered as tentatively anterior to Tertullian, and is therefore first to be analysed in this study of the Latin apologists in the African tradition. The specific dating range of the *Octauius* is difficult to pinpoint, but a pre-197 location is taken as the necessary starting-point in its surrounding milieu.

[1] In spite of the relative uncertainty of its dating and contextualisation, the *Octauius* has enjoyed a number of modern editions. In English, the translation by G. H. Rendall in the Loeb Classical Library (1931, repr. 2003) is useful for the parallel Latin-English text, but reliance upon this version is not recommended due to the divergence in internal textual layout that occurs between chapters 21–25. Although the difficulties resolve themselves at chapter 25, the format of the four chapters in question suffers from a confused progression. A possible explanation could be Rendall's usage of J. P. Waltzing's Teubner edition (1926) as the base text, while later editors such as G. W. Clarke have based their own translations on Jean Beaujeu's text in the Budé series (1964). The more critically recognised format of the text is that of Jean Beaujeu, and so citation of these chapters in question should follow his progression. Since the work of G. W. Clarke in the field of Minucian study during the 1960s and 70s, Rendall has been surpassed in English by Clarke's translation and detailed commentary in the Ancient Christian Writers series (1974). In French, the edition of Jean Beaujeu presents a highly insightful parallel text with analysis, and Beaujeu's introductory comments and textual footnotes continue to be of great utility. B. Kytzler's version in the Teubner series (1992) provides the base text of the *Octauius* used throughout this work.

It seems likely that Minucius follows Aulus Gellius and Fronto, and possibly the reign of Commodus, but is also a potential source for Tertullian's *Apologeticum*, so an approximate period of post-192 but pre-197 could be a plausible time span following this criteria. Minucius Felix would thus become the earliest extant Latin apologist. However, in view of the highly problematic dating situation, Minucius could equally have followed Tertullian, and therefore would only be dated firmly between the *Apologeticum* and the *Quod idola dii non sint* of the Cyprianic corpus.

Minucius is generally placed at Rome, on his own testimony that is followed by Lactantius and Jerome.[2] He is traditionally also identified as having an African connection; perhaps as a place of birth. This is primarily due to the established tradition of Latin apologetics originating in North Africa,[3] the numerous close similarities of the *Octauius* with Tertullian's *Apologeticum* and *Ad nationes*, and the more general prevalence of Greek over Latin at this period of Rome's intellectual history. The reference in the *Octauius* to M. Cornelius Fronto as *tuus Fronto*,[4] often used in support of an African provenance, should actually be taken to regard the shared religious standpoints with Caecilius Natalis of the dialogue, and not as a pointer towards location. The issue of Minucius' origin remains open, but personal testimony must carry the greatest weight. Minucius is also clear regarding his occupation. The debate of the *Octauius* is set during a period of relief from his *iudiciariam curam*,[5] and following this, he is portrayed by Lactantius and Jerome as *causidicus* at Rome.[6] Minucius' personal character takes on the role of arbiter in his debate, and his judicial *métier* is made explicit from the outset. It is expressly stated for a deliberate reason, and prefigures the highly educated nature of the text. Like Lactantius over a century later, Minucius has compiled a highly sophisticated literary work. The *Octauius* embodies an intentional Christian imitation of Cicero, and particularly his *De natura deorum*. It achieves this purpose both by continual direct citations, and also by more subtle echoes

---

[2] *Octauius*, 2: 1. Against this, read T. D. Barnes on the *Octauius* as 'almost certainly written in Carthage (rather than either Rome or Cirta)'. *Early Christian Hagiography and Roman History*, p. 54.

[3] As an example, G. W. Clarke has justified the argument for 'an ultimately African provenance' as making 'sound literary sense'. *The Octavius of Marcus Minucius Felix*, p. 7.

[4] *Octauius*, 31: 2.

[5] 'Judicial responsibilities'. *Octauius*, 2: 3.

[6] *Diuinae institutiones*, 5: 1; 22, Jerome *De uiris illustribus*, 58, and *Epistula*, 70: 5.

of Cicero's well regarded Latinity. Cicero's encapsulation of multiple philosophical standpoints in the *De natura* provides the backbone for much of Minucius' arguments on both sides of his religious debate. He is Minucius' greatest influence in style and argument, and the *Octauius* is possibly the most rhetorically stylised piece of Christian Latin extant from the Patristic period. Minucius also shares Cicero's attitude of disdain for the theological contributions of the poets,[7] and praises a multitude of philosophical personalities and tenets by comparison, even in his Christian argument. The strong engagement with the poets and philosophers takes on an overt precedence, and becomes the most marked feature of the *Octauius* as a whole. By contrast, the Scriptures are never directly cited, Jesus is never discussed, and Christian teachings are instead presented from moral and philosophical perspectives. Minucius endeavours throughout to make Christianity more palatable to the educated non-Christian reader, through a continual recourse to classical authorities. The *Octauius* is the central archetype of this quality that is most peculiar to Latin apologetics, also being present in Tertullian's *Apologeticum* and *Ad nationes*, the more obscure *Quod idola dii non sint*, Arnobius of Sicca's *Aduersus nationes*, and Lactantius' *Diuinae institutiones*. They represent a desire to reconcile the doctrines of Christianity with the philosophical currents of the Roman world, through a Christian appropriation of the great works of poetry and philosophy. Although relatively brief in itself, the *Octauius* provides a significant contribution to Latin apologetics, and is the pick of the field as the standout work of style and description.

Its setting at Ostia during the legal vacation provides the backdrop for a cultured religious debate; it is primarily an apologetic work, but is also at once picturesque, well-crafted, and evocative of its early-morning stroll on a beautiful coastline. The setting of the scene is fundamentally relevant. Minucius is directly referring to the dialogue recorded by Aulus Gellius in his *Noctes Atticae*;[8] where the philosopher Favorinus presides over a debate between a Peripatetic and a Stoic. This dialogue is also set during a walk along the shore at Ostia, and is

---

[7] *Octauius*, 23, and Cicero, *De natura deorum*, 1: 16. The corresponding treatment by Tertullian is *Apologeticum*, 14: 1–6.

[8] *Noctes Atticae*, 18: 1. The dating of Gellius' work is problematic, and therefore any conclusions regarding the *Noctes Atticae* as possibly contributing to the *terminus post quem* for the *Octauius* must be restricted. However, following the dating evidence and argument of Leofranc Holford-Strevens, the *Noctes Atticae* is likely to be approximately dated to the 'joint or sole reign of Commodus' (177–192). *Aulus Gellius: An Antonine Scholar and his Achievement*, p. 21.

deliberately reminiscent in the opening of the *Octauius*. Minucius is not essentially responding to Gellius throughout the *Octauius*, but it is incontrovertible that his employment of the similar setting is measured, and would have been a well-recognised philosophical motif by his contemporary audience. Although it has been suggested that this could point towards the date of the *Octauius* as relatively soon after Gellius' work,[9] it would be a mistake to read too much into Minucius' reference. A more supportable conclusion would be to line the Gellius reference alongside the numerous other philosophical citations and allusions of Minucius' writing; it is another reference in a long list of many textual recourses.

This study of the *Octauius* explores a number of issues. The question of whether Minucius is responding to the anti-Christian rhetoric of Marcus Cornelius Fronto is first considered, followed by a discussion of a possible textual allusion to Commodus, and the bearing that this could have on the *Octauius* dating issue. The central aspect of this study of Minucius Felix is an exploration into the picture of the theological and practical life of the Church that can be observed from analysis of the *Octauius* as potentially the earliest extant document of Latin apologetics.

2. To what extent is the *Octauius* a response to Fronto?

The relationship of Fronto and the *Octauius* is evident, although the particular degree is more difficult to pinpoint. G. W. Clarke concedes that 'on this subject much remains idle speculation',[10] while on the other hand, Simon Price has utilised the Frontonian dimension as an argument in an effort of roughly dating the work to the second century.[11] But the definite location, contextualisation, and even formulation of Fronto's anti-Christian statements are practically unattainable, and the only surviving extracts seem to be Caecilius' citations in the *Octauius* text. Edward Champlin has reinforced the idea of a supposed 'Oration Against the Christians' as being actually non-specific, and instead part of the forensic speech *In Pelopem*.[12]

---

[9] Simon Price, 'Latin Christian Apologetics', in *Apologetics in the Roman Empire*, p. 112.

[10] *The Octavius of Marcus Minucius Felix*, p. 223, n. 123.

[11] 'Latin Christian Apologetics', p. 112.

[12] *Fronto and Antonine Rome*, pp. 64–6.

Champlin's argument is based primarily upon the brief mention of Fronto by the fifth-century bishop Sidonius Apollinaris, whose admiring reference singles out *In Pelopem* as the rhetor's finest work.[13] Champlin points towards Fronto's usage of the colourful history of the mythological Pelops as a suitable academic metaphor, under which the infamous practices attributed to the Christians would be described. Champlin follows Sidonius in depicting *In Pelopem* as Fronto's most renowned work, therefore supporting Minucius' response to comparatively well-known arguments.[14] Whether Fronto indeed composed a specific piece against the Christians, or otherwise employed attacks on the Church as part of a speech against Pelops, is too uncertain to yield much further conclusion. Champlin's reasoning is not the final word on the subject, even if it does fit well with the possibilities thrown up by the scant nature of the evidence. It appears to be the most likely scenario, and if nothing else provides sufficient grounding for a departure from the once-commonplace idea of Fronto's specific 'Oration against the Christians'.

On the face of it, the *Octauius* only contains two allusions to Fronto: the *Cirtensis nostri* depiction by Caecilius,[15] and the later *tuus Fronto* retort by Octavius.[16] These brief references hardly provide substantial evidence for the question of Minucius' relationship to Fronto, and are seemingly most likely explained by the identification of Caecilius and Fronto as comrades in their anti-Christian contentions. Perhaps Minucius' character Caecilius also originated from Cirta, but even this is surplus to the explanation of either remark. The allusions do not suggest any particular range of dating, and neither betray nor preclude Fronto's contemporaneity to the setting of the *Octauius* dialogue. But they do certainly point towards an engagement with Fronto's arguments, and therefore provide the signpost for an exploration into the possible areas of Frontonian influence.

Caecilius' recounting of the popular accusations of incestuous immorality taking place under the sanctified visage of Christian ritual

---

[13] *M. Fronto cum reliquis orationibus emineret, in Pelopem se sibi praetulit.* 'Although Marcus Fronto may excel in his surviving speeches, he surpassed himself with *Against Pelops*'. *Epistula*, 8: 10; 3. Latin text in Paul Mohr ed., *C. Sollius Apollinaris Sidonius.*

[14] *Fronto and Antonine Rome*, p. 66.

[15] *Octauius*, 9: 6.

[16] *Octauius*, 31: 2.

reads like a direct quotation from Fronto in its entirety.[17] It immediately follows from the introductory remark *id etiam Cirtensis nostri testatur oratio*,[18] and is included as a corroborating voice in Caecilius' foundation of a case against Christian morality. Octavius' corresponding retaliation ultimately makes it clear that Caecilius has adapted the contentions of the famous orator, and that Octavius himself is responding in kind. Fronto's original accusations would thus have included the imputation of sexually immoral banqueting at the organized Christian gatherings, where incestuous depravity masquerades under the cover of religious celebration. The infamous story of a dog initiating the lustful activities by upsetting the ceremonial lamp is a particularly notorious inclusion. The popular accusation centred around a dog chained to a lampstand being enticed to pull it over upon being thrown a morsel of food, in order to absolve any particular reveller of the responsibility of starting the forthcoming acts of incest and immorality. Octavius summarises the Christian defence with a complete denial of any such practice, and casts Fronto in the light of a courtroom-slanderer rather than an advocate utilising precise evidence: *tuus Fronto non ut adfirmator testimonium fecit, sed conuicium ut orator adspersit.*[19] It seems likely that this area of the anti-Christian accusations has its inspiration in Fronto, and it is not stretching the evidence too much to allow for a certain degree of Fronto's arguments providing influence for Caecilius' other attacks in the course of his anti-Christian tirade. Indeed, the most part of the assault on the Church of chapter 9 could be reminiscent of the influence of Fronto, occurring as it does immediately before the first reference to *Cirtensis nostri* as possibly one overall allusion, rather than the Frontonian reference solely preceding the recourse to his arguments. Also, later in the text, immediately following Caecilius' final summation of the non-Christian viewpoint of the dialogue, Minucius interjects with an oration on the dangers of persuasive rhetorical language in the impact of argument.[20] This serves the dual purpose of bridging the two sides in the debate, while also providing a thinly-veiled reference to the stylistic eloquence of the classical works in comparison with the terseness and lack of elegance of

---

[17] *Octauius*, 9: 6–7.

[18] 'As the speech of our Cirtensian testifies'. *Octauius*, 9: 6.

[19] 'Your Fronto did not give evidence as a proven witness, but cast abuse as an orator'. *Octauius*, 31: 2.

[20] *Octauius*, 14.

the Christian Scriptures.[21] But if much of the general flow of Caecilius' argument bears the influence of Fronto, then Minucius' statements regarding the enticing speech of the great masters of language takes on a double meaning. Fronto was highly regarded as a gifted rhetorical speaker, while the barbarous language of the Christian Scriptures presented an undistinguished opposition – Fronto could therefore be the specific embodiment of Minucius' cautionary remarks. In this sense, Minucius' words of praise after Octavius' Christian defence in the closing chapters of the work would also refer back to Fronto as the personification of one of the *maleuoli* who attack the Christians with accusation and insult.[22] A Christian riposte to Fronto's accusations would naturally be valid, and perhaps the *Octauius* is actually an attempt at a fluid encapsulation of Fronto's arguments with their concurrent Christian defence – coupled together as a more subtle formulation of an 'Against Fronto' literary response.

A further reminiscence of Fronto, if albeit a tentative one, is Minucius' description of Socrates as *sapientiae principem*.[23] Similar pronouncements of epithets referring to Socrates can be found in the numerous sources in the library of the *Octauius*, notably *principe philosophiae*[24] and *parentem philosophiae*[25] in Cicero's *De natura deorum*. But the closest parallel of Minucius' *sapientiae principem* is Fronto's *princeps ille sapientiae simul atque eloquentiae* from his correspondence with Marcus Aurelius.[26] The possible explanations would be either that it is coincidental in view of the similar descriptions of Socrates in other textual sources, or even perhaps that Minucius has borrowed this particular articulation from Fronto. This would not necessarily demand Minucius' awareness of Fronto's letter to Marcus Aurelius, but instead suggest the prospect of Fronto's depiction of Socrates as *princeps … sapientiae* as potentially occurring elsewhere, specifically in his anti-Christian rhetoric that the *Octauius* is engaging with. The Frontonian influence here would be conceivable, but necessarily remains hypothetical due to the lack of

---

[21] See Clarke, *The Octavius of Marcus Minucius Felix*, p. 245, n. 173.

[22] *Octauius*, 39.

[23] 'Master of wisdom'. *Octauius*, 13: 1.

[24] *De natura deorum*, 2: 66.

[25] *De natura deorum*, 1: 93.

[26] 'That master of wisdom as well as eloquence'. *Ad M. Caes.*, 3: 15. Latin text in C. R. Haines ed., *The Correspondence of Marcus Cornelius Fronto with Marcus Aurelius Antoninus, Lucius Verus, Antoninus Pius, and Various Friends*, Vol. 1.

other corroborating sources. The survival of a text of Fronto's anti-Christian diatribe would have greatly aided the contextualisation of the *Octauius*. Very much like Gellius' *Noctes Atticae*, the dating range of Fronto's anti-Christian attack is impossible to isolate. This, in turn, affects the contextualisation of the *Octauius* by preventing the formulation of even an estimated *terminus post quem*, as conjecture can advance no further than the general area of the 160s for the location of Fronto's *In Pelopem*, if such is the source of his anti-Christian statements. The *terminus ante quem* for the *Octauius* of 197 with the *Apologeticum* of Tertullian could potentially be established, leaving an approximate 30 year period for Minucius' composition. However, it is also possible that Minucius has provided another hint of his surrounding circumstances, which would betray a further allusion to the background events in the corroboration of the textual dating.

3. Minucius Felix and Commodus?

During Octavius' retort to the anti-Christian arguments of Caecilius, he presents a response to the issue of the theological justification of non-Christian men ostensibly blessed by God with temporal power and riches.[27] At first glance it reads as a broad critique of ostentatious displays of power, wealth and earthly adornments, as part of Minucius' greater address of the innate divergence of Christianity with aspects of Roman culture. Building upon this, Minucius departs from his depiction of the role of Christians within public society, and specifies an archetype of the dissolute and earthly heathen ruler. It achieves a balanced literary aside from the main flow of the text, and postulates an attacking retort against an embodied Christian opponent amidst the wider current of general apologetic defence of Christian practice. There are numerous parallels with the life of the Antonine emperor Commodus (180–192), which can be observed from a point-by-point study of Minucius' text with the extant historical sources for the life and character of Commodus. The bearing that this possibility could have on the dating scenario of the *Octauius* merits its further exploration. In the continuing

[27] Advanced by Caecilius regarding the indiscriminate blessings of good fortune upon men of questionable personal morality. *Octauius*, 5: 11–12.

attempt at contextualising the text, its evidence would be of use. In the passage in question, Minucius argues:[28]

> Perhaps it deceives you that men who are unaware of God abound in wealth, flourish with honours, and exert great power. These wretched people are raised this high so they might fall the deeper. For they are like animals fattened for the slaughter; like victims garlanded for punishment. Indeed, they are raised with supreme power (*imperiis*) and domination so that these degenerates may freely market their reason for license and power.[29] For where there is death, what foundation can happiness have without acquaintance with God? Like a dream, before it is grasped it slips away. Are you king? Yet you fear as much as you are feared, and however large is your bodyguard surrounding you, in the face of danger you are alone. Are you rich? Yet wealth is ill-trusted, and many provisions on the short journey of life only burden, and do not provide for you. Do you pride yourself on fasces and purples? It is a vain error of man, and an empty decoration of office; to gleam in purple and be sordid in mind. Are you of famous noble descent? Do you praise your parentage? Yet all men are born equal; only virtue distinguishes us.[30]

Although it first appears to be more of a broad condemnation of secular power and authority, the hints at a particularly specific denouncement are there to be seen. The character in question occupies the imperial throne itself; the mentions of *fasces*, *purpurae*, and the question *rex es?* all contribute to the picture of someone raised to the *imperium*; the highest position of the empire. Pride in the trappings of public office forms the core of the critique, alongside an equal self-superiority of noble ancestry. Regardless of any large imperial retinue, Minucius warns that danger finds even such a supposedly great man completely alone. If Minucius is deliberately alluding to an individual in the historical background to the *Octauius*, then the field of possibilities would thus be already reduced significantly. If an historical incarnation is to be sought for, the personality of Commodus comes to the fore.

Although the extant sources for Commodus' life and character are marred by varying degrees of unreliability, the picture that emerges

---

[28] This lengthy citation has been immediately rendered into English, in the interest of greater ease of engagement.

[29] The Latin *ut ingenium eorum perditae mentis licentiae potestatis libere nundinentur* has proved continually difficult to translate. For a catalogue of several attempts thus far, see Clarke, *The Octavius of Marcus Minucius Felix*, p. 121, n. 630.

[30] *Octauius*, 37: 7–10.

is always one of a profligate contrast with his widely respected father Marcus Aurelius. The biographies of Cassius Dio and Herodian focus on his numerous failings, and his twelve-year reign is unfavourably compared with the worst of any pestilence in Roman history.[31] He is portrayed as a lamentable dark spot in the imperial tradition. If Minucius' text does indeed refer to Commodus, then he would also have the dubious honour of being detested by both Christian and non-Christian alike. Multiple incidents of murder and tyranny litter the historical accounts, and although some level of bad feeling is to be expected from the inevitable comparison with his seemingly universally popular father, Commodus' lifestyle enters the annals of Cassius Dio and Herodian marked by innumerable acts of gross injustice. Cassius Dio's *Historia Romana* records the attempt by the Roman populace to dismember Commodus' corpse after his eventual declaration as a public enemy.[32] The key points of Minucius' critique are all present in these corroborating sources for the character of Commodus. Irrespective of his high official status, Commodus' own personality is degenerate and corrupt, and he is a slave to his passions.[33] His particular ambition to be feared by the populace is noted,[34] and also contrasted with his own level of personal fear; one that even caused him to be labelled a coward.[35] This would be echoed by Minucius' *tam times quam timeris*.[36] Commodus' delight in the paraphernalia of state office becomes an object of ridicule,[37] and Minucius' admonition of pride in ancestry is reminiscent of his noble Antonine heritage. His warning to flee the burdens of wealth, *magno uiatico breue uitae iter non instruitur, sed oneratur*,[38] in a specific articulation of a more general concept from earlier in the text,[39] is brought home with a direct meaning. Minucius' line *quamlibet sis multo comitatu stipatus,*

---

[31] Cassius Dio, *Historia Romana*, 73: 15; 1.

[32] 74: 2; 1.

[33] *Octauius*, 37: 7, Herodian, *Historia*, 1: 13; 7.

[34] *Octauius*, 37: 9, Herodian, *Historia*, 1: 14; 9.

[35] Cassius Dio, *Historia Romana*, 73: 1; 1, 73: 13; 6.

[36] 'You fear as much as you are feared'. *Octauius*, 37: 9.

[37] *Octauius*, 37: 10, Cassius Dio, *Historia Romana*, 73: 17; 3.

[38] 'Many provisions on the short journey of life only burden, and do not provide for you'. *Octauius*, 37: 9.

[39] *Octauius* 36: 6; *igitur ut qui uiam terit, eo felicior quo leuior incedit, ita beatior in hoc itinere uiuendi, qui paupertate se subleuat, non sub diuitiarum onere suspirat.* 'As a man walks on a road, he is happier who travels lighter. So too is he happier on this journey of life who lightens himself by poverty, and does not pant under the burden of riches'.

ad periculum tamen solus es,[40] is strongly evocative of the futility of Commodus' bodyguard when he faces death while bathing alone.[41] Although it is also intended as a reference to the ultimate isolation of every single individual in the judgement of God, the potential identification with Commodus would give the term a much more immediate meaning. Minucius' aphorism *fulgere purpura, mente sordescere*,[42] succinctly encapsulates the crux of the denunciation, and would also fit well with the condemnations of Commodus' non-Christian biographers. It captures the perceived duality at the heart of Commodus' personality. Although born of Marcus Aurelius and possessing many of the key attributes required of a successful Roman ruler, his various despotic acts pointed towards an underlying dissolute mind.

If Minucius is attempting a specific personification of his critique, Commodus fits this archetype of the degenerate secular ruler better than any other candidate from the late second century. And if, for the purposes of argument, it is accepted that Commodus is indeed the target, then Minucius' line *quamlibet sis multo comitatu stipatus, ad periculum tamen solus es* would be an implied allusion to Commodus' notorious form of death at the end of December 192. This would necessarily follow a post-192 dating, and would narrow the period of production to post-193. Coupled with Minucius' probable location at Rome, this could be a potential contribution to the contextualisation of the *Octauius*. Needless to say, if Minucius is actually intending a more general interpretation of the worldliness of secular rulers, then the *terminus post quem* must remain with Gellius and Fronto of the late 160s/early 170s. The issue is open to discussion, but the personality of Commodus echoes in Minucius' words to a degree that is undoubtedly unsurpassed by the other occupants of the imperial throne in the years immediately predating Tertullian's *Apologeticum*.

4. The Christianity of the *Octauius*

If a pre-197 dating period for the *Octauius* is accepted as the necessary starting-point, then Minucius Felix becomes the earliest extant voice

---

[40] 'However large is your bodyguard surrounding you, in the face of danger you are alone'. *Octauius*, 37: 9.

[41] Cassius Dio, *Historia Romana*, 73: 22, Herodian, *Historia*, 1: 17; 11–12.

[42] 'To gleam in purple and be sordid in mind'. *Octauius*, 37: 10.

of Latin Christianity after the *Passio sanctorum Scillitanorum*, which in itself is dated to soon after the events of July 17ᵗʰ 180. Elucidation of the glimpse of the life of the Church presented in the *Octauius* now takes on further importance as the evidence of potentially the first document of Latin apologetics. But the *Octauius* is not detailed theology, and the general problem with the interpretation of apologetics as a genre lies in its comparatively minor level of insight into Christian practice. Minucius is more concerned with defending the beliefs of the Church by recourse to classical literature, and explaining Christian practice through analogies of well-known precedent. The *Octauius* never claims to be a complete portrayal of Christian life. As such, practical insights are often only indirect references, and much has to be deduced from strains of thought within the text. But nevertheless, the picture of the Church that can be expressed is a positive contribution to the situation of pre-Tertullianic Latin Christianity. This exploration is concerned with several key features. The structure is divided into the 'external' and 'internal' aspects of Minucius' Christianity; the outward perceptions of the Church in non-Christian eyes, and the forms of theological belief that occupied its inner life, and are brought out in the apologetic argument. Key to this theology is the presentation of the character of God, and the formulation of Christian eschatology.

For the following discussion, the *terminus ante quem* of 197 is assumed, while the *terminus post quem* of 193 is taken as the most likely possibility. The tentative contextualisation of the Christianity represented by the *Octauius* can thus be located at Rome, c. 193–197. The period is under the imperium of Septimius Severus after the tumultuous 'year of the five emperors' of 193, and the episcopate of Victor I of Rome. This latter observation is highly relevant. In his brief biographical information on Victor in the *De uiris illustribus*, Jerome mentions a work of his entitled *Super quaestione paschae*,[43] and suggests a strongly Latin provenance. Victor precedes Tertullian in Jerome's reference to the main Latin writers, where a level of distinction is clearly intended: *Tertullianus presbyter, nunc demum primus post Uictorem et Apollonium Latinorum ponitur.*[44] Victor is testifying to the existence of Latin as a viable mode of expression at this point in Christian literature, and more specifically at Rome itself. While this

---

[43] *De uiris illustribus*, 34.

[44] 'Tertullian the presbyter, now counted as first of the Latins after Victor and Apollonius'. *De uiris illustribus*, 53. The Latin text of the *De uiris illustribus* used throughout this work is Wilhelm Herding ed., *Hieronymi: De Viris Inlustribus Liber.*

is not sufficient evidence alone to postulate an influential movement from Greek into Latin at Rome during this period, it is certainly suggestive of Minucius' possible location in this setting. It helps to situate documents of Christian Latin in the years immediately prior to Tertullian's *Apologeticum*, and is specifically useful in relating Minucius' *Octauius* to another Latin work in the further location of late second century Roman Christianity. The *Octauius* would thus become less of an obscure text in an epoch of the Church that is more generally vocalised in Greek.

The public image of the Church

One of the central themes in the overall landscape of the *Octauius* is the address of common perceptions of Christianity, and its corresponding portrayal of the position of the Church within Roman culture. The attacks of Caecilius, combined with Octavius' Christian defence, can be examined to elucidate some of the key characteristics of Minucius' Church. In particular, there are several unambiguous references to the low social status of the early Christians. The recurrence of this theme throughout the *Octauius* points toward the likelihood of its being a prevalent smear within the anti-Christian arguments of Minucius' contemporaries. Caecilius sneeringly defines the Church as *homines... deploratae inlicitae ac desperatae factionis*,[45] and contends that the majority of Christian believers are encountered *de ultima faece*.[46] They refuse to accept the trappings of secular office, and can even be publicly recognised by their basic attire; an aspect hinted at in the derisive statement *honores et purpuras despiciunt, ipsi seminudi*.[47] From the perspective of the educated opponents of Christianity, represented here in the *Octauius* debate by the character of Caecilius, the Church is a rabble of illiterate paupers;[48] a gang of only semi-lawful people whose boorish behaviour is reflective of their senseless religious belief. A deliberately patronising tone is employed in assessing the place of Christian philosophical and theological exploration: *satis est pro pedibus aspicere, maxime indoctis inpolitis rudibus agrestibus; quibus non est datum intellegere ciuilia, multo magis denegatum*

---

[45] 'A gang of miserable and desperate criminals'. *Octauius*, 8: 3.

[46] 'From the farthest dregs of society'. *Octauius*, 8: 4. See also *de ultima statim plebe consistimus*, 'we take our place among the lowest class'. *Octauius*, 31: 6.

[47] 'Themselves half-naked, they despise honours and the purple robes of office'. *Octauius*, 8: 4.

[48] See also the Christian response, at *Octauius*, 16: 5.

est disserere diuina.[49] This can be linked with Minucius' ever-present need to confine his premises to the classical sources, as the Christians' general lack of education would have proved to be an almost insurmountable stumbling-block for intellectual religious dialogue. The Church is quite specifically being viewed in some quarters as socially inferior. Caecilius' attacks on the Christians may certainly read as snobbish in tone, but they emanate from a more widespread suspicion of the Church that is primarily based upon the undesirable public appearance of Christianity. It also becomes far easier to construct rumour and slander against such a group when their outward persona is so ill-respected. Much of the edifice of Caecilius' argument is built upon this position; the Church is so lowly in status, yet claims the sole support of God, and regardless of its poor appearance has the audacity to preach impending judgment against even the highest secular authorities.[50] Octavius' defence addresses the accusations of poverty and intellectual ignorance, but maintains the image that the Christians occupy some of the lowest rungs of Roman society. No embarrassment is displayed at this situation, but is instead replaced by a thorough awareness of repackaging the worldly impoverishment of the Christian believers as a natural counterpart of their divine favour.[51] There are two notable thematic strains in the textual current: true intellect is unaffected by earthly distinction,[52] and excessive possessions with temporal responsibilities only burden the human soul on its journey through life.[53] Minucius' Christian Octavius testifies to an almost ascetic glorification in worldly poverty: *ceterum quod plerique pauperes dicimur, non est infamia nostra, sed gloria; animus enim ut luxu soluitur, ita frugalitate firmatur.*[54] This relatively low social position is presented as a thoroughly positive characteristic of the Church, and while it allows Minucius to commend the glories of worldly poverty, it is still potentially reflective of the contemporary situation to a certain degree. Octavius' refusal to deny that many Christians are

---

[49] 'It is enough for the unlearned and unpolished, the uncultured and rude, to contemplate the things under their feet. Those to whom it is not given understanding of civic things, are much more denied the discussion of things divine'. *Octauius*, 12: 7.

[50] *Octauius*, 11: 1.

[51] Expressly defined in the New Testament at 1 Cor 1: 26–28.

[52] *Octauius*, 16: 5–6, 35: 5.

[53] *Octauius*, 36: 6, 37: 9.

[54] 'And as far as the majority of us are said to be poor, it is not to our disgrace, but to our glory. For as the mind is relaxed by luxury, so it is strengthened by frugality'. *Octauius*, 36: 3.

impoverished members of the lowest classes adds to the hint of the general public appearance of the Church in the popular perception. He repeats some common imputations of the Christian believers; they are *inliteratos, pauperes, inperitos*,[55] who have the impudence to *de rebus caelestibus disputare*.[56] The essence of the Christian response is that as humanity is born with nothing,[57] so too is reason and intellect restricted from no-one. Even the great philosophers themselves were previously ordinary men in like status with the Christians; something Octavius phrases with deliberate usage of Caecilius' terminology, as *plebeios, indoctos, seminudos*.[58] The heart of the issue is the innate equality of every human creation before God, as part of an argument that deals with the Christians' general lack of respectable philosophical education:

> *Unde apparet ingenium non dari facultatibus nec studio parari, sed cum ipsa mentis formatione generari. Nihil itaque indignandum uel dolendum, si quicumque de diuinis quaerat sentiat proferat, cum non disputantis auctoritas, sed disputationis ipsius ueritas requiratur.*[59]

Even though Minucius himself is the prime example of a highly educated Christian believer, the fact that Octavius does not attempt to deny that most Christians are *pauperes*, even *inliteratos*, is a manifestation of the social status of the late second century Latin Church. The actual state of affairs behind the *Octauius* text is impossible to pinpoint exactly, but some key observations can be made. It is likely that inasmuch as Caecilius' accusations of poverty and illegality against the Church are designed to blacken it in the eyes of its opponents, so too is Octavius' refusal to deny the social aspects of the argument a by-product of an existent Christian agenda. That is to say that the imputations of poverty actually play into the Christians' hands. Numerous statements in the documents that were slowly acquiring the status of 'Scripture' for the Christians deal with the subject of keeping oneself

---

[55] 'Illiterate, poor, ignorant'. *Octauius*, 16: 5.

[56] 'To discuss heavenly things'. *Octauius*, 16: 5.

[57] *Octauius*, 16: 5, 36: 5.

[58] 'Ignorant, half naked plebeians'. *Octauius*, 16: 5, following the Christians being depicted as *seminudos* at 8: 4 for refusing the robes of office.

[59] 'It is apparent that mental power is neither to be bought nor obtained through study, but is produced with the formation of the mind. And so there is no reason for indignation, or to be pained if anyone whatsoever inquires, thinks, or advances anything regarding divine things. For it is not about the authority of the disputant, but it is the truth of the disputation that is sought after'. *Octauius*, 16: 5–6.

unstained from the world.[60] In short, the Church is proud of its low status, and values the ideal of temporal poverty in the search for celestial wealth. Although Minucius' reticence in alluding to the Scriptures is a predominant feature of his text, the Scriptural inferences behind his treatment of Christian poverty can be traced. During the course of a justification of worldly frugality, Octavius argued: *aues sine patrimonio uiuunt et in diem pecua pascuntur: et haec nobis tamen nata sunt, qui omnia, si non concupiscimus, possidemus.*[61] This bears the likely influence of the Gospel injunctions regarding temporal anxieties:

Ἐμβλέψατε εἰς τὰ πετεινὰ τοῦ οὐρανοῦ ὅτι οὐ σπείρουσιν οὐδὲ θερίζουσιν οὐδὲ συνάγουσιν εἰς ἀποθήκας, καὶ ὁ πατὴρ ὑμῶν ὁ οὐράνιος τρέφει αὐτά·…μὴ οὖν μεριμνήσητε λέγοντες, Τί φάγωμεν; ἤ, Τί πίωμεν; ἤ, Τί περιβαλώμεθα; πάντα γὰρ ταῦτα τὰ ἔθνη ἐπιζητοῦσιν· οἶδεν γὰρ ὁ πατὴρ ὑμῶν ὁ οὐράνιος ὅτι χρῄζετε τούτων ἁπάντων. ζητεῖτε δὲ πρῶτον τὴν βασιλείαν [τοῦ θεοῦ] καὶ τὴν δικαιοσύνην αὐτοῦ, καὶ ταῦτα πάντα προστεθήσεται ὑμῖν.[62]

Minucius' Christianity is testifying to its pride in following the advice on possessions and wealth. There is also a distinct impression of rebellion against traditional social categories, emanating from the Scriptural precepts of remaining separate from the world. But Octavius' refusal to deny the generally low social status of the Church is not tantamount to admitting that every Christian was strictly impoverished. The imputations of the Church as being a religion of the *ultima faece* are not restricted to aspects of poverty, and the stains of Christian illegality further underlie its identification with the very lowest criminal classes. Such is the core of the connection with the *ultima faece*, and the abhorrence which Caecilius employs within his castigation of the Church of the *Octauius* debate. His anti-Christian invective prompts the identification of a veritable smear campaign.

The assault on Christianity, represented in the speech of Caecilius, revolves around several key accusations. The Church is described as

---

[60] Jas 1: 27. See also Mt 6: 24–33, Jn 15: 18–19, and 1 Tim 6: 10.

[61] 'Birds live without inheritance; cattle are fed day by day, and these things are produced for us. We possess every such thing, if we do not covet more'. *Octauius*, 36: 5.

[62] 'Look at the birds of the air; they do not sow, nor reap, nor gather into barns, but your Father in heaven feeds them…Therefore do not worry, saying "what will we eat?", or "what will we drink?" or "what will we wear?". For the Gentiles seek after all these things, and your Father in heaven knows that you need all these things. But first seek the kingdom [of God] and its righteousness, and all these things will be added to you'. Mt 6: 26–33.

a haven of incest, immorality, and illegality; where the secret covers of religion conceal a dangerous and growing perversion. The secrecy itself is a serious issue for the non-Christians looking in. The obscurity and impenetrability of Christian ritual contributes to its classification as *praua religio*.[63] In essence, this is part of the broad foundation of Christian apologetics. It becomes easier to advance the immoral slurs when the true system of worship is unknown; preparing the way for the elucidation of the apologist. The *Octauius* would be immediately redundant if it addressed non-existent issues in the religious controversies, and Caecilius' critique reads throughout as representations of prevalent arguments:

> *Cur etenim occultare et abscondere quicquid illud colunt magnopere nituntur, cum honesta semper publico gaudeant, scelera secreta sint? Cur nullas aras habent, templa nulla, nulla nota simulacra, numquam palam loqui, numquam libere congregari, nisi illud, quod colunt et interprimunt, aut puniendum est aut pudendum?*[64]

This betrays the deep privacy maintained by the Christian believers towards the Roman world, and there is a clear sense of a divide between the members of the Church and the surrounding populace. In Christian eyes they are the people of the *nationes*, the *gentes*; the Scriptural warnings of over-familiarity with non-believers[65] underlie a definition of the Christian world-view. A direct indicator of this is the Christian aversion to the public games and the theatre; dismissed by Octavius as *noxia blandimenta*.[66] A picture of the Church as a distinct entity within Roman culture is emerging,[67] fostered by the signs with which they may be distinguished. The contention *occultis se notis et insignibus noscunt*,[68] points towards the usage of recognised Christian emblems, and even the sign of the cross. The latter possibility is perhaps a likely inference.

---

[63] 'Perverse religion'. *Octauius*, 10: 1.

[64] 'Why do they struggle with great effort to hide and conceal whatever things they worship, when upright things always rejoice in public, and crimes exist in secret? Why do they have no altars, no temples, no familiar images, never talk in public, never assemble in the open, unless what they worship – and suppress – is either punishable or shameful'. *Octauius*, 10: 2.

[65] 2 Cor 6: 14–16.

[66] 'Offensive delights'. *Octauius*, 37: 11.

[67] *Non spectacula uisitis, non pompis interestis; conuiuia publica absque uobis.* 'You do not visit the shows, you take no part in the processions, you stay away from the public feasts'. *Octauius*, 12: 5.

[68] 'They recognise each other by secret signs and marks'. *Octauius*, 9: 2.

Tertullian testified to the practice of tracing the sign of the cross upon the forehead in the *De corona*; vouching for its usage in Latin Christianity potentially fifteen years after the *Octauius*:[69] *ad omnem progressum atque promotum, ad omnem aditum et exitum, ad uestitum, ad calciatum, ad lauacra, ad mensas, ad lumina, ad cubilia, ad sedilia, quacumque nos conuersatio exercet, frontem signaculo terimus.*[70] Both Tertullian's given details and the hint in the *Octauius* point towards the prominence of the sign of the cross in the Christian life. It is also further reflected in the physical posture of the Christian believer at prayer in the orant style.[71] On a more civic level, the comparatively primitive nature of the Church at the time of Minucius' writing is alluded to with the statement *nullas aras habent, templa nulla* – a possible sign that Christian structures are far from notable in the public sphere at late second century Rome. The common Christian practice of meeting at night further compounds the shrouded obscurity of the mysterious rites.[72] This secrecy provides the necessary grounding for the more colourful accusations present in Caecilius' critique. That the Christians referred to each other as *fratres* under the symbolic understanding of the believers as brothers and sisters,[73] is associated with the connection of incestuous affairs with Christian ceremony.[74] The observance of the Eucharist is perhaps alluded to by Caecilius with a garbled interpolation of child-killing and cannibalism at the heart of the *inhumanis cibis* practiced by the Church.[75] Accusations of infanticide are embodied with a gory depiction of the murder of a child encased in bread, followed by its ritual consumption. Caecilius' voicing of such allegations presupposes a certain degree of popularity in the contemporary situation, along

[69] Following the early 208 dating for the *De corona* of T. D. Barnes, *Tertullian*, p. 55.

[70] 'At every advance and forward step, at every entrance and exit, when putting on clothing and shoes, when bathing and sitting at table, in lighting lamps, lying in bed, sitting down, and at whatever regular activities we are employed with, we mark the sign upon the forehead'. *De corona*, 3: 4. Although Tertullian does not specifically refer to the cross under the *signaculo*, it is the most probable explanation.

[71] *Octauius*, 29: 8.

[72] *Octauius*, 8: 4. Pliny the Younger commented in his well-known letter to Trajan on the Christian practice of nocturnal meeting: *essent soliti stato die ante lucem conuenire*; 'they were in the habit of meeting together before dawn on an appointed day'. *Epistula*, 10: 96. Latin text in Betty Radice ed., *Pliny: Letters, Panegyricus*, Vol. 2.

[73] *Fratres uocamus*. *Octauius*, 31: 8. Caecilius also refers to the Christian usage of *fratres et sorores*, at *Octauius*, 9: 2.

[74] *Octauius*, 9: 2, 6–7.

[75] 'Inhuman meals'. *Octauius*, 8: 4.

with the accompanying denouncement *haec sacra sacrilegiis omnibus taetriora.*[76] Minucius seems to be responding to pre-existent contentions; the issue of the presence of Jesus at the Eucharist has very possibly been embellished by Christian opponents into imputations of ritual cannibalism.[77] If the case, this would betray some degree of dissemination of the rumours surrounding the Eucharist, as grains of truth elaborated on from the source of the body and blood of Jesus represented in the Christian celebration.

Octavius' counterblasts are concerned with establishing an acceptable system of Christian morality in direct opposition to the various anti-Christian slurs of Caecilius' forerunning diatribe. The virtues of chastity and monogamy are exalted,[78] and a radically divergent picture of Christian ceremony is painted. Octavius' rejection of the allegations of infant sacrifice prefigures one of the key structures in his vindication of the truth of Christian worship:

> *Illum iam uelim conuenire, qui initiari nos dicit aut credit de caede infantis et sanguine. Putas posse fieri, ut tam molle, tam paruulum corpus fata uulnerum capiat? Ut quisquam illum rudem sanguinem nouelli et uixdum hominis caedat fundat exhauriat? Nemo hoc potest credere nisi qui possit audere.*[79]

The statement *nemo hoc potest credere nisi qui possit audere* directly poses the opening of the *tu quoque* arm of his Christian defence. The *tu quoque* is a recurrent feature throughout Latin apologetics, and originates with this primary occurrence of Octavius' response to the accusations of infanticide and incest.[80] It is the most self-assured for-

---

[76] 'These "sacred rites" are more foul than all sacrilege'. *Octauius*, 9: 5.

[77] However, for another interpretation of the imputations of cannibalism aimed at the Christian feasts, see Andrew McGowan, 'Eating People: Accusations of Cannibalism Against Christians in the Second Century'. McGowan specifically deals with the contribution of Minucius at pp. 420–21.

[78] *Unius matrimonii uinculo libenter inhaeremus, cupiditate procreandi aut unam scimus aut nullam.* 'We gladly adhere to the bond of a single marriage; with desire for procreation we know either one woman or none'. *Octauius*, 31: 5. Also present at *Octauius*, 35: 6.

[79] 'Now I would like to address the man who either says or believes that we are initiated by the murder and blood of a child. Do you think it possible that someone can injure its tender, tiny body with fatal wounds? That anyone should chop up, pour, and drain the innocent blood of a young babe only just born? No-one can believe it, unless capable of doing it'. *Octauius*, 30: 1.

[80] *Octauius*, 30–31.

mula of the apologetic defence, and exemplifies the Christian advocate at ease in the use of secular sources and precedents. From this perspective, the character of Minucius Felix himself betrays much about his contemporary Church. He is both highly educated and fully comfortable with Christianity in spite of the imputations of low social status, and the poor rhetorical quality of the Scriptural writings. He is the strongest piece of evidence that Christianity was spreading to the intellectual classes, regardless of the primitive status of the public image of the Church. The actual degree of the membership growth of Christianity cannot be specifically identified, but can be noted from comments in the *Octauius* debate. Caecilius disparagingly remarks that *per uniuersum orbem sacraria ista taeterrima impiae coitionis adolescunt.*[81] Octavius' corresponding treatment *et quod in dies nostri numerus augetur,*[82] points toward to the identification of a steadily, and noticeably, developing Christian minority.

The *Octauius* also provides several insights into the Christian understanding of death, along with its attendant ritual and ceremonial practices. Caecilius refers to the Christians' noticeable lack of fear of death as nothing more than a perversely illogical reaction to the prospect of mortality; *dum mori post mortem timent, interim mori non timent.*[83] Their attitude towards death is presented as little short of bewildering to this manifestation of the non-Christian observer. He also mentions a Christian avoidance of cremation from theological principles, which is again condemned for its illogicality, due to the unavoidable decomposition of the earthly body.[84] Christian eschatology is then ridiculed for its acceptance of bodily resurrection.[85] Octavius addresses these issues in turn, and denies any purported Christian aversion to cremation; he mentions no specific theological problems with the practice, but advocates the Christian support for inhumation instead.[86] A desire on the part of the Christians to depart from the customs and ceremony of Roman burial is tangible. Such are the funeral pyres, and ostentatious pub-

---

[81] 'Throughout the whole world the foul shrines of this impious conspiracy increase'. *Octauius*, 9: 1.

[82] 'And as far as our numbers increase daily'. *Octauius*, 31: 7.

[83] 'While death after death they fear, they are not afraid of death in the present'. *Octauius*, 8: 5.

[84] *Octauius*, 11: 4.

[85] *Octauius*, 11: 7. Discussed below, pp. 61–2.

[86] *Octauius*, 34: 10.

lic displays of mourning. In direct opposition to this, the Christian burial rites are solemn, quiet, and as free from the traditional funerary paraphernalia as possible.[87] The clash between grief at losing a fellow-believer, but also controlled joy in anticipation of the righteous judgment of God, leads to a demure and withdrawn Christian attitude. It is another aspect in the reserved public image of Christianity:

> At enim nos exsequias adornamus eadem tranquillitate qua uiuimus, nec adnectimus arescentem coronam, sed a deo aeternis floribus uiuidam sustinemus, quieti modesti, dei nostri liberalitate securi, spem futurae felicitatis, fide praesentis eius maiestatis animamur.[88]

This follows from Caecilius' assault on Christian funerary rites,[89] which specifically pinpointed and criticised the meagre conventions accompanying the body of the deceased. The impression throughout Octavius' Christian response is that the Church is deliberately departing from the traditional ceremonial attached to bodily death, in favour of a more transcendent understanding; something made manifest in the dearth of attendant Christian rituals, with the emphasis instead being on the salvific work of God. The numerous references to the Christian perception of death throughout the *Octauius* are suggestive of its prominence in the key areas of noticeable difference between the Christians and their non-Christian counterparts. In effect, the divergent understanding of death provides a window into the relationship between Christianity and the traditional customs of Roman religion. The complete Christian aversion to death is such that their abhorrence of all forms of slaughter leads them to refuse to attend the arena, and even to use animal blood within food preparation.[90] This is directly reminiscent of the commands to the Gentile believers at the so-called 'Council of Jerusalem' in the Lukan Acts narrative: ἀπέχεσθαι εἰδωλοθύτων καὶ αἵματος καὶ πνικτῶν

---

[87] *Octauius*, 38: 3–4.

[88] 'We prepare our funeral rites with the same tranquillity in which we live; we do not tie a garland that withers, but by God we sustain the lively garland of everlasting flowers. With quietness and restraint, secure in the kindness of our God, we animate our hope for future happiness by faith in his present majesty'. *Octauius*, 38: 4.

[89] *Octauius*, 12: 6.

[90] *Octauius*, 30: 6.

καὶ πορνείας, ἐξ ὧν διατηροῦντες ἑαυτοὺς εὖ πράξετε.[91] The command to abstain from food sacrificed to idols can also be traced within the *Octauius*,[92] alongside the Christian censure of fornication.[93]

A picture of Minucius' Christianity can be constructed from the evidence of the *Octauius* debate. The Church appears as a withdrawn and mysterious religious society, that combines with its low social status in contributing to the imputation of numerous criminal acts. Criminality is the crucial smear, and more specific accusations descend from this overriding theme. But inside, the Church glories in its worldly poverty, and remains faithful to its intellectually-condemned Scriptures. Regarding the methodology of the *Octauius* as a whole, although the Scriptural references may not be explicit, they still lie at the heart of the expounded beliefs and practices. Minucius himself testifies to the flourishing intellectual component of the community; and although the terse and unpolished Scriptures are best avoided for his argument, they nevertheless provide the ultimate grounding of his belief. He also represents Christianity in a period of substantial growth and development – the increase in numbers reflects a growing dissemination into Roman society, even if statements such as *nullas aras habent, templa nulla, nulla nota simulacra, numquam palam loqui, numquam libere congregari*,[94] reference a still obscure status. It is this insecure position that feels the effects of the continued dangers of persecution. Yet the Church is not cowed, and Minucius applauds the courage of the victims of persecution and assault. Any feeling of pathos at the loss of religious compatriots is immediately dispelled; the execution of a Christian is instead a *pulchrum spectaculum*,[95] in the eyes of both God and the Church. The dominant analogy is to the trials of war; *quis non miles sub oculis imperatoris audacius periculum prouocet?*[96] And although the Christian victim may seem *miser*,[97] Minucius reverts the terminology back on the accusers; the true *miseri*,[98]

---

[91] 'That you abstain from what has been sacrificed to idols, and from blood, from what has been strangled, and from fornication; by observing these things you will do well'. Act 15: 29.

[92] *Octauius*, 38: 1, possibly reflective of the influence of 1 Cor 10: 14–21.

[93] *Octauius*, 31: 5.

[94] *Octauius*, 10: 2.

[95] 'A beautiful spectacle'. *Octauius*, 37: 1.

[96] 'What soldier would not challenge danger more boldly under the eyes of the general?'. *Octauius*, 37: 2.

[97] 'Miserable/unfortunate'. *Octauius*, 37: 3.

[98] *Octauius*, 37: 6.

contrasted with the victorious Christian *dei miles*.[99] Another possible Scriptural allusion could lie underneath the surface of Minucius' statement *itaque ut aurum ignibus, sic nos discriminibus arguimur.*[100] In spite of the external difficulties, internally the Church is thriving. Minucius portrays the Church as one comfortable with both the classics and the Scriptures; philosophical and theological exploration united in the Christian worldview. Theologies are developing, and a Christian understanding of purpose is taking root, emphasised by the external implications of its eschatology in particular. Following is a exploration of some of the theological tenets alluded to in the *Octauius*. The articulation of God is first to be considered, followed by the insights provided by Minucius into Christian eschatology.

God

After the distinctive incidence that the *Octauius* never mentions the person of Jesus by name, the presentation of the character and attributes of God becomes the key hallmark of Christian theology. Neither is the economy of salvation explicitly discussed, cementing Christian monotheism as the fundamental issue in the theological argument. The particulars of Minucius' debate point towards the centrality of such topics as monotheism, providence, and predestination in the surrounding religious dialogue. The theological principles of the *Octauius* take on a high degree of significance as possibly the earliest extant Latin contribution in the field of the evolution of early Christian theology.

Caecilius exemplifies a scornful understanding of the precepts of monotheism and providence, and formulates a deliberately ridiculous picture of the Christian God. The singular *deus unicus* is satirically depicted as *solitarius, destitutus*;[101] a mocking exhibition of a supposedly omnipotent deity. The lofty Christian description of one God alone is disdainfully reduced to a somewhat forlorn and lonely figure. This monotheistic tenet appears in the *Octauius* to represent a divisive bone of contention between Christian belief and the traditional gods

---

[99] 'Soldier of God'. *Octauius*, 37: 3.

[100] 'And so, like gold with fire, we are proven by ordeals'. *Octauius*, 36: 9. There could be an allusion to 1 Pet 1: 7, but the general metaphor of gold being refined by fire is not a purely Christian one. See elsewhere with Seneca, *De prouidentia*, 5: 10; *ignis aurum probat, miseria fortes uiros.* 'Fire tests gold; suffering brave men'. Latin text in John W. Basore ed., *Seneca: De Providentia*. See further the note of Clarke, *The Octavius of Marcus Minucius Felix*, p. 120, n. 619.

[101] 'Solitary, destitute'. *Octauius*, 10: 3.

of Roman religion. Within a religious worldview that is ultimately based upon the propitiation of numerous conspicuous deities, the more intangible prospect of Christian monotheism poses an almost unbridgeable jump from Caecilius' perspective. Octavius' employment of an argument from the natural world is intended to achieve the recognition that society relies upon a sole leader for survival, and is thus reflective of the overall sovereignty of God.[102] Numerous examples are quoted as evidence of the innate autocracy of natural life, contrasted with the inevitable conflict that occurs between rivals for supreme power; *quando umquam regni societas aut cum fide coepit aut sine cruore discessit?*[103] These are incidences often cited as Minucius' denunciation of joint imperial Roman rule, with the resulting tentative conclusions as to possible dating scenarios. But they should rather be viewed solely as proofs in his monotheistic establishment, with less direct bearing on the contemporary imperial situation. The only implicit argument is the criticism of polytheistic belief that naturally corresponds with the advocacy of monotheism; *tu in caelo summam potestatem diuidi credas.*[104]

Under the ideological conviction that the Roman empire occupied the farthest reaches of the civilised world,[105] one relatively obscure deity claiming prominence over the multiplicity of well-known characters in traditional Roman worship is a staggering prospect. Caecilius directs a question towards the Christian expression of the power of God; *nonne Romani sine uestro deo imperant regnant, fruuntur orbe toto uestrique dominantur?*[106] Octavius characteristically responds by focusing primarily on the association of philosophy with the Christian standpoints, in order to diminish the sense of novelty encountered with the anti-Christian contentions.[107] The gulf between the opposing articulations

---

[102] *Octauius*, 18: 5–7.

[103] 'When did joint monarchy ever begin with trust, or end without bloodshed?'. *Octauius*, 18: 6.

[104] 'Do you believe that in heaven the greatest power is divided?'. *Octauius*, 18: 7.

[105] A situation commonly ascribed to its piety; *sic dum uniuersarum gentium sacra suscipiunt, etiam regna meruerunt.* 'Thus, because they observe the sacred rites of every people, they gain sovereignty'. *Octauius*, 6: 3.

[106] 'Surely the Romans without your God reign, rule, enjoy the whole world, and are masters of you?'. *Octauius*, 12: 5. The origin of the Christian God is also questioned by Caecilius; as *quem non gens libera, non regna, non saltem Romana superstitio nouerunt?*. 'Whom no free nation, no kingdom, even no Roman superstition knows?'. *Octauius*, 10: 3.

[107] *Octauius*, 19.

of the divine character is evident from Caecilius' sardonic treatment of Christian providence:

> *At etiam Christiani quanta monstra, quae portenta confingunt! Deum illum suum, quem nec ostendere possunt nec uidere, in omnium mores, actus omnium, uerba denique et occultas cogitationes diligenter inquirere, discurrentem scilicet atque ubique praesentem; molestum illum uolunt, inquietum, inpudenter etiam curiosum, siquidem adstat factis omnibus, locis omnibus intererrat, cum nec singulis inseruire possit per uniuersa districtus nec uniuersis sufficere in singulis occupatus.*[108]

Although this depiction of God almost borders on slapstick in its frivolity, it nevertheless addresses a deeply important concern in Christian theology. Faith in God's providential involvement in the world is one of the vital principles upon which Octavius' theological establishment is based, reflecting its central location in Christian belief. The interjectory statement *erras, o homo, et falleris*,[109] is employed to add weight to Octavius' refutation of the impotence of God; a noticeable feature in itself within a Christian speech that otherwise reads as generally calm and considered, and lacking in such interjectory outbursts. God is portrayed as all-encompassing, therefore able to be present everywhere at once. The common metaphorical image is that of the sun, whose rays shine over the whole earth; *pariter praesens ubique interest et miscetur omnibus*.[110] It is hardly a watertight analogy, but is fit for the purpose – God is *quanto magis*[111] than even the life-giving rays of the sun. The usage of arguments from the natural world is a continual theme in Octavius' development of Christian precepts; the recalcitrance to overtly cite Scripture is replaced by naturalistic philosophical reasoning, where God can be traced throughout aspects of creation. The other notable analogy in the *Octauius'* defence of God and creation is that of the well-organized house,

---

[108] 'But still what extravagant tales the Christians fabricate! That god of theirs, whom they can neither show nor see, diligently scrutinises the habits and actions of all men, indeed even into their words and hidden thoughts, dashing around to be present everywhere. They are willing for him to be troublesome, restless, to pry shamelessly and assist in everything that is done, wandering through every place. He can neither take care of particulars because he is distracted by universal things, and is not capable of managing these because he is occupied by the particulars'. *Octauius*, 10: 5.

[109] 'You err, o man, and are deceived'. *Octauius*, 32: 7.

[110] 'Equally present everywhere, and intermingled with all things'. *Octauius*, 32: 8.

[111] 'How much more'. *Octauius*, 32: 9.

which consequently points towards its far greater designer.[112] God is not a remote deity out of the reach of humanity, but is omnipresent; transcendent through *omnia caelestia terrenaque*.[113] The Scriptural basis for the Christian doctrine of providence is strongly linked with the sovereignty of God, and Octavius' argument follows along similar lines. God is the *speculator omnium*,[114] who is even *interest cogitationibus nostris*.[115] Far from the interfering nuisance of Caecilius' mocking critique, the character of God is that of a beloved sovereign ruler. Yet the two articulations remain highly similar; a fact that testifies to the ever-present complication on the subject of Christian providence. For Minucius, however, the ubiquitous assistance of God is no annoyance, and actually lies behind the composition of the *Octauius* itself. The eloquence of Octavius' Christian defence is expressly traced to its providential underpinning, with the words *habet dei munus eximium a quo et inspiratus orauit et obtinuit adiutus*.[116] The permeation of the sovereignty of God into human life is a deeply significant tenet, and one of the key insights provided by Minucius into personal Christian belief. The proximity of God is a critical aspect of faith, voiced by Octavius with the dictum *non tantum sub illo agimus, sed et cum illo, ut prope dixerim, uiuimus*.[117] This is further associated in the *Octauius* debate with the joint concepts of fate and predestination. In the course of his attempted establishment of chance as the fundamental law of the universe,[118] Caecilius poses the loaded questions of indiscriminate natural disasters, seemingly arbitrary fatal accidents, and the blessings of good fortune upon ill-deserving men.[119] He attacks the perception of the *iniquum iudicem*,[120] who unfairly punishes those whom he himself has left without any

---

[112] *Octauius*, 18: 4.

[113] 'All things in heaven and earth'. *Octauius*, 32: 7.

[114] 'The observer of all'. *Octauius*, 32: 9.

[115] 'Present in our thoughts'. *Octauius*, 32: 9.

[116] 'He has an exceptional gift from God, by whose breath he speaks and by whose aid he prevails'. *Octauius*, 40: 3.

[117] 'Not only do we act under him, but I may almost say, we live with him'. *Octauius*, 32: 9.

[118] *Uariis et lubricis casibus soluta legibus fortuna dominatur.* 'With various and inconstant accidents, and by unbridled laws, chance is in control'. *Octauius*, 5: 13.

[119] *Octauius*, 5: 9–13.

[120] 'The unjust judge'. *Octauius*, 11: 6.

other choice in life.[121] Much of the argument is directly lifted and summarised from Cicero's *De natura deorum*, and the general course of Cotta's attack on Stoic ideals of providence.[122] Octavius' response is to dismiss the prospect of injustice, and instead to advance the contention that everyone is judged according to his own personal action. The complications of any expression of predestination and free-will are present, and Octavius advocates God's prior knowledge of the personal characters of each individual in his ultimate tabling of retributive punishment.[123] There is a tension in Caecilius' argument of the unjust judge, which reveals itself in Octavius' response. The role of human action is not at all clearly defined in the Christian understanding of salvation and judgment. The discussion of fate and predestination is deliberately brief, and the reader is pointed towards the other work of Minucius Felix, now unfortunately lost to history.[124]

The primary concern of the *Octauius* is to ally Christian belief with cultural and philosophical precedents, and so to dispel any notions of Christianity as either novel or unnatural using recognised philosophical terminology. The immediate expression of this throughout the text is the continually reinforced appropriation of secular philosophical positions in support of Christian principles. Many of the arguments can be found originally in Cicero's *De natura deorum*;[125] selectively copied into Minucius' Christian framework in order to form the necessary evidence in his researched defence of Christianity. The philosophical examples are utilised essentially as incidences of proto-Christian belief, and can be reduced to point towards Minucius' theological intentions. They can be isolated to define some important insights into the theological tenets under consideration. In the

---

[121] *Qui sortem in hominibus puniat, non uoluntatem.* 'Who inflicts punishment on men for their lot in life, rather than their will'. *Octauius*, 11: 6.

[122] *De natura deorum*, 3: 32–39.

[123] *Octauius*, 36: 2.

[124] *Ac de fato satis uel, si pauca pro tempore, disputaturi alias et uerius et plenius.* 'A few words are enough on fate for this occasion; it will be discussed more fully and completely elsewhere'. *Octauius*, 36: 2. Jerome mentions a treatise circulating under the title *De fato* or *Contra mathematicos*, purportedly of the authorship of Minucius, but rejects it as authentic on the grounds of a stylistic comparison with the *Octauius*. He wrote: *qui, cum sit et ipse diserti hominis, non mihi uidetur cum superioris libri stylo conuenire.* 'Although it is itself the work of an eloquent man, it does not seem to me to fit with the style of the above book'. *De uiris illustribus*, 58. It is also mentioned elsewhere by Jerome, at *Epistula*, 70: 5, with a similar description of its questionable authenticity.

[125] *De natura deorum*, 1: 25ff.

Christian theological understanding, God is primarily the universal Father; *patrem diuum atque hominum.*[126] A famous citation from Homer is employed in the depiction of God as *parens omnium.*[127] The continual purpose of the Christian appropriation of philosophical sources is to enforce the understanding of the omnipresence and universality of God; he is *mens et ratio et spiritus,*[128] *animus per uniuersam rerum naturam commeans et intentus.*[129] He is infinite,[130] and the creator of everything existent in the natural world,[131] including the falsely-titled gods of Roman religion.[132] Minucius is fully at home in the usage of such philosophical terms as *aethera,*[133] *ratio,*[134] and *naturalis lex*[135] to contribute to his Christian articulation of God. An allusion from Plato's *Timaeus* is portrayed as most akin to the Christian theological perspectives, and Plato himself is almost wholly appropriated for the Christian cause: *Platoni apertior de deo et rebus ipsis et nominibus oratio est et quae tota esset caelestis, nisi persuasionis ciuilis nonnunquam admixtione sordesceret.*[136] This is Minucius' concern of reconciling Christianity with philosophy at its most focused. By his perpetual recourse to philosophical sources, Minucius has constructed a Christian definition of the divine character without the usage of partisan Christian texts. The concluding words of Octavius after citing the examples are *eadem fere et ista, quae nostra sunt,*[137] and the Christian presentation of

---

[126] 'Father of gods and men'. *Octauius,* 19: 1.

[127] 'Parent of all'. *Octauius,* 19: 1. The Homeric reference is to *Odyssey,* 18: 136.

[128] 'Mind, reason and spirit'. *Octauius,* 19: 2.

[129] '[He is] soul, permeating and extended throughout the entire nature of things'. *Octauius,* 19: 6. Other English translations, such as Clarke (1974) and Rendall (1931) have rendered *per uniuersam rerum naturam* as 'throughout the entire universe of nature' and 'through the entire nature of nature' respectively. Both have failed to include the genitive plural *rerum* in the translation; creating the rather obscure concept in English of the 'universe of nature'. Another possible translation of Minucius' Latin could be 'the entire nature of things', suggesting God's pervading of all created matter as the universal Soul.

[130] *Octauius,* 19: 7.

[131] *Octauius,* 19: 14.

[132] *Octauius,* 19: 8. Elsewhere they are defined as demons mistaken for gods, with their worship being nothing short of sacrilege. *Octauius,* 26: 8–27: 8.

[133] 'Ether'. *Octauius,* 19: 10.

[134] 'Reason'. *Octauius,* 19: 10.

[135] 'Natural law'. *Octauius,* 19: 10.

[136] 'The discourse of Plato is clearer regarding God with actual facts and names, and could be altogether divine, were it not tarnished by the occasional mixture with political beliefs'. *Octauius,* 19: 14.

[137] 'These [opinions] are almost the same as our own'. *Octauius,* 19: 15.

God is thus established. This also forms an effective cross-section of the purpose of the *Octauius* itself; although the understanding of God is the key hallmark of Christian belief in the absence of any Christology, even this is solely supported by non-Christian evidences.

Another key characteristic in the articulation of God is the prevalence of apophasis in the explanation of the divine character. It is a fairly common mode of expression in early Latin apologetic, and can be particularly noted elsewhere with Tertullian and Arnobius of Sicca.[138] Classical precedence is cited in support of God being *infinitum et inmensum*,[139] and that the true divine form can never be adequately grasped by human comprehension.[140] If mankind is incapable of viewing even the sun, how much brighter is the magnitude of God?[141] The employment of a commonly-used Platonic reference[142] is included as further justification of the apophatic argument.[143] The centrality of apophasis is made evident in the most specific wording of the character of God in the *Octauius*:

> *Hic nec uideri potest: uisu clarior est; nec conprehendi potest nec aestimari:*[144] *sensibus maior est, infinitus inmensus et soli sibi tantus, quantus est, notus. Nobis uero ad intellectum pectus angustum est, et ideo sic eum digne aestimamus, dum inaestimabilem dicimus. Eloquar quemadmodum sentio: magnitudinem dei qui se putat nosse, minuit, qui non uult minuere, non nouit.*[145]

This apophatic description of God originates from a well justified Scriptural foundation, and is one of the clearest vestiges of the influ-

---

[138] Tertullian, *Apologeticum*, 17: 2–3. Arnobius, *Aduersus nationes*, 1: 31; 1–2, 3: 12; 3, 7: 34.

[139] 'Infinite and immeasurable'. *Octauius*, 19: 5.

[140] *Octauius*, 19: 13–14.

[141] *Octauius*, 32: 5–6.

[142] *Timaeus*, 28C. See also below, pp. 95–6.

[143] *Octauius*, 19: 14.

[144] The other formulation of *nec conprehendi potest nec aestimari*, is *nec conprehendi: tactu purior est; nec aestimari*. I have adhered to the former, and the accompanying critical apparatus in the edition of Kytzler (1992).

[145] 'God cannot be seen; he is too bright for sight. Neither can he be comprehended or measured; he is too great for our senses. Infinite, immeasurable; of such great magnitude known to himself alone. Our heart is too small to truly understand, so therefore we only measure him appropriately when we call him immeasurable. I speak just as I feel – whoever thinks he knows the greatness of God, is diminishing it. Whoever is not willing to diminish it, does not know it'. *Octauius*, 18: 8–9.

ence of Old Testament theology within Minucius' presentation of Christian belief. Aside from the anthropomorphisms of the early Genesis narratives,[146] imputations of God carrying a human persona are elsewhere quashed.[147] The picture of human encounters with the divine are shrouded in symbolic gestures of purity, as God is so wholly 'other' to human comprehension.[148] Minucius' address of the unfathomable *magnitudinem dei* is reminiscent of a prior Scriptural formulation.[149] It is not necessarily a direct allusion, but does point towards the influence of a pre-existent theological tradition, which originates in turn from its Scriptural definition. This Christian apophasis demonstrates the extent of its divergence from some key aspects of traditional Roman polytheistic belief; the depiction of God as *infinitum et inmensum* could scarcely be further removed from the humanised qualities of the pantheon of Roman deities. This contrast also lies at the heart of Minucius' elevation of the classical philosophers over the poets within a system of theological merit. The contribution of the poets to theological development is seen as nothing more than a worthless assemblage of *fabulas et errores*,[150] while the selected citations from the philosophers are undergoing a period of positive Christian appropriation. Minucius is building a clear order of distinction between the rival systems of belief; Christianity attains prominence for the closest proximity in truly relating the character of the divine, the philosophers are led by Plato in almost arriving at the similar level of understanding, while the poets are yet still weighed down by their childish representations of heavenly matters. At the very bottom of the order of distinction, the gods of Roman religion follow the stories of the poets.

But there is also a theological dichotomy between the apophatic depiction of God on the one hand, and the concept of the *imago dei* on the other. It comes to the fore of Octavius' speech in his address of the Christian refusal to construct statues representing the divine character. It would be redundant to attempt the building of a statue of God, Octavius argues, since *sit dei homo ipse simulacrum*.[151] The

---

[146] The very human image of God walking in the garden in the evening breeze. Gen 3: 8.

[147] As, for example, at Num 23: 19.

[148] As in the theophanic narratives of Ex 3: 2–15, and 19: 9–24.

[149] Job 11: 7–9.

[150] 'Fables and errors'. *Octauius*, 23: 1.

[151] 'Man himself is an image of God'. *Octauius*, 32: 1. Compare Gen 1: 26.

Scriptural origins closely underlie the surface of the text. However, there is no attempt in the *Octauius* to reconcile the apophatic presentation of God with the implications of the *imago dei*; its inclusion in Octavius' defensive encapsulation is solely in relation to the lack of a Christian iconography of God. The various approaches to the character of God in the *Octauius* can be isolated to provide some important insights into its underlying Christian theological belief. There is a clear sense of divergence from traditional Roman sacrificial understandings of the divine, in favour of a far more remote and transcendent deity. Yet the articulation of providence allows for a more complete extent of divine influence in the world, and a level of permeation that far surpasses the anthropomorphised gods of Roman religion. Christianity is *lucem sapientiae et ueritatis*,[152] with the great philosophers of antiquity as its ultimate forbears. The association of Christianity with Judaism is dismissed,[153] and never used in support of Christian origins to the degree of the appropriation of philosophical sources. This dual heritage of Christianity is only united by the contention that the philosophers were influenced by the ancient prophets.[154] The *Octauius* testifies to a sense of pride in the lack of Christian *delubra et aras*,[155] and postulates instead the true unadulterated worship of the universal God; *idem enim omnium deus est.*[156] The departure from the traditional constructions of sacrifice and propitiation in religious devotion leads to a description of Christian worship as the continual action of a consecrated life. It is another doctrine with a strong Scriptural foundation.[157] The demands, achievements, and implications of religious worship are comprehensively re-defined:

> *Igitur, qui innocentiam colit, deo supplicat; qui iustitiam, deo libat;*
> *qui fraudibus abstinet, propitiat deum; qui hominem periculo subripit,*

---

[152] 'The light of wisdom and truth'. *Octauius*, 1: 4.

[153] *Ita prius eos deseruisse conprehendes quam esse desertos.* 'You will understand that they deserted [God] first before they were deserted'. *Octauius*, 33: 5.

[154] *De diuinis praedicationibus prophetarum umbram interpolatae ueritatis imitati sint.* 'They have imitated and distorted a shadow of truth from the divine predictions of the prophets'. *Octauius*, 34: 5.

[155] 'Shrines and altars'. *Octauius*, 32: 1.

[156] 'For he is the same God of all'. *Octauius*, 33: 3.

[157] As examples, see Mt 9: 13, and Mk 12: 32–34.

optimam uictimam caedit. Haec nostra sacrificia, haec dei sacra sunt; sic apud nos religiosior est ille qui iustior.[158]

Since the *Octauius* deliberately refrains from mentioning the name of Jesus, it is these theological particulars that form the prominent features of Christian belief. Key tenets like monotheism, providence, and predestination support the Christian belief in the nature-pervading universal God. Although God cannot be described as anything other than *infinitum* or *inmensum*, humanity bears the created marks of his *simulacrum*, and exists inexpressibly bound up with him.[159] Christianity is charged with the responsibility of representing God to the errant world, and in turn, the task of the apologist is to articulate the divine persona using recognisable imagery and terminology.

Eschatology

Following from the apologetic elucidation of the character of God, the other primary theological issue addressed in the *Octauius* is the Christian perspective on the end of the world. It is prominent in Minucius' debate due to its significance in the question of the relationship of Christianity and Roman society; such issues as judgement, damnation, and the ultimate destruction of the earth are often key aspects in inter-religious dialogue. But the implications of eschatology are not solely confined to the theological or philosophical spheres, and Minucius' address of these eschatological principles speaks to a controversy at the heart of the Christian understanding of its location in the surrounding non-Christian world. Within the arguments of the debate between Caecilius and Octavius, Minucius broaches the topics of the destruction of the universe by fire, the Christian conception of salvation/damnation, and the consequences of the acceptance of the doctrine of bodily resurrection.

---

[158] 'Therefore whoever cultivates innocence supplicates God, whoever practices justice offers libations to God, and whoever abstains from deceit propitiates God. Whoever rescues his fellow-man from danger slays the perfect offering. These are our sacrifices; these our sacred rites to God. Thus, with us, the most religious person is whoever is most just'. *Octauius*, 32: 3. A more theologically developed understanding of the Christian *uir iustus* is a subject of Lactantius, at *Diuinae institutiones*, 6: 12. See below, pp. 195–7.

[159] *Ubique non tantum nobis proximus, sed infusus est.* 'Not only is he near to us everywhere, but he is infused within us'. *Octauius*, 32: 7.

The Christian pronouncement of fiery destruction upon the entirety of the natural world is condemned by Caecilius as impudent and offensive; nothing more than a *furiosa opinione*.[160] Christian perceptions are castigated by the shameful likening to ridiculous *aniles fabulas*,[161] in prophesying the eventual annihilation of the universe irrespective of the transient position of humanity: *anceps malum et gemina dementia, caelo et astris, quae sic relinquimus ut inuenimus, interitum denuntiare, sibi mortuis exstinctis, qui sic ut nascimur et interimus, aeternitatem repromittere.*[162] Octavius' response characteristically employs philosophical allusions in the Christian defence, and firmly endorses the prospect of universal destruction as a necessary act of God.[163] It is very much a core Christian doctrine, which is reflected in the incidences of Scriptural foundation.[164] But in typical Minucian style, the Scriptural support remains under the surface, and is subordinated to the selective mentions of the theories of Stoics, Epicureans, and Plato. The Christian position is that the end of the universe will be brought about in a fiery blaze,[165] with the final intervention of the Creator. This is then interlinked with the concept of divine retributive judgement. The exclusivity of Christian claims of eternal salvation is denounced by Caecilius,[166] and he urges the Christians to rather judge the basis of their afterlife on their situation in the present; how can they be so eternally blessed when they are so forsaken as mortals? The Christian *miseri* are thus condemned as tragically doomed to enjoy neither present nor future life.[167] Octavius dismisses these particular claims with the common Christian response of the positive effects of worldly trials; *fortitudo*

---

[160] 'Wild idea'. *Octauius*, 11: 2.

[161] 'Old wives tales'. *Octauius*, 11: 2.

[162] 'It is a twofold evil, a double madness, to denounce destruction on the sky and the stars which we leave just as we find them, and to guarantee eternity for themselves when they are dead and destroyed, though we die just as we are born'. *Octauius*, 11: 3.

[163] *Ita nihil mirum est, si ista moles ab eo, quo exstructa est, destruatur.* 'Therefore it is not at all surprising, if this massive structure should be destroyed by whom it was made'. *Octauius*, 34: 4.

[164] 2 Pet 3: 12. See also Is 66: 15–16, 2 Thes 1: 5–8, Apoc 18: 8.

[165] *In uim ignis abiturum.* 'Disappearing in the power of fire'. *Octauius*, 34: 2.

[166] *Hoc errore decepti beatam sibi, ut bonis, et perpetem uitam mortui pollicentur, ceteris, ut iniustis, poenam sempiternam.* 'By this error they are led astray. They promise themselves, as the just, a blessed everlasting life; for the others, as the unjust, everlasting punishment'. *Octauius*, 11: 5.

[167] *Ita nec resurgitis miseri nec interim uiuitis.* 'Therefore, poor fools, you neither rise again nor live in the meantime'. *Octauius*, 12: 6.

enim infirmitatibus roboratur.[168] Divine judgment on the world is upheld as a universal doctrine in spite of the comparative obscurity of Christianity, and the celebrated Roman *pietas* will not lessen the depth of eternal punishment against the unconverted individual:

> *Eos autem merito torqueri, qui deum nesciunt, ut impios, ut iniustos, nisi profanus nemo deliberat, cum parentem omnium et omnium dominum non minoris sceleris sit ignorare quam laedere. Et quamquam inperitia dei sufficiat ad poenam, ita ut notitia prosit ad ueniam, tamen si uobiscum Christiani comparemur, quamuis in nonnullis disciplina nostra minor est, multo tamen uobis meliores deprehendemur.*[169]

Although Octavius is articulating a form of the Christian doctrine of salvation, Scripture is of course never referred to. It remains an explanation of justification without even a mention of Jesus, and all cited arguments are again mythological and literary.[170] Throughout the entire theological scope of the *Octauius*, this understanding of salvation and judgement represents the most peculiarly Christian doctrine that is supported by the sole use of secular evidences. In spite of its components being predominantly Christological, they are put aside to allow for its inclusion in Octavius' Christian defence. This incidence attests Minucius' fidelity to his apologetic aims; the *Octauius* is not a work of theology, and therefore no further elucidation of a specifically Christian dogma is required for the purposes of the apologetic debate. This is not a proactive establishment of Christian principle, but a response to common criticisms of religious error, impiety, and novelty.

Following judgement on humanity and the destruction of the world by fire, the concept of bodily resurrection is the other central eschatological belief to be discussed by the protagonists of the *Octauius*. The topic of bodily resurrection was already a prominent issue in Christian writing,[171] and although its inclusion in Minucius'

---

[168] 'For strength is braced by weakness'. *Octauius*, 36: 8.

[169] 'But that those who have no knowledge of God do not deserve to be tortured as impious and unjust, no one but the irreligious considers, when it is no less of a crime to be ignorant of – as to wrong – the parent and lord of all. And although ignorance of God suffices for punishment, just as knowledge helps for pardon, yet if we Christians are compared with you, although a few may fall short of our teaching, we will be recognised as a great deal better than you'. *Octauius*, 35: 4–5.

[170] *Octauius*, 35: 1–2.

[171] Testified to by such works as the *De resurrectione* of Justin, Athenagoras' *De resurrectione mortuorum*, and Tertullian's *De resurrectione carnis*.

debate is comparatively brief, it was a highly sensitive issue in contemporary Christian theological discourse. It is also stoutly defended though the *Octauius* debate. Caecilius denounces the Christian hope of total bodily renewal from an intensely rational standpoint; there is no logical reason to believe that a decomposed or destroyed corpse can fully reanimate, and there is neither precedent nor proof: *et tamen tanta aetas abiit, saecula innumera fluxerunt: quis unus ullus ab inferis uel Protesilai sorte remeauit, horarum saltem permisso commeatu, uel ut exemplo crederemus?*[172] Octavius responds by pointing towards the power of God; if humanity can originally be created *de nihilo*,[173] then by extension it could also be reformed. The basic elements, and the fundamental blueprint of each human individual, remain under the protection of God. The heart of the Christian belief in bodily resurrection surrounds the omnipotence of God, that can reform and renew humanity at will.[174] Octavius utilises a metaphorical example from the natural world; *ita corpus in saeculo, ut arbores in hiberno.*[175] He refuses to admit the inference that the Christian avoidance of cremation can be traced to this hope of resurrection, and favours a less strictly physical interpretation of the concept of bodily renewal.[176] The doctrine of bodily resurrection is a crucial piece within Minucius' eschatology due to its integral place with the Christian hope of eternal life, and is strongly defended within the *Octauius*.

The Christians are smeared by Caecilius as *tu, qui inmortalitatem postumam somnias*,[177] whose delusion unfortunately prevents them from enjoying their temporal situation. But from the Christian side of Octavius, the concept of eternal reward enforces a distaste for harmful earthly pleasures, and *pompis uestris et spectaculis abstinemus.*[178] In contrast with the propitiatory cults of Roman religion, the Christian God is the universal transcendence of such worldly matters and *superstitiosis uanitatibus.*[179] Octavius rhetorically asks; *nonne melius in*

---

[172] 'And yet so much time has passed, innumerable ages have flown by; what one man has returned from the dead – either with the fortune of Protesilaus, permitted so much as a few hours leave, or an example that we might believe?'. *Octauius*, 11: 8.

[173] 'From nothing'. *Octauius*, 34: 9.

[174] Also present at Justin, *De resurrectione*, 6, Athenagoras, *De resurrectione mortuorum*, 3, and Tertullian, *De resurrectione carnis*, 11.

[175] 'The body in the world is as trees in winter'. *Octauius*, 34: 11.

[176] *Octauius*, 34: 10.

[177] 'You, who dream of posthumous immortality'. *Octauius*, 12: 3.

[178] 'We abstain from your processions and spectacles'. *Octauius*, 37: 11.

[179] 'Superstitious vanities'. *Octauius*, 1: 5.

nostra dedicandus est mente, in nostro immo consecrandus est pectore?[180] An analysis of the theological and eschatological principles of the *Octauius* emphasises the degree of the divergence of Christianity from the surrounding Roman culture, even if Minucius couches his doctrines with non-Christian philosophical terminology. The philosophical parallels exist in the Christian worldview to be exploited for the purpose of argument in the service of the *ueram religionem*.[181] This is the most marked feature of Minucius' apologetic, and is nowhere more ambitious than in the establishment of the core principles of Christian theology and eschatology.

5. Conclusion: The apologetic of the *Octauius*

A potential dating period of 193-197 would naturally require a substantial change in our understanding of early Latin apologetics. The *Octauius* would become the earliest extant text, and its interpretation takes on a greater importance as the evidence of the primary witness of the group. Despite the imputations of great swathes of believers being *pauperes*, even *inliteratos*, Minucius has articulated a piece of highly educated Christian apologetic, permeated throughout with skilled touches of educated rhetorical flair. It is Christian Latin at its most elegant, and the ultimate antithesis of any imputations of illiteracy and poverty. Minucius himself is the strongest manifestation of a highly sophisticated Latin mode of expression of early Christianity.

The depth of theology is generally considered the main weakness of the *Octauius*. Yet this problem lies not with Minucius alone, but with the entire genre of apologetics. The *Octauius* is no exception to the apologetic expedient of choosing relevance and conciseness over thorough theological argument and explanation. The greatest strength of the *Octauius*, on the other hand, lies in Minucius' concern with redefining the common perceptions of the Church, in order to reconcile the doctrines of Christianity with conventional philosophical terminology. He endeavours throughout to present Christianity as more akin to a philosophical school, rather than a

---

[180] 'Surely our mind would be a better place of dedication? Is not our heart a better place of consecration?'. *Octauius*, 32: 2.

[181] 'True religion'. *Octauius*, 1: 5.

new religious cult. It is also the mode of expression found in the *Apologeticum*, where Tertullian utilises the terminology of a *secta* in reference to the Christian community.[182] The assertion that the Church has *nullas aras, templa nulla* should also not be slavishly taken as the hint at an almost totally undeveloped Christian era, when it is more likely another argument in the establishment of the universality and earthly transcendence of Christian worship. Although the Christians may well have had furniture and property connected with aspects of ritual and ceremony, the sacrificial nature of the terms *ara* and *templum* play no part in the customs of Christian worship described by Minucius. He is continually keen to downplay the material and physical elements in favour of the truly spiritual aspects of devotion. With some of the final words of his Christian defence, Octavius expresses the heart of the Christian understanding of its own meaning:

> *Nos non habitu sapientiam sed mente praeferimus, non eloquimur magna sed uiuimus, gloriamur nos consecutos, quod illi summa intentione quae-siuerunt nec inuenire potuerunt... Fruamur bono nostro et recti senten-tiam temperemus: cohibeatur superstitio, inpietas expietur, uera religio reseruetur.*[183]

The purpose of apologetics is to dispel the notions of impiety, novelty, and immorality, and to justify the beleaguered religious practices by extension. Minucius achieves this without a particularly detailed explanation of the Christian life, but instead with a contemptuous dismissal of the most notorious immoral accusations,[184] and an accompanying construction of the virtuous principles of the misunderstood Christian minority. The Church continues to remain marked by a high level of public obscurity, and a deliberate refusal to take part in the traditional religious ceremonies of Roman culture. But in spite of this, the *Octauius* symbolises something of a bridge between Christianity and Rome. Minucius has chosen to defend his religion through a secular medium, and has achieved a

---

[182] 'School/Party'. *Apologeticum*, 21: 1.

[183] 'We do not show off wisdom in our outward dress, but in the mind; we do not speak great things, but live them. We pride ourselves in having achieved what those with the highest effort have searched for, but could not discover. Let us delight in our good, and regulate our understanding of virtue: that superstition may be curbed, that impiety may be expiated, that true religion may be held onto'. *Octauius*, 38: 6–7.

[184] *Octauius*, 28: 10–11, 29: 1.

sense of compatibility with the philosophical authorities through the eloquent argument of his Christian protagonist. Before Lactantius' later attempt at fully describing Christianity as the sole guardian of the *uera sapientia*, Minucius' *Octauius* represents a significant step in the undertaking.

TERTULLIAN

1. Introduction

Little is known of Quintus Septimius Florens Tertullianus' life (c. 155–c. 222) outside of what is gleaned from his own writings, but his work has left an indelible mark on the Christian Church.[1] He is, in many ways, the central figure of early Latin Christian theology before Augustine of Hippo, and from the dual perspective of defending the Church from its attackers while reinforcing the faith of the persecuted, the place of apologetic in Tertullian's Christian era is vital. His apologetic corpus includes both defensive encapsulation and fiery polemical argument, and is effectively microcosmic of the character of Latin apologetic literature as a whole. Even though the earlier dating of Minucius Felix is maintained throughout this study, the significance of Tertullian within early Latin apologetics cannot be undermined in any way. His *Apologeticum* remains the cardinal Latin apology before the production of Lactantius' *Diuinae institutiones*.

Although Tertullian produced a copious amount of apologetic, doctrinal and theological works, he rarely divulges personal details. Only on a few occasions does he close a particular work with his own name; something which is received with great value by the commentator engaged in the often desperate search for autobiographical information.[2] On the question of Tertullian's dating range, Jerome wrote *sub Seuero principe et Antonino Caracalla maxime floruit*,[3] isolating a

---

[1] Tertullian's *Opera* exists in a two-volume set in the Corpus Christianorum Series Latina, ed. by E. Dekkers, and provides the source text for all textual citations used within this work.

[2] At *De uelandis uirginibus*, 17, and *De baptismo*, 20.

[3] 'He flourished chiefly in the reign of Severus and Antoninus Caracalla'. Jerome, *De uiris illustribus*, 53.

loose timeline spanning 193–217 for the bulk of his work. But outside of the biographical snippets of Jerome's *De uiris illustribus*, identifying Tertullian the individual behind Tertullian the apologist is difficult. He can be located at Carthage from the opening of the *De pallio*, where he addresses the men of the city in response to popular insults of his chosen form of dress.[4] Also, like so many other Christians of his era, Tertullian was a convert. It becomes clear from a wider reading of his work that he lived and wrote during a period of intermittent persecution for Christianity,[5] and his apologetic is highly responsive to the contemporary situation. Tertullian's apologetic corpus manifests some of the key issues in the religious and ideological conflict between Christianity and Rome at the opening of the third century. But Tertullian's theological character is historically contentious, due to the extent of his association with the schismatic *Noua Prophetia* of Montanus. Some of his later work seems to exhibit a certain breach with the 'Catholic' Christianity of his earlier years, and the particulars of the intra-Christian controversy from his own perspective are marked by a sense of theological rigour.[6] His *De ieiunio*, in particular, points toward a divisive relationship between the two groups – generally rather broadly defined as 'Catholic' and 'Montanist' – but called by Tertullian *Psychici* and *Spiritales*.[7] His forceful critique of the laxity of the *Psychici* on the issue of fasting, added to their deplorable validation of the practice of second marriage, is said to be at the centre of a serious doctrinal conflict. Tertullian provides unique insight into the level of divergence between the two groups, and argues:

Hi paracleto controuersiam faciunt; propter hoc nouae prophetiae recusantur; non quod alium deum praedicent Montanus et Priscilla et Maximilla,

---

[4] *De pallio*, 1.

[5] Chiefly noted in the background to his apologetic works, but also as the primary setting and purpose behind *De fuga* and *Scorpiace*.

[6] Prominent examples are *De monogamia*, *De pudicitia*, and *De ieiunio*. However, tracing Tertullian's developing theological rigour purely to the arrival on the scene of Montanism is not necessarily as simple as cause and effect. Tertullian's rigour could well have been a natural feature of his own theological evolution, with Montanism being an appealing outlet of similar theological standpoints. It borders on anachronism to presume that upon Tertullian's acceptance of Montanistic tenets, he became theologically and doctrinally rigorous.

[7] 'Carnal' and 'Spiritual'. *De monogamia*, 1. See the use of the term φυχικὸς at 1 Cor 2: 14, referring to the 'unspiritual' non-believers unable to comprehend the spiritual gifts bestowed by God upon the Church.

nec quod Iesum Christum soluant, nec quod aliquam fidei aut spei regulam euertant, sed quod plane doceant saepius ieiunare quam nubere.[8]

Some level of discord is clearly in operation, but the essentials of the relationship between 'Catholic' and 'Montanist' at Carthage come down almost wholly to the interpretation of Tertullian's words, and the construction of any hypothesis on the basis of one partisan argument alone is always problematic. But as unravelling the exact nature of the Montanist party at Carthage is rife with difficulty, so too is ascribing the actual extent of Tertullian's 'heretical' connections. Jerome's concept of an organized and actively proselytising 'heresy' that so captivated Tertullian that *ad Montani dogma delapsus*,[9] seems to be an overstatement of the evidence. It has to be noted that the biographical vignettes of the *De uiris illustribus* were penned at the much later date of 392–3, and the nature of Jerome's evidence for Tertullian's details has now been acutely questioned. While Tertullian's acceptance of Montanist principles is still evident from his writings, the modern school of thought is moving away from a black-and-white definition of his becoming a 'heretic', and instead allows that certain Montanist principles could perhaps have cohabited at some level within the 'Catholic' Christianity it sprung from. As an example, David Rankin has compared this to the contemporary 'Charismatic Renewal movement within certain Western churches – Catholic and Protestant alike',[10] as opposed to the far less subtle picture of a radical 'heresy' claiming converts from the more 'orthodox' Church of its origin. It stands as a potentially more rational picture of the circumstances of Tertullian's Church, and could also do much to repair his posthumous reputation.[11] Furthermore, since the seminal work of T. D. Barnes on the subject,[12] Tertullianic study has moved on from

---

[8] 'It is these who raise controversy with the Paraclete; on this account the new prophecies are rejected; not that Montanus and Priscilla and Maximilla proclaim another God, nor that they detach Jesus Christ [from God], nor that they overturn any certain rule of faith or hope, but that they plainly teach more frequent fasting than marrying'. *De ieiunio*, 1: 3.

[9] 'He lapsed into the doctrine of Montanus'. *De uiris illustribus*. 53.

[10] David Rankin, *Tertullian and the Church*, p. 41, n. 1.

[11] For example, away from such sweeping generalisations as: 'it was this unrestrained impulsiveness of nature that soon beguiled him to break away from the wise moderation of the Church and to embrace the heresy of Montanus, – a Phrygian fanatic'. T. Herbert Bindley, *The Apology of Tertullian for the Christians*, p. viii.

[12] *Tertullian: A Historical and Literary Study* (1971, repr. 1985). (Henceforth *Tertullian*).

its previous dependence on the words of Jerome. Barnes' critical reflection on aspects of Tertullian's life and thought has heralded a wider re-evaluation of Jerome's biographical criteria. Personal incidences like the traditional position of Tertullian's father as a proconsular centurion have been dismissed,[13] the dating of Tertullian's textual corpus has been comprehensively reworked, and the late-twentieth century picture of Tertullian has emerged as a very different one.

Tertullian's apologetic writings

The *Apologeticum* stands out as Tertullian's most influential contribution, in view of its legacy as the prime text of the early Latin apologetic tradition. His other works of apologetic alongside this are *Ad natiunes*, *De testimonio animae*, and *Ad Scapulam*. The *De pallio* also fits into most of the conventional aspects in the broader template of apologetic: it is aimed at a non-Christian audience and is defensive of a particular practice, but for its sole concern with one single issue (Tertullian's attachment to the *pallium*) it holds a comparatively minor position in the overall classification of Tertullian's apologetic work. This study is restricted to Tertullian's four principal apologetic texts, without the inclusion of the *De pallio*. Following the dating scenario of Barnes, the *Ad nationes* and the *Apologeticum* are placed at 197, with the *De testimonio animae* likely following shortly afterwards, even at around 198.[14] *Ad Scapulam* must originate from the period of the African proconsulship of Scapula (211–213), and probably towards the end of the year 212.[15]

Tertullian's literary style is his own, and continues to be the focus of discussion. It has divided opinion since its inception, and attracted reviews from the polar extremities of personal taste. Philip Schaff concluded on Tertullian's key stylistic qualities in a manner that merits being repeated, if only for the breathless flow and picturesque mass of adjectives used in explanation:

> His style is exceedingly characteristic, and corresponds with his thought.
> It is terse, abrupt, laconic, sententious, nervous, figurative, full of hyperbole, sudden turns, legal technicalities, African provincialisms, or rather

---

[13] Tracing the sole 'evidence' to a likely corrupt source in Jerome's text of Tertullian's *Apologeticum*, Barnes has concluded that 'there is no valid evidence whatever that Tertullian's father was a soldier'. *Tertullian*, p. 21.

[14] See Barnes' chronological table, at *Tertullian*, p. 55.

[15] Ibid., p. 38.

antiquated or vulgar Latinisms. It abounds in Latinised Greek words, and new expressions, in roughnesses, angles, and obscurities; sometimes, like a great volcanic eruption, belching precious stones and dross in strange confusion; or like the foaming torrent tumbling over the precipice of rocks and sweeping all before it.[16]

Schaff's description is intended to be highly complimentary, regardless of his use of the term 'belching', and 'sweeping all before it' has become a dominant metaphorical image within Tertullianic study. Tertullian is often admired for his idiosyncratic yet innovative linguistic medium, even if this does tends to work against the elegance of a more balanced stylistic flow. Lactantius, one of Tertullian's successors in Latin apologetics, unfavourably contrasted Tertullian's literary eloquence with that of Minucius Felix and Cyprian: *Septimius quoque Tertullianus fuit omni genere litterarum peritus, sed in eloquendo parum facilis et minus comptus et multum obscurus fuit.*[17] This comparison with the articulate Latinity of Minucius Felix is frequently employed, and even sometimes seems almost obligatory, but is an unfair slight on the style of Tertullian. Minucius' *Octauius* is relatively brief, remarkably well studied, and a highly developed piece of rhetorical polish, whereas Tertullian's writings are often aggressive, passionate, forceful, and highly theologically technical. This is not to make excuses, but instead to defend the possibility that creating a work of stylistic and rhetorical panache was secondary to advocating his cause under consideration, and in turn made more penetrating by his unrestrained linguistic style. Tertullian's most enduring characteristic is not the commendable mastery of his own Latin medium, like Minucius Felix, but rather his genius in theological originality; even forcing a novel comparison with Genghis Kahn on the part of one eminent scholar, by virtue of his singular character and personality.[18]

This chapter undertakes an exploration into some of the key issues surrounding Tertullian's use of apologetic. The texts referred to are his four primary apologetic works; the *Apologeticum*, *De testimonio animae*, *Ad nationes*, and *Ad Scapulam*. These are considered

---

[16] Schaff, *Ante-Nicene Christianity*, Vol. 2, pp. 824–5.

[17] 'Septimius Tertullian was also skilled in every kind of literature, but unready in eloquence, not elegant at all, and very unclear'. *Diuinae institutiones*, 5: 1; 23. The Latin text of the *Diuinae institutiones* used throughout this work is *Lactantius: Divinarum Institutionum Libri Septem*, Eberhad Heck and Antonie Wlosok eds.

[18] 'He is an intellectual Genghis Khan, who explores the bible and classical culture, yet manages to present antiquarian, scientific, medical and philosophical material in an original way'. Eric Osborn, *Tertullian, First Theologian of the West*, p. 255.

individually in order to address some of the main concerns of each piece, and the varying threads of Tertullian's apologetic corpus can therefore be addressed in turn. This is followed by the beginnings of an examination into Tertullian's place in the Christian literary tradition that preceded his own work, through a study of his potential Christian textual sources. Following the starting-point of the tentatively anterior dating of Minucius Felix's *Octauius*, a contribution to the picture of Tertullian as one of the prime movers in Latin apologetics, rather than strictly as the sole 'father' of the field, can be formulated.

2. Tertullian's apologetic

This examination of Tertullian's apologetic work is concerned with identifying the key features which pervade each individual text. The dual legal and religious dimension of the *Apologeticum* is explored, the purpose of the *De testimonio animae* is discussed, and the central meaning of *Ad nationes* reconsidered. It is argued that *Ad nationes* is not merely the survivor of an intermediate stage in the compilation of the more polished *Apologeticum*, but perhaps a collection of arguments deliberately assembled for the purpose of current and future apologetic utilisation, and an important step in bridging the gap between defensive apologetic and exoteric polemical discourse. The epistolary nature of *Ad Scapulam* and its close proximity to the *Apologeticum* closes the discussion. It is well fitting that Tertullian's final and most mature piece of apologetic literature is compiled in a manner of direct focus to an individual with predominant influence over his contemporary society.

Apologeticum

The *Apologeticum* is addressed to the *Romani imperii antistites*,[19] and *Ad Scapulam* to a North African governor, while the named recipients

---

[19] 'Overseers of the Roman empire'. *Apologeticum*, 1: 1. For a brief discussion of *antistes* in the *Apologeticum*, see Simon Price, 'Latin Christian Apologetics', pp. 109-10. The usage of the term is also testified to in Minucius' *Octauius*, where the leader of Christian ritual is referred to as *antistitis ac sacerdotis* by Caecilius, at *Octauius*, 9: 4. See further J. H. Waszink, 'Minuciana', p. 129. *Antistes* develops into common usage as a Latin formula for a bishop, and carries its meaning well into the Early Modern period. As an example, the 1538 Latin dictionary of Thomas Elyot confirms this definition as a 'prelate'. 'Antistes', in Thomas Elyot, *Dictionary*, p. vii.

of *Ad nationes* are the generalised people of the *nationes* – the generic non-Christian populace. A clear contrast in the legal and social status of the recipients is evident. Tertullian is addressing a whole social level within the *Apologeticum*; one with clear judicial and religious significance, and a correspondingly high social status. Although the terminology of address is more general than with the particular governor of *Ad Scapulam*, the address of the *Apologeticum* can be immediately contrasted with the more universal direction of the *Ad nationes*. After a relatively brief introduction which outlines the plan of the text, Tertullian summarises the public grievances against Christianity before proceeding to respond. The Christian religion is defended by means of explaining the truth behind any controversial practices, emphasising the unimpeachable morality at the heart of the Church in spite of the accusations, and countering the existent criticism with specific ripostes. The life of the Church is elucidated from a defensive standpoint with constant recourse to the rational justification of Christian practice, and the Christian refusal to participate in the imperial cult is clarified.

Along with its point-by-point rejoinders and continual appeals to traditional precedent and classical culture, the *Apologeticum* bears explicit witness to its legal character throughout. The opening lines of the text represent the introductory remarks of the defence counsel in a court case, and is Tertullian beginning to launch into his role as the Christian advocate.[20] But Tertullian's defence is not on legal terms alone, and the *Apologeticum* is ultimately more concerned with the religious justification of the Christian faith, underneath the framework of its appeal at judicial vindication. As part of this, the legal metaphor as a speech for the defence is employed as an appropriate schema within which Tertullian can work to ensure his points are adequately detailed. He writes of the unreasonableness of the Christian trials, where standard judicial conventions are shirked. At the heart of the absurdity lies the contention *in omnibus nos aliter*

---

[20] So Quasten, 'he was an expert in law and gained a reputation for himself as an advocate at Rome. Most probably he is to be identified with the jurist Tertullianus'. *Patrology*, Vol. 2, p. 246. But although the legal terminology is integral within the wider concept of the *apologia* format, Tertullian's awareness of legal schema does not necessitate his actual occupation as a lawyer. Following the reasoning of T. D. Barnes, the traditional identification of the apologist Tertullian with the contemporary African jurist of the same name is hardly a conclusive connection. See Barnes, *Tertullian*, pp. 22–29.

disponitis quam ceteros nocentes;[21] the inequality of treatment between Christians and everyone else, which even extends into making the criminality of Christianity a totally distinct form in itself.[22] Against this, Tertullian constructs a defence of the Christians' innocence of all criminal charges, using terminology that deliberately rings with legal influence: *iam de causa innocentiae consistam; nec tantum refutabo quae nobis obiciuntur, sed etiam in ipsos retorquebo qui obiciunt.*[23] This also doubles as a succinct definition of the whole course of the *Apologeticum* itself. The legal mode of expression is indispensable for the meaning of the work, as Tertullian's confident depiction of the plan of the case is deliberately reminiscent of the opening remarks of a counsel. Tertullian's entire apologetic concern is borne out of a sense of injustice in the treatment of Christians by the Roman authorities, and he intends to respond to each prevalent criticism in turn. He writes with the aim *respondebimus ad singula*[24] in reference to the alleged crimes of Christian practice. His main technique in doing this is an employment of a mode of attacking retort – the *tu quoque*. This approach is a more prominent feature of the *Ad nationes*, but is also a key component within the methodology of the *Apologeticum*. Tertullian introduces it with a helpful definition: *haec quo magis refutauerim, a uobis fieri ostendam partim in aperto, partim in occulto, per quod forsitan et de nobis credidistis.*[25] This polemical element becomes a major part of Tertullian's apologetic. It is a logical progression from his depiction of the legal absurdities inherent in the Christian condemnation, and represents Tertullian's further attempt to cast doubt on the foundations of anti-Christian persecution. The Christians are being persecuted for the very things *a uobis fieri*; which should require across-the-board punitive measures by extension. The crux of the issue is the personal and public morality of the Christians, and the hypocrisy inherent in punishing one group while overlooking the same vices in another. While Tertullian would certainly have been aware that Christians were not

[21] 'In everything you treat us differently from other criminals'. *Apologeticum*, 2: 18.

[22] Also a feature with Cyprian, at *Ad Demetrianum*, 12: 5.

[23] 'Now I will stand for the cause of innocence. I will not only refute the things which are cast against us, but I will also cast them back against those who present them'. *Apologeticum*, 4: 1.

[24] 'I will respond to every [accusation]'. *Apologeticum*, 4: 2.

[25] 'Therefore, in order to further refute these things [the accusations], I will show that they are done by you, some in the open and others in secret. Because of this, perhaps, you believe them of us'. *Apologeticum*, 9: 1.

actually persecuted for being incestuous or cannibalistic, but rather due to more general imputations of treason, sedition, and impiety,[26] his address of the notorious smears of immorality serves an important purpose. When the focus of the *Apologeticum* develops into the constructive explanation of the life of the Church, Tertullian grounds his standpoints on the successfully refuted immoral and irreligious accusations; *quo minus mala refutauerim, bona ostendam.*[27] With such a literary flourish, he can vindicate his Church in direct and explicit reaction to the immoral accusations. The Christian believers can be defined as the acute opposite to the negative allegations, and the Church celebrated for its fidelity to discipline, love, and unity.[28] The unfairness of the punishments for being Christian is drawn in view of the apposite purity of the Christian gatherings; *in cuius perniciem aliquando conuenimus?*[29]

But even as the format of a defensive *apologia* in a courtroom setting provides the structure within which Tertullian sets out his argument, the issue of religious identity is the central matter in question.[30] This is not to pose a dichotomy between the legal and religious aspects of the text as being two disparate themes, but to suggest that Tertullian used the one as the crucial means of unfolding the other. The *Apologeticum* is by its nature a fundamentally religious work. For Tertullian, existing alongside the judicial inequality facing Christianity was a corresponding state of religious inequality, manifested in the difference between the conduct of the opposing religions. His argument revolves around the public immorality of traditional Roman rites; the Christians are so much more moral and rational, yet they are the ones who are condemned with trumped-up charges

---

[26] Much scholarly literature exists on the foundations for the persecution of Christianity. See in particular W. H. C. Frend, *Martyrdom and Persecution in the Early Church*, Paul Keresztes, 'The Imperial Roman Government and the Christian Church', and G. E. M. de Ste. Croix, 'Why Were The Early Christians Persecuted?'.

[27] 'Where I have refuted what is bad, I will exhibit what is good'. *Apologeticum*, 39: 1.

[28] *Apologeticum*, 39.

[29] 'To whose ruin have we ever met?'. *Apologeticum*, 39: 21.

[30] On a further, specifically historical, dimension of the *Apologeticum*, see Mark S. Burrows, 'Christianity in the Roman Forum: Tertullian and the Apologetic Use of History'. Burrows' interpretation views the *Apologeticum* as 'an historiographical treatise, an extended consideration of "origins" which applies the force of history squarely to the apologetic task'. Ibid., p. 231. Burrows' argument poses another positive means of reading Tertullian's methodological concerns in the *Apologeticum*.

of criminality. Tertullian is making the contrast as stark as possible, by praising the restrained virtue of the Church in opposition to the excesses of traditional public ceremonies.[31] His depiction of the irrational absurdities of Roman worship reaches a verbal crescendo with an attack on the veneration of idols:

> *O impiae uoces, o sacrilega conuicia! Infrendite, inspumate! Iidem estis, qui Senecam aliquem pluribus et amarioribus de uestra superstitione perorantem probetis. Igitur si statuas et imagines frigidas, mortuorum uestrorum simillimas, non adoramus, quas milui et mures et aranei intellegunt, nonne laudem magis quam poenam merebatur repudium agniti erroris?*[32]

The interjections *o impiae uoces, o sacrilega conuicia!* raise the tone of the text in preparation for the judgement which follows; image-worship is condemned as sacrilegious and misguided error. Tertullian also condemns the Roman priests as corrupt and motivated only by financial gain, swiping *circuit cauponas religio mendicans.*[33] This is then directly contrasted with the voluntary nature of Christian monetary offerings.[34] Such marked duality is one of the main features of the *Apologeticum*, as Tertullian is throughout concerned with responding to every accusation with its positive Christian actuality. The ultimate grounding for his statements originates from an attack on the values of his opponents, utilised in order to disprove the foundation of the accusations of immorality by contrast. The criminal imputations of

[31] *Apologeticum*, 6: 2; Tertullian's criticism of the extravagant and wasteful spending of ostentations public festivals. See also 9: 10–12; the bloodthirsty rites of the arena.

[32] 'O impious words. O sacrilegious abuse! Grind your teeth, vent your spittle! You are the same [people], who approve of a certain Seneca, who summed up your superstitions with many more bitter words. Therefore if we do not adore statues and lifeless images, the very likenesses of your dead men – something which the kites, mice, and spiders understand – then surely praise rather than punishment is earned for the rejection of recognised error?'. *Apologeticum*, 12: 6–7. Tertullian's reference to the *milui et mures et araneae* crawling all over the statues represents an attempt to postulate evidence in support of his religious attacks, but as with any religious debate, proof for the existence of one deity over another is by nature difficult to elucidate. His analogy of the kites, mice and spiders who know the true character of the statues is simplistic, but fits the purpose well enough. The commonplaces with *Octauius* 24: 9–10 are too close to point towards anything other than Minucius' prior influence. See below, pp. 102–3. This citation is one of the key textual incidences employed for the analysis of the *Apologeticum* in this chapter.

[33] 'Religion goes around the taverns begging'. *Apologeticum*, 13: 6.

[34] *Apologeticum*, 39: 5–6.

the Church are thus re-directed to pose the essential introductions in Tertullian's establishment of virtuous Christian attributes.

The *Apologeticum* is the literary expression of Christianity on trial. The legal format is present throughout as a structure within which the Christian religion is defended, and provides a fitting template to help Tertullian set out his argument. This is underlined by the very last lines of the text, where the joint play on the legal and religious dimension is made obvious: *ut est aemulatio diuinae rei et humanae, cum damnamur a uobis, a deo absoluimur.*[35] The passive verbs *damnamur... absoluimur* are to be rendered into English as 'we are condemned... we are acquitted', with the legal aspects of the terms highlighted as the central meaning in the clause. Yet the corresponding religious significance inherent in the verbal meanings is unmistakeable. 'Damned' and 'absolved' are expressions which carry the highest importance for Christian belief. This mode of ending the *Apologeticum* emphasises the close proximity of the legal and religious aspects within Tertullian's work, but is also brought to a specific focus by the issue of persecution. The Christians were punished not solely for following strange or novel religious practices, but for their entire dissension from traditional Roman religious understanding. When faced with punitive action for refusing to repent, the only Christian hope lay in the inexpressible differences between the authority of the Roman judicial system and the authority of the judicial office of God; the *aemulatio diuinae rei et humanae.*

De testimonio animae

The brief *De testimonio animae* is markedly different from Tertullian's other works not only in terms of direction, but also in style and subject matter. Although it is concerned primarily with a rhetorical conversation with the soul, the vocative form of address by the narrator moves between the universal persona of the soul itself, and the generic form of the opponent of Christianity. Tertullian is unable to classify the soul as Christian by nature, as a result of the crucial importance of personal conversion in becoming Christian.[36] Instead, monotheism,[37] the demonic origin of Roman gods,[38] and the soul's commonly-held immortality,[39]

---

[35] 'But there is a rivalry in the things of God and man. Although we are condemned by you, we are acquitted by God'. *Apologeticum*, 50: 16.

[36] *De testimonio animae*, 1: 7.

[37] *De testimonio animae*, 2.

[38] *De testimonio animae*, 3.

[39] *De testimonio animae*, 4.

are employed as markers to point towards the implicit truth of Christianity. The soul itself secretly worships the Christian God and prays in Christian words, regardless of the religion of the human individual, and due to the universal nature of the truth of Christian worship.[40] The *De testimonio animae* is an ambitious work, but the apologetic principles that underlie the surface point towards a relative simplicity of intention. It is designed as another theoretical witness for the Christian faith; one idealistically free from the differing interpretations of philosophical texts, and untarnished by previous religious dialogue. The core argument hinges around the desire to create a source that can be shared by every perspective in the religious conflict, and can therefore be in itself the very validation of objectivity and truth. For Tertullian, the existence of such an authoritative testimony would be a great weight in the contemporary religious and philosophical debate, where all current sources already possess their own individual failings. Tertullian is hesitant to recommend the classics of philosophy to his readers, but also writes of the general unawareness of the Christian Scriptures outside the boundaries of the Church.[41] Following this, an appeal to a common authority is required, and the archetype of the human soul is brought forward as an appropriate witness. The *De testimonio animae* is Tertullian's attempt at outlining the evidence of a voice that is inherently divine, but still somehow inseparable from humanity.[42] The apologetic methodology is identifiable, and can be taken to refer back to Tertullian's apologetic concern in the broader picture. This ambition is highlighted from the opening lines of the text:

> *Magna curiositate et maiore longe memoria opus est ad studendum, si qui uelit ex litteris receptissimis quibusque philosophorum uel poetarum uel quorumlibet doctrinae ac sapientiae saecularis magistrorum testimonia excerpere Christianae ueritatis, ut aemuli persecutoresque eius de suo proprio instrumento et erroris in se et iniquitatis in nos rei reuincantur.*[43]

---

[40] *De testimonio animae*, 6: 2.

[41] *De testimonio animae*, 1: 4.

[42] Also developed by Tertullian at *De anima*, 51–53.

[43] 'Great curiosity and a much greater memory are needed by anyone who wishes to select from the most popular works of the philosophers, poets, or any other books of doctrine and wisdom from the testimony of worldly teachers, so that as persecutors and rivals of Christian truth, of error in themselves and injustice towards us, they may be refuted using their own apparatus'. *De testimonio animae*, 1: 1.

Tertullian's key point is to draw attention to the centrality of a common source in the religious debate. It is very much like along the lines of the legal appeal to a respected and ostensibly objective judicial authority, in line with the character of the *Apologeticum*. It may be that the *De testimonio animae* is not quite on the level of significance of the *Apologeticum* or the *Ad nationes*, but it does maintain an important position for its contribution to Tertullian's overall apologetic corpus. It is the positive interpretation of the necessary authorities that lies at the heart of a successful apologetic argument, and the *De testimonio animae* is representative of a Christian need to postulate new sources for use within the religious dialogue, in order to move away from the sole engagement with either the classics or the Scriptures.

Ad nationes

The *Apologeticum* and *Ad Scapulam* are often considered together for their similar appeals to those in possession of judicial authority. Both the *antistites* and Scapula himself are held responsible in a large degree for the legal status of the Christians, and the works addressed to them bear the marks of appeals to high judicial and social authority. As such, a level of restraint in aggression and divisiveness would be an expected component within each work. But with the *Ad nationes*, Tertullian moves from the defensive position of the *Apologeticum* into a lengthy and elaborate confrontational retort. There is a very clear structure to the two books of the work; the first is concerned with establishing the morality and legality of Christianity in a way that can be defined as a reaction against popular public opinion,[44] while the second moves on to a barbarous demolition of the key aspects of non-Christian worship, pulling no punches in a lengthy series of pointed criticisms. Tertullian is keen to hammer his point home. A more condescending tone in the vocative address is also evident in some parts of the *Ad nationes*,[45] something not as marked in either the *Apologeticum* or *Ad Scapulam*. But perhaps in a situation of intermittent yet harsh persecution such as that facing Tertullian's Christian communities, merely defensive explanations of the persecuted Church could be improved upon. In such a case, a more active response would be to go on the attack and call the morality of the prevailing public religion into question. The *Ad nationes* achieves this through its concerted focus in drawing the elements of

---

[44] *Ad nationes*, 1: 7 ff.

[45] In its address to the *miserandae nationes*. *Ad nationes*, 1: 7; 29, and 2: 1; 1.

unpunished acts of immorality,[46] unfaithfulness to the law,[47] and the naivety of popular religious belief,[48] into a panoramic image of hypocrisy that is embarrassed by the virtue of the Christian individuals. Although many of these concerns are also mentioned in the *Apologeticum*, they are present in a much more vociferous sense in the *Ad nationes*.

Following the results of I. L. S. Balfour's study of Tertullian's terminology, *nationes* can be shown to be his 'favourite word for the heathen'.[49] A contrast of the *nationes* with the *antistites* is noted throughout the work, and a case could possibly be made for a difference in tone as an implication of its intended readership. The *Apologeticum* is more strongly characterised by the style of a legal defence, and it is made clear that the *antistites* of the address are responsible for the punitive action against the Christians.[50] This is also evident in *Ad Scapulam*.[51] Therefore, Tertullian's greater stress on the moral and legal defence of Christianity as opposed to a larger volume of attack can certainly be understood, and possibly even expected. But it is not to say that Tertullian completely refrains from taking the fight to the enemy in the *Apologeticum* and *Ad Scapulam*, however. While the *Apologeticum* is essentially a response to the pre-existent moral and philosophical criticisms of Christianity, it still contains its own attacks on the religious values of the opponents of the Church.[52] But the general impression of the tone of the *Apologeticum* is one of a primarily defensive justification of Christianity, rather than such an aggressive attack as can be found in the *Ad nationes*. The judicial appeals of the *Apologeticum* are replaced in the *Ad nationes* by a greater focus on the personal morality

---

[46] Accusations of infanticide and incest are countered by charging his opponents with the very same acts. *Ad nationes*, 1: 15–16.

[47] His argument on the absurdity of the judiciary system in persecuting Christians leads to a call for the abandonment of such farcical trials (*seposita forma iudicandi*), as they are so rife with abuse. *Ad nationes*, 1: 2; 8.

[48] Tertullian's casting of the traditional Roman deities as nothing more than deified humans is a recurring theme throughout his apologetic work, but occurs particularly at *Ad nationes*, 2: 13.

[49] 'Tertullian's Description of the Heathen', p. 786.

[50] *Apologeticum*, 44.

[51] *Ad Scapulam*, 4.

[52] *Quantum igitur deis uestris, nomina solummodo uideo quorundam ueterum mortuorum, et fabulas audio, et sacra de fabulis recognosco.* 'So much, therefore for your gods. I see only names of dead men of old, I hear fables, and from the fables I recognise the sacred rites'. *Apologeticum*, 12: 1.

of the Christians in response to popular smears of immorality.[53] Although distinguishing a colloquial tone would probably be an over-statement, there is a far greater emphasis on the popular perception of Christians than in Tertullian's other apologetic texts. The virtuous Christian believer as the natural archetype of his personal religion is defended on a very human level, in order to achieve the moral vin-dication of each individual Christian victim from physical assault. An attempt at establishing a more positive complexion for the public image of Christianity is being employed:

Quid enim insigne praeferimus, nisi primam sapientiam, qua friuola humanae manus opera non adoramus; abstinentiam, qua ab alieno tem-peramus; pudicitiam quam nec oculis contaminamus; misericordiam, qua super indigentes flectimur.[54]

In direct opposition to accusations of immorality and impiety, Tertul-lian is concerned with re-identifying the Christian archetype as wise, pure, chaste and compassionate, and the very model human individual.[55]

Tertullian's *tu quoque* form of defence by retort, already encoun-tered in the *Apologeticum*, comes into its own in the *Ad nationes*. The work launches into a raging defence of Christianity from its very outset, due to the regrettable absence of any conventional style of introduction in the extant manuscripts. Tertullian opens by attack-ing the injustices suffered by the Church for its adherence to the name of Christ. Of the crime with which the Christians are accused, he contends *nullum criminis nomen extat, nisi nominis crimen est.*[56] As is so often present elsewhere in his work, Tertullian's argument swarms with pithy dictums and turns of phrase. Also, his motivation for writing is characteristically engendered by sentiments of unfair-ness and inequality; the term *iniustus* is recurring, and its theme frequently addressed. The absurdity of Christian trials is again

[53] Introduced by such statements as *quod ergo dicitis*, for example. 'On account of what you are saying'. *Ad nationes*, 1: 5; 1.

[54] 'For what mark do we display, except the prime wisdom, by which we do not worship the trifling works of the human hand; the abstinence, by which we keep from taking another's property; the chastity, which we corrupt not even with our eyes; the compassion, with which we help the needy'. *Ad nationes*, 1: 4; 15.

[55] See also the comment of P. C. Finney, 'Idols in Second and Third Century Apology', p. 686: 'apology pits the philosophical Christians against the common louts who drag civilisation into the gutter with their obscene and superstitious cults'.

[56] 'No name of a crime exists, but the crime of a name'. *Ad nationes*, 1: 3; 2.

highlighted, along with the unjust passing of laws solely concerned with responding to the Christian issue. The phrase *legis iniustae honor nullus est*[57] represents a plea to a universal belief in the idealised fairness of the Roman legal system, and reads as a succinct maxim. It is then directly followed by Tertullian's own personal standpoint; *ut opinor autem*,[58] that the treatment of Christianity is inescapably unjust. From this perspective, the *Ad nationes* and the *Apologeticum* are closely linked in terms of motivation and message. Their pose an united appeal for proper justice for the Christian cause, emblematic of Tertullian's overall apologetic aim, and summed up by his incisive *haec est iniquitas, ut gnari ab ignaris, absoluti a reis iudicemur.*[59]

But the most distinctive feature of the *Ad nationes* lies in the ferocious polemical attack on contemporary Roman religion. Tertullian invites the audience of the *iniquissimae nationes* to investigate the controversial matters at hand;[60] he has concentrated on vindicating the practices of the Church up to the end of book one, and is about to really tear into the positions of his opponents. His employment of sarcasm is scarcely more evident anywhere else than in his invitation to fellowship with the Christians accused of gross immorality: *quia non odistis quod estis, date dextras potius, compingite oscula, miscete complexus, cruenti cum cruentis, incesti cum incestis, coniurati cum coniuratis, obstinati et uani cum aequalibus.*[61] Book two provides a torrent of criticisms and accusations levelled at the rites, customs and beliefs of Tertullian's religious adversaries. It is an opportunity for him to engage with the poets and philosophers, and to expound the great pieces of classical literature within a deconstructionist argument. The measured attacks on the historical and philosophical standpoints of his opponents are grounded by the perspective of rational inquiry.[62] He disparages the anthropomorphic gods described by the poets, and particularly by Homer, and writes with forceful irony regarding their

---

[57] 'There is no honour in an unjust law'. *Ad nationes*, 1: 6; 7.

[58] 'But in my opinion'. *Ad nationes*, 1: 6; 7.

[59] 'This is the injustice; that we who are knowledgeable and innocent, should be judged by the ignorant and guilty'. *Ad nationes*, 1: 20; 11.

[60] *Ad nationes*, 1: 20; 1.

[61] 'Because you don't hate what you are, rather give us your right hands, join in kisses, mingle in embraces; bloodthirsty with the bloodthirsty, unchaste with the unchaste, conspirators with conspirators, the obstinate and false with their equals'. *Ad nationes*, 1: 20; 2.

[62] *Ad nationes*, 2: 1.

supposedly divine qualities. Their veneration has become nothing more than embodied hypocrisy:

> *Atquin horretis et auersamini uagos, exules, infirmos, debiles, sordide natos, inhoneste institutos; contra incestos, adulteros, raptores, parricidas etiam legibus exarendis. Ridendum an irascendum sit, tales deos credi quales homines esse non debeant?*[63]

This is also as much a social critique as it is a religious one. Tertullian's Christians are presented as being more socially-conscious as well as religiously righteous, while their unbelieving counterparts create a drastically opposing picture of both public and private immorality. But his central point is always the denunciation of Roman religion, and the characters of the gods are vilified as a means of further embarrassing their followers. The gospel allusion is reminiscent: they are the blind leading the blind.[64] In Tertullian's damning condemnation of great Roman historical figures, even the great Aeneas himself is not spared,[65] capping the acutely brazen nature of the work as a whole.

The text also ends as abruptly as it began. As it started by launching into an argument from its very opening, so it terminates in almost mid-flow of a refutation of the providential abilities of the Roman gods. Tertullian's final words constitute a warning that the power and authority currently enjoyed by the empire is fleeting and insecure.[66] In response to all accusations to the contrary, the Christians cannot be to blame for the disasters and calamities felt by the empire. Culpability lies instead with the failure of the public; the people of the *nationes*, to propitiate the true God.[67] The *Ad nationes* marks an invaluable contribution to the early stages of Latin apologetic for its inclusion of an exhaustive series of polemical attacks. It also lends itself very easily to reproduction and citation, due to its compartmentalised structure in

---

[63] 'But you shrink from and shun the wanderers, the exiles, the sick, the weak, the poorly-born and the lower classes; yet conversely even by law you honour the unchaste, adulterers, robbers and traitors. It is either a matter of laughter or of anger – should that sort of men be accepted as so excellent gods?'. *Ad nationes*, 2: 7; 7.

[64] Lk 6: 39.

[65] *Ad nationes*, 2: 9.

[66] *Ad nationes*, 2: 17. The subject of regulated time under the ultimate control of God himself; the *lex dei*, is further developed by Cyprian at *Ad Demetrianum*, 3: 3.

[67] *Ad nationes*, 2: 17. The issue of blame for instances of public suffering also forms the explicit purpose of Cyprian's *Ad Demetrianum*.

systematically deconstructing men, gods, poets, heroes, and philosophers. It is, in effect, almost a 'scrap-book' of polemical statements. While it is hardly encyclopaedic, it still comprises a lengthy and accessible body of re-usable apologetic and polemical arguments. And even if the tone is decidedly polemical, it still poses an important bridge with apologetic. The two styles of argument need not be considered as completely separate entities. Polemic is the attacking mode necessary in any good defence, and the *Ad nationes* supplies Latin apologetics with the most audacious textual justification of its early history.

Ad Scapulam

The relatively brief *Ad Scapulam* conveys a personal request in the manner of an epistolary appeal to the African governor Scapula for the relaxation of the persecutions.[68] Tertullian is intentionally candid, and faithful to the prime concern of his earlier apologetic works; the Christians are innocent of all accusations placed upon them, and the persecutions need to be ceased for the sake of all parties involved. The situation of Scapula as the named addressee influences the text in as much as what is written is absolutely fundamental to Tertullian's plea on behalf of the Christians. The text does not embark on lengthy digressions, and maintains direct focus throughout. The issues that are brought forth speak of the genuine feelings of Tertullian's community. But rather than immediately articulating the apologetic nature that underlies the text, Tertullian explains the *Ad Scapulam* as originating from the motives of Christian charity; the piece is a forthright attempt at saving the governor's soul.[69] There is also a noticeable eschatological current in operation, which is more marked than in his other apologetic texts. These elements combine in Tertullian's outline of his plan for the achievements of the work: *qui ergo dolemus de ignorantia uestra, et miseremur erroris humani, et futura prospicimus, et signa eorum cottidie intentari uidemus, necesse est uel hoc modo erumpere ad proponenda uobis ea quae palam non uultis audire.*[70] Fidelity to this concept of a defence of Christianity

---

[68] For a comprehensive explanation of the rhetorical elements used within the work, see Geoffrey D. Dunn, 'Rhetorical Structure in Tertullian's "Ad Scapulam"'.

[69] *Ad Scapulam*, I: 3.

[70] 'Therefore we grieve over your ignorance, we have pity on human error, and we provide for the future as every day we see its threatening signs. It is necessary to issue forth in this way, to relate to you what you are not willing to hear in public'. *Ad Scapulam*, I: 4.

on a more intimate level outside of the public sphere is also evident in the mention of the *occulta uia tacitarum litterarum*,[71] referred to in the opening statements of the *Apologeticum*. The fifteen-year time span that separated the two works has had little effect on changing Tertullian's apologetic motivation. The two texts are related pieces within his overall apologetic concern, as the *Ad Scapulam* condenses much of the material from Tertullian's earlier work, in order to support an exclusive plea to end the persecutions carried out in Scapula's name. Tertullian formulates a cry for the universal freedom of worship, within a passionate call to halt the suffering of the Christians.[72] He interjects with a plea for mercy, representing the expressive crescendo of the text before its end; *parce ergo tibi, si non nobis. Parce Carthagini, si non tibi.*[73] This is then followed by a personalised warning of the consequences of serving men over God; *ceterum quos putas tibi magistros, homines sunt et ipsi morituri quandoque.*[74] Although the Christians may be judged by men in the present, their accusers will be eternally judged by God.[75]

The principal feature of the *Ad Scapulam* is the epistolary nature which gives a direct force to Tertullian's broader appeals for justice and equality. The *antistites* of the *Apologeticum* and the *miserandae nationes* of the *Ad nationes* were never directly named, and as such they exist only as generic personalities in the background of the works. The *Ad Scapulam* adds a very present intensity to Tertullian's contentions which would otherwise be lacking in his wider apologetic corpus. Comparatively passing side-notes such as the allusion to recent events at Carthage,[76] and contemporary persecutions in Legio and Mauritania,[77] refer to the state of relations between Christian Church and Roman State in the early third century, and serve to contextualise Tertullian's present appeal. Although the *Ad Scapulam* is a shorter work in comparison with Tertullian's other apologetic texts, it also stands out as the most focused. Considering its late place in Tertullian's literary career, it could also be argued

---

[71] 'The hidden path of silent literature'. *Apologeticum*, 1: 1.

[72] *Ad Scapulam*, 2: 2.

[73] 'Spare yourself, if not us! Spare Carthage, if not yourself!'. *Ad Scapulam*, 5: 3.

[74] 'All the rest whom you believe to be your masters are men, and at some time or another they themselves will die'. *Ad Scapulam*, 5: 4.

[75] *Ad Scapulam*, 2: 10.

[76] *Ad Scapulam*, 3: 2.

[77] *Ad Scapulam*, 4: 8.

to represent the maturation of his apologetic thinking. From the polished *Apologeticum* and the brash *Ad nationes* of his earlier work, Tertullian's final extant composition is this candid piece of driven apologetic aimed at the governor of his province.

Conclusion

At its most basic level it could be argued that Tertullian employs a different style in addressing the *nationes*, emphasised by the more substantial defences of personal Christian virtue alongside a more vehement polemical argument. But this would leave the greatest part of the evidence untouched. In view of the circumstance that so much of Tertullian's apologetic material is recycled in order to suit changing purposes in each different work, so a larger picture of his apologetic concern as a whole can be drawn up. In the case of the *Apologeticum* and the *Ad nationes*, the latter is far more than just a preliminary draft of the former. The greater body of Tertullian's apologetic begins with the *Apologeticum*, and ends with *Ad Scapulam*, but transcends the texts individually and becomes part of a greater apologetic corpus which Tertullian continually borrows from and adds to. In this sense, the essence of Tertullian's apologetic motivation is the continuing defence of Christianity against an enemy that may occupy different social and religious positions, but still remains intrinsically the same. Whether his opponents are *antistites* or not, they are all part of the wider and more universal *nationes*. The judicial power held by the addressees of the *Apologeticum* and *Ad Scapulam* allows for the opportunity to emphasise such Christian virtues as fidelity to the law, support for the offices of the state, and non-treasonous motives for failing to sacrifice to the emperor, but the overall dimensions of each work essentially correspond. It is a consideration of the subtle differences between Tertullian's apologetic works that defines the homogeneity of them all. It is in this sense that Tertullian effectively creates a genre of apologetic within his own work; one which can be continually tweaked to respond to multiple opponents of Christianity. But just as he would redeploy concepts from the *Apologeticum* in the *Ad nationes*, and later in the *Ad Scapulam*, so too would succeeding generations of Latin apologetic writers, and Tertullian's developing genre would continue to be reworked for the same core motivations.

3. Tertullian's Christian sources

Even a theologian of such influence as Tertullian has his predecessors. He is neither the first Christian apologist, nor the first Christian Latinist, and although his works are remarkable for a great degree of originality, not all is completely without influence. Yet as he neglects to name any textual sources apart from what the classical authorities he is keen to engage with, so any connections with Christians of earlier generations have to be traced solely through textual allusions. This study is restricted to apologetic sources alone, as potentially contributory steps in the development of Tertullian's own forms of apologetic. The results of such a study are important for the location of Tertullian's apologetic work in front of a specifically Christian textual background, and in the evaluation of his framework of influence. An identification of his forbears is essential in the placement of Tertullian within the overall apologetic scene of early Christianity. In this section it is argued that Tertullian testifies to his awareness of some of these Christian works through a variety of uses of argument and modes of expression. The works included in this discussion are the *Apologia prima* and *secunda* of Justin Martyr, the anonymous *Epistula ad Diognetum*, the *Legatio* of Athenagoras, the *Passio sanctorum Scillitanorum*, and the *Octauius* of Minucius Felix; in line with his possibly earlier location. If the dating of Minucius could be shown to be conclusively later than Tertullian, then any such textual borrowings would naturally be traced to the priority of the *Apologeticum*, with Minucius as the copyist instead.

Scripture

One of the most pronounced features of Tertullian's theological corpus is his reliance on the interpretation of both the Old and New Testaments. Scriptural dependence as the primary foundation for his theological principles is markedly evident from his doctrinal writings. Scriptural analysis is ever-present in his doctrinal and anti-heretical works, and although toned down for his apologetic work, the allusions are there under the surface. Tracing every such influence would naturally form more than enough material for a lengthy study in itself, and the subject cannot be adequately treated within this discussion of Tertullian's apologetic. However, one key point can be included in order to broach the issue of Scriptural influences within his apologetic work; the explicitly evangelical motivation that fuels the meaning of

86

Ad Scapulam. The Gospel command ἀγαπᾶτε τοὺς ἐχθροὺς ὑμῶν καὶ προσεύχεσθε ὑπὲρ τῶν διωκόντων ὑμᾶς,[78] is taken by Tertullian to justify the composition of an attempt to save Scapula's soul.[79] In a similar vein as the purpose of the legal structure behind the framework of the *Apologeticum,* so too it is the Scriptural 'pray for those who persecute you' tenet that underlies the explicit motivation of the plea of *Ad Scapulam.* It is one of the most pronounced usages of a Scriptural allusion throughout his entire apologetic corpus. But otherwise, Tertullian is in line with one of the most characteristic features in the wider spectrum of Latin apologetics. The Scriptures are pushed into the textual undercurrent, and generally withdrawn from the apologetic argument.[80] In the engagement with an audience possessing little awareness of the Scriptures, let alone much respect for them as viable textual authorities, they cannot serve as the foundation for principles of belief developed in the apologetic argument. Commonplaces from which to construct bases of argument must instead originate from a commonly-respected philosophical authority, or a shared moral position. Under the demands of apologetic, Tertullian must hold back the texts of the Church in favour of the writings of Greece and Rome. In the *Ad natiores* in particular, any allusions to Scripture are rare occurrences,[81] and the purpose of the *De testimonio animae* is to create another outlet of textual recourse in the theological argument; *tanto abest, ut nostris litteris annuant homines, ad quas nemo uenit nisi iam Christianus.*[82] In the *Apologeticum,* he repeats a common satirical portrait of the God of the Christian believers,[83] which illustrates his dilemma through a simple but telling allegory: *is erat auribus asininis, altero pede ungulatus, librum gestans et togatus. Risimus et nomen*

---

[78] 'Love your enemies, and pray for those who persecute you'. Mt 5: 44. See also Rom 12: 14.

[79] *Ad Scapulam,* 1: 3.

[80] Especially with Minucius Felix and Arnobius, but compare Lactantius' more sophisticated deployment of multiple textual authorities, even to the inclusion of the Scriptures as evidence when required.

[81] One of the few examples would be the deployment of a proverb traditionally attributed to Solomon, referring to true wisdom as solely developing from the fear of God. *Ad nationes,* 2: 2. See Prov 9: 10, Ps 111: 10.

[82] 'So much less do men assent to our books; to which no-one comes unless already Christian'. *De testimonio animae,* 1: 4.

[83] Recurring in an anti-Christian derisory graffito found scrawled on a wall on the Palatine Hill, depicting a male figure worshipping before a crucified man with the head of an ass. For a sketch of the graffito with a brief explanation, see Graydon F. Snyder, *Ante Pacem: Archaeological Evidence of Church Life Before Constantine,* pp. 27–8.

et formam.[84] As it represents the importance of the Scriptures to the typical Christian believers, so it emphasises their more personal meaning for Tertullian himself. His dependence upon the Scriptures is one of the most marked features of his broader theological output, and his affectation for the pallium was ridiculed to the point of his great personal frustration.[85] Essentially, Tertullian personifies the Christian man *librum gestans et togatus*, carrying the Scriptures that form the crucial basis for his doctrinal principles. But it still stands that it is this deliberate shirking of the Scriptural foundation that lies behind Tertullian's apologetic collection as a whole, and his most influential single piece of work; the *Apologeticum.*

Justin Martyr

The entire genre of Christian apologetic seems to have its roots with the *Apologia prima* and *secunda* of Justin Martyr. Notwithstanding the problems surrounding the status of the two documents that now make up Justin's overall apology for Christianity, they remain as passionate and tenacious pieces of literature, and are among the most significant documents of the Church from the post-Apostolic age. Justin's presence can be felt throughout Latin apologetics for his position as the archetype of the entire Christian apologetic genre itself; it is his initial *Apologia* that brings forth the primary conceptual framework followed by the succeeding generations of Christian apologetic writings. But the focus of Justin's apologetic work is considerably different from that of Tertullian. Justin goes to greater lengths to support his theological standpoints, and cites directly from the Scriptures throughout. His apologetic works become as a result not only defences of Christianity, but also include the theological justification of Christian practices. Justin's positive vindication of Christian belief is a key part of his apologetic. Furthermore, Justin's utilisation of the Old Testament writings as evidence for the prophetically-ordained mission of Jesus and the Church takes up a sizeable part of his work.[86] Tertullian, on the other hand, has moved away from overt Scriptural usage within his attempt to present Christian apologetic on more neutral ground. Tertullian's depiction of particular areas of Christian

---

[84] 'It had asses' ears, a hoof for one foot, carrying a book and wearing a toga. We laughed at its name and appearance'. *Apologeticum*, 16: 12.

[85] Hence the *De pallio.*

[86] *Apologia prima*, 30–53.

theology, and his explanation of the life of the Church, also occupy more minor roles. Again, Justin's critique of the traditional Roman deities is minimal compared with Tertullian's devotion of virtually the entire *Ad nationes* to their attack. In like manner runs Justin's response to the infamous accusations of sexual immorality at Christian meetings; they are merely dismissed out of hand.[87] Compared with Tertullian's point-by-point refutation of the same accusations, Justin refers to them almost in passing within an overall assertion of the unimpeachable righteousness of the Church. The strength of Justin's apologetic lies in its exposition of some of the key controversial issues in Christian belief,[88] and in an engagement with the prophecies of the Old Testament to defend the theological heart of Christianity. Justin is highly aware of the value of the Hebrew prophets, but also conscious that an introduction is required before he can focus on their interpretation in identifying the prophetical foretelling of Jesus.[89] He appeals to established history and antiquity, and traces the inspiration of Plato to Moses as part of an attempt to validate the cited Old Testament statements.[90] They are recognised as an important step in the justification of Christian origins, and defended accordingly. In contrast, the strength of Tertullian's apologetic lies in the more practical justification of the inherent innocence of the Christians from all their criminal accusations. The dual legal and moral defence of Christianity as part of a plea for judicial equality is both the central aim of the *Apologeticum* itself, and a recurring feature in Tertullian's broader apologetic concern. But even if both sets of apologetic work have different key considerations, Justin's influence upon Tertullian can still be strongly felt.

One issue is the subject of the statue at Rome supposedly consecrated to the worship of Simon Magus, taken up with typically biting rhetoric by both apologists. Justin gives the inscription in Latin as *Simoni Deo Sancto*,[91] while Tertullian relates the dedication slightly changed as *Sancti Dei*.[92] Justin also gives the specific location of the statue,

---

[87] *Apologia prima*, 26.

[88] For example, as with the sacraments and weekly worship, *Apologia prima*, 65–67.

[89] *Apologia prima*, 31.

[90] *Apologia prima*, 59.

[91] *Apologia prima*, 26. For an overview of the subject of the monument itself, see Leslie W. Barnard, *St. Justin Martyr: The First and Second Apologies*, p. 136, n. 181.

[92] *Apologeticum*, 13: 9.

as ἐν τῷ Τίβερι ποταμῷ μεταξὺ τῶν δύο γεφυρῶν.[93] For Justin, the apparent veneration of Simon Magus proves that the people of Rome have elected to venerate a magician who operated under the influence of demons, and has been later deplorably raised to the honour of a god. For Tertullian, the Simon Magus connection is just another example in a long list of mistakenly-identified gods; as the Romans even honour Larentina the prostitute, so they have awarded Simon Magus the statue and inscription of a venerated deity. This seemingly innocuous usage of a shared argument provides an interesting piece of evidence in the evaluation of the extent of Justin's influence over Tertullian. Both apologists are conventionally considered to have mistaken in ascribing the origin of this statue to Simon Magus, instead of recognising its correct identification with the Sabine deity Semo Sancus. Although this could potentially have been a general bone of contention for late second century Christians, the more likely explanation is that Tertullian is testifying to his dependence upon Justin. Essentially, Justin made the original error of misinterpreting the inscription, and Tertullian later followed without verifying the truth behind the actual dedication. This theory would be supported by the conclusions of T. D. Barnes, in his attempt to reconstruct many of the aspects of Tertullian's life that seem to be based on incorrect traditional assumptions. Barnes has specifically called Tertullian's presence at Rome into question,[94] and it now seems a strong possibility that Tertullian never spent any time at Rome itself, and would thus have never personally seen the inscription. If correct, then Tertullian's chance of committing the Semo Sancus error by dependence on Justin's *Apologia* is far greater. Tertullian would have recognised the apologetic value in the Simon Magus incidence, and redeployed it for use in his own argument; unwittingly following the error first committed by the earlier apologist.

Both apologists also work to de-sensitise their non-Christian audience to the symbolism of the cross. This carries the additional purpose of reconciling its adoration in the Christian mind, with a more universal foundation where the cross is more than just an instrument of torture and violent death. Justin's depiction occurs in chapter 55 of the *Apologia prima*; after his establishment of the prophetic ordination of Jesus, and directly within his attack on the demonic forces beneath the harassment of Christians. His argument of the extended

---

[93] 'On the river Tiber, between the two bridges'. *Apologia prima*, 26. Greek text in A. W. F. Blunt ed., *The Apologies of Justin Martyr*.

[94] Barnes, *Tertullian*, pp. 243–5.

universality of the crucifical form comprises a specific illustration inside Justin's more general construction of the natural grounding for Christian tenets. Justin focuses on the likeness of the cross to the sail of a ship, and points toward the importance of the cruciform shape in tools and instruments. In his key argument, the cross becomes a representation of the gloried form of humanity itself, in the upright posture that separates mankind from the animal world.[95] But if this is the more philosophical placement of the cross, then its everyday usage is in the banners and standards of both military and public authority, under which even the emperors themselves are consecrated.[96] Justin's reasoning on the subject of the cross signifies a need to re-establish one of the key symbols of Christianity as a vitally positive concept, rather than a shameful object of suffering. Approximately forty years later, Tertullian takes up the argument with characteristic enthusiasm. He restrains himself in the *Apologeticum* to drawing comparisons with constructions of idols as standing-logs, the cross-beam structure used in the sculpture of statues, and the standards and trophies of state and military honour.[97] His trademark sarcastic expressiveness is again in operation, highlighted in the ridiculing remark of *laudo diligentiam: noluistis incultas et nudas cruces consecrare.*[98] Tertullian is underlining the place of the cross in Roman public life, presented as seemingly hitherto unnoticed by the detractors of Christianity. His more detailed address on the subject of the veneration of the cross occurs in the polemic of the *Ad nationes*. From the outset, it runs along the same lines as its corresponding passage in the *Apologeticum*, and even in parts as a word-for-word confluence. But then Tertullian includes a portrayal of the cross as a structure with deep significance for the human form, where the upright posture with outstretched arms betrays its underlying cruciform influence.[99] This is then followed by a likening of the cross to traditional banners and standards once again. The similarities between the depictions used by the two apologists are too strong to be completely independent of each other.

[95] The interpretation of upright posture is a highly recognisable motif in the Latin apologists. See Minucius Felix, *Octauius*, 17: 2, 11, Cyprian, *Ad Demetrianum*, 16, and Lactantius, *Diuinae institutiones*, 2: 1; 14–19, 2: 2; 23, 2: 18.

[96] *Apologia prima*, 55.

[97] *Apologeticum*, 16: 6–8.

[98] 'I applaud your diligence; you have not been willing to consecrate bare or uncultivated crosses'. *Apologeticum*, 16: 8.

[99] *Ad nationes*, 1: 12; 7.

In view of the date of production of the *Apologia prima* before the *Apologeticum* and *Ad nationes*, and following these brief examples, Tertullian's apologetic work can be shown to exhibit clear evidence of the influence of Justin.

Ad Diognetum

The obscure piece of Christian epistolary apologetic known as the *Epistula ad Diognetum* is conventionally placed as a product of either the second or third century, but even loose contextualisation is highly problematic. The text itself remained in almost total oblivion until its publication as a lesser epistle of Justin in an edition of 1592,[100] and due in no small part to these unclear origins, its place among the Patristic writings is difficult to define. It would be an interesting prospect to unite the Diognetus of the textual address with the tutor of Marcus Aurelius of the same name,[101] but therein lies the sole evidence for the argument. To address an apology for the Christians to the personal teacher of the emperor of Rome would certainly stand well in line with the more general tradition of directing Christian apologetic towards intellectuals of high social standing, but the lack of contextualising evidence restricts the basis for further supposition. The thesis of P. Andriessen relating the *Ad Diognetum* with the lost work of the early apologist Quadratus imparts a highly plausible contribution to the debate of the nature of the text, and is not improbable given the lack of many other alternatives.[102]

Tertullian's own relationship with the work is possible, but unlikely. There are several features of argument held in common between the *Ad Diognetum* and the *Apologeticum* in particular, but similar topics of discussion alone do not necessitate prior textual influence. Such elements would be the defences of Christians as equally ordinary men and women as everyone else,[103] and the unintentionally positive contribution of the persecutions to the life of the Church.[104] The primary candidate for evidence of textual dependence would be the critique of the futilities of idol-worship, articulated by both apologies along similar lines. The arguments

---

[100] See Philip Schaff, *Ante-Nicene Christianity*, Vol. 2, p. 699.

[101] Mentioned by Marcus Aurelius, *Commentariorum*, 1: 6.

[102] P. Andriessen, 'The authorship of the Epistula ad Diognetum', pp. 129–36.

[103] *Ad Diognetum*, 5: 1–6, compare *Apologeticum*, 42.

[104] *Ad Diognetum*, 6: 9, compare *Apologeticum*, 50.

hinge around the contention that as religious statues are created by humanity out of earthly materials, so it follows that their cultic adoration is therefore tragically misplaced. The *Ad Diognetum* deconstructs the stone, bronze, wood, silver and earthenware materials used in the construction of statues and images by comparing them with their more mundane usages,[105] while Tertullian's employment of the argument serves as the force behind his disdaining encapsulation of the impotence of the idols of Roman religion.[106] The interjection of the *Ad Diognetum* ταῦτα θεοὺς καλεῖτε[107] immediately after its verbal assault on the materialistic attributes of the idols, is echoed by Tertullian's corresponding *sed nobis dei sunt, inquis.*[108] This literary device of an engagement with the apparent interjection of a polemicised idol-worshipper introduces the crux of the argument, and also anticipates the most shared feature of the texts. A brief comparative analysis can bring out the key elements in question:

Ὑμεῖς γὰρ οἱ νῦν νομίζοντες καὶ οἰόμενοι, οὐ πολὺ πλέον αὐτῶν καταφρονεῖτε; οὐ πολὺ μᾶλλον αὐτοὺς χλευάζετε καὶ ὑβρίζετε, τοὺς μὲν λιθίνους καὶ ὀστρακίνους σέβοντες ἀφυλάκτους, τοὺς δὲ ἀργυρέους καὶ χρυσοῦς ἐγκλείοντες ταῖς νυξὶ καὶ ταῖς ἡμέραις φύλακας παρακαθιστάντες, ἵνα μὴ κλαπῶσιν;[109]

Et quomodo uos e contrario, impii et sacrilegi et irreligiosi erga deos deprehendimini, qui quos praesumitis esse, neglegitis, quos timetis, destruitis, quos etiam uindicatis, inluditis?[110]

---

[105] *Ad Diognetum*, 2: 1–4.

[106] *Apologeticum*, 12: 7.

[107] 'These things you call gods'. *Ad Diognetum*, 2: 5. Greek text in J. J. Thierry ed., *The Epistle to Diognetus*.

[108] 'But to us they are gods, you say'. *Apologeticum*, 13: 1.

[109] 'For although you believe and suppose that you are praising the gods, how much more are you actually disdaining them? Are you not much rather mocking and insulting them; worshipping those of stone and earthenware left unguarded, while those of silver and gold are locked up at night, and by day you set guards beside them lest they be stolen?'. *Ad Diognetum*, 2: 7.

[110] 'And how, because of this contrast, are you found to be impious, sacrilegious and irreligious towards the gods? You ignore those whom you presume to be gods, you destroy those whom you fear; you mock even those whom you champion'. *Apologeticum*, 13: 1–2.

The connection of professing to honour the created idols while actually mocking the deities they represent is concurrent, along with the
inequality of exalting some deities at the expense of others based on
materialistic value alone. The argument achieves a swipe at the illogical fallacies connected with the prevalent customs of Roman image-
worship, from the Christian perspective of its own transcendence of
the materialistic elements of religion. The critique of the earthly origin
of the statues, followed by the shared interjectory remark, concluding
with the theological hypocrisies inseparable from such forms of worship, and then further followed by an attack on the establishment of
a preferential hierarchy, all combine to pose similar features held in
common between the texts.

However, this instance is as likely to be too much a natural feature
of apologetic literature to justify any further conclusions. The example
of martyrs providing the public show of fortitude that encourages the
strength in conviction of the Church is another such particularly common feature,[111] along with the claims of injustice inherent in the public
hatred of the Christian name.[112] Utilising these issues as evidence in an
attempt to establish textual dependence would be mistaken. Even the
seemingly most probable example – the nature of the attack on idol-
worship cited above – cannot be cited as proof of prior textual influence. Two separate expressions of such a key issue within apologetic
writing as the veneration of idols, and only running along the broadest
lines of similarity, cannot provide adequate support for a case of literary dependence. From this perspective, there is not sufficient textual
support to ground the construction of a theory of influence of the *Ad
Diognetum* upon Tertullian's *Apologeticum*. Even if Tertullian's critique
still sounds reminiscent of *Ad Diognetum* 2: 7, it is overshadowed in
the same lines of argument by the far more likely influence of *Octauius*
24: 5-10;[113] provided the anterior dating of Minucius Felix can be
accepted. Tertullian's own formulation of the argument against image-
worship shares many more features in common with the *Octauius* than
the *Ad Diognetum*, and to such degree that the influence of Minucius
Felix would be inescapable, if the *Octauius* conclusively predates the
Apologeticum and *Ad nationes*.

---

[111] Justin, *Dialogus cum Tryphone*, 110.

[112] *Ad Diognetum*, 5: 11–17.

[113] Discussed below, pp. 102–3.

Athenagoras

Approximately twenty years before the date of Tertullian's *Apologeticum*, possibly along the coastal road of Roman North Africa at Alexandria,[114] Athenagoras was producing his own Christian apology. So little is conclusively known of Athenagoras that it is difficult to contextualise him adequately, but a dating period for the *Legatio* that ranges between November 176 and March 180 seems justifiable.[115] And very much like the *Ad Diognetum*, the relative anonymity of the author does little to affect the particular attributes of the work. The *Legatio* shows the touch of a well-educated Christian writer, confident in the use of the classics as well as the Scriptures, and highly able in his creation of a sophisticated piece of apologetic literature. If directly compared with Tertullian, and putting the latter's doctrinal works aside, Athenagoras gives the greater insight into Christian theology within the confines of an apologetic argument on its own. Alongside his unashamed usage of the Scriptures, Athenagoras mentions such theological issues as the Christian doctrine of God,[116] the Trinity,[117] and the Resurrection of the dead.[118]

Several apparently similar features of argument exist between the *Legatio* and the *Apologeticum*. One such could be the common usage by Justin, Athenagoras, Minucius Felix and Tertullian of a sentence from Plato's *Timaeus*. All five apologists employ an extract from *Timaeus* 28C in the establishment of a Christian doctrine of God, of particular utility for the apologetic setting.[119] Referring to the condition of God as uncreated and unknowable, the philosopher Timaeus of Locri in Plato's dialogue argued: τὸν μὲν οὖν ποιητὴν καὶ πατέρα τοῦδε τοῦ παντὸς εὑρεῖν τε ἔργον καὶ εὑρόντα εἰς πάντας ἀδύνατον

[114] Athenagoras seems to have been born an Athenian, but became head of the Christian catechetical school of Alexandria, and produced his work at this location. See Leslie W. Barnard, *Athenagoras: A Study in Second Century Christian Apologetic*, pp. 13–17, and Joseph Hugh Crehan, *Athenagoras: Embassy for the Christians, The Resurrection of the Dead*, pp. 4–8. For an introduction to Roman North African infrastructure, and the coastal road itself, see John Wilkes, 'Provinces and Frontiers', in *The Cambridge Ancient History*, Vol. 12, p. 241.

[115] Barnard, *Athenagoras*, p. 21.

[116] *Legatio*, 4, 7.

[117] *Legatio*, 10.

[118] *Legatio*, 36.

[119] Justin, *Apologia secunda*, 10: 6; Athenagoras, *Legatio*, 6; Minucius Felix, *Octauius*, 19: 14; Tertullian, *Apologeticum*, 46: 9.

λέγειν.[120] This extract is taken by the apologists as a suitable definition of the apophatic character of God, intended to be made more acceptable to the philosophical opponent of Christianity by virtue of its appropriated Platonic foundation. As can be noted from its first employment by Justin, and through the further usage of his successors, this citation from Plato's *Timaeus* became a common piece of Christian evidence in the apologetic depiction of the inherent unfamiliarity of God.[121] It is used to stand in support of the Christian opposition to the anthropomorphised qualities of the traditional gods. Justin utilises it to prefigure the revelatory work of Jesus, and Athenagoras to describe the sole and uncreated unity of God. For Minucius, it is another philosophical opinion in a list of many, drawn together in his painting of a picture of the divine attributes. Tertullian cites it to refer to the action of the Christian believer in revealing the true personality of God; somehow Plato has struck onto an acceptable mode of describing God from a Christian perspective, despite his worldliness as a human philosopher.[122] The Christians, on the other hand, are the only genuine seekers of truth.[123] The question as to the origin of the Platonic citation brings up the usage of doxographical texts; compilations of sentences from the great philosophers of antiquity. Athenagoras was certainly in possession of one such work,[124] and it is probable that Justin, Minucius, and Tertullian were also. Given the established priority of Justin's *Apologia*, and added to the possible anteriority of Minucius, Tertullian is probably testifying to his reading of either, or both. The usage of the same citation by Athenagoras does not point towards Tertullian's dependence on the *Legatio*, in view of his more solidly established textual relationship with Justin and Minucius Felix.

Other similar features between the texts would be the contention that Christians are of all men the most faithful to God and the emperor,[125] contrasted with the injustice of grounding persecution on

[120] 'But the maker and father of all this is difficult to find out, and when found, to speak of him to all men is impossible'. Plato, *Timaeus*, 28C. Greek text in R. D. Archer-Hind ed., *The Timaeus of Plato*.

[121] See even further, for example, its later usage by Gregory of Nazianzus, at *Orationes*, 28: 4. Gregory does not need to reference Plato as the source directly, but its ultimate influence is manifest. The *Timaeus* citation has become an essential element in the Christian apophatic demonstration of the character of God.

[122] *Apologeticum*, 46: 7, 18.

[123] *Apologeticum*, 46: 7.

[124] *Legatio*, 6. See also Barnard, *Athenagoras*, pp. 41–2.

[125] *Legatio*, 1, *Apologeticum*, 30–36.

the basis of the Christian name alone.[126] Legal imagery is also freely used by both apologists, and Roman religion is criticised along similar lines. But such details do not necessarily point towards literary dependence, and stem instead from fundamentally similar surrounding contexts. That the persecutions would be considered unjust is a relatively commonplace observation to make, along with the need for a refutation of the fabricated charges of sexual immorality, cannibalism, and the like. Specifically writing against the source of the Christian name alone as sufficient grounds for punishment is also to be expected, and would be a natural part of any defensive apologetic text. Although Carthage and Alexandria were in relative proximity on both the shipping routes and overland roadways of the infrastructure of Roman Africa, it must be said that Tertullian seems to bear no direct trace of Athenagoras' *Legatio*. The common themes between the works are evidence only of Justin, their common apologetic forbear, and the similar circumstances of late second-century Africa where they lived and wrote. It appears that Athenagoras' *Legatio* was either unknown, or at least relatively unimportant in the formation of Tertullian's apologetic, even if there are scattered modes of argument between the two texts that do initially seem to resemble each other.

The Scillitan martyrs

The *Passio sanctorum Scillitanorum* is possibly the earliest surviving text referring to Latin Christianity. Although brief, it concisely recounts the events of the trial and martyrdom of twelve North African Christians under the proconsul P. Vigellius Saturninus in July 180.[127] It is likely that the town of Scillium (or Scilli) was somewhere reasonably close to Carthage,[128] and therefore conceivably known by Tertullian geographically. The date of the piece itself cannot be fixed with any real conviction outside of its probable location in the general period following the recorded events, and is most likely to be fixed at 180. The work itself a remarkable document within early Christian literature for many reasons. Its style is throughout short, terse and official, and reads as though it could be an adaptation of the court record of the events of the trial, eventually developed into the primary

---

[126] *Legatio*, 2, *Apologeticum*, 1: 4-5, 18–19.

[127] Parallel Latin and English text, and brief introduction to the MS tradition in Herbert Musurillo ed., *The Acts of the Christian Martyrs*, pp. xxii–xxiii, 86–89.

[128] Following W. H. C. Frend, *Martyrdom and Persecution in the Early Church*, p. 313.

source of a Christian witness. Due to its relation of an event that can be dated to 180, it could well be the earliest datable textual witness of the establishment of Christianity in Africa. Also, it contains perhaps the earliest extant reference by a Latin Christian to the epistles of Paul, maybe even already rendered into Latin by this point. The usage of beheading as the manner of execution points towards the accused being Roman citizens, notwithstanding the Punic origin of the name of at least one of the company, Nartzalus.[129] When the proconsul Saturninus, officiating at the trial, asks Speratus, the unquestioned spokesperson for the group, what is inside his case, he replies *libri et epistulae Pauli uiri iusti*.[130] Speratus is the accepted leader of the Christians group, although any other information as to his particular identity is not given. Saturninus' plea to the others only as *ceteris* to *desinite huius esse persuasionis*,[131] also seems to corroborate him as the figure at the forefront of the accused. The Christian group go on to decline the official offer of reconsideration, and amidst cries of *Deo gratias*,[132] they are led away to death and martyrdom. The most significant recorded event in the early history of Christianity near Carthage takes place with their execution.

Evaluating the degree of influence of the *Passio sanctorum Scillitanorum* on Tertullian's apologetic requires a different mode of interpretation than with the other Christian sources. That the story of the Scillitan martyrs would have remained in the Church around Carthage is to be expected, and considering the relatively short length of elapsed time, the particular details would probably not have been forgotten. As such, although there is of course a possibility that Tertullian never had access to the text itself, his awareness at least of anecdotal evidence of the martyrdoms must be considered as likely. Furthermore, in his depiction in the *Ad Scapulam* of the divine retribution that has overtaken the persecutors of the Church, Tertullian shows his familiarity with the proconsul Vigellius Saturninus, *qui primus hic gladium in nos egit*.[133] The deserved punishment for his actions in condemning

---

[129] Henry Chadwick, *The Church in Ancient Society*, p. 118. The full list of the names of the seven men and five women is recorded at the very end of the *Passio sanctorum Scillitanorum* text.

[130] 'Books and letters of Paul, a just man'. *Passio sanctorum Scillitanorum*, 12.

[131] 'Cease to be of this persuasion'. *Passio sanctorum Scillitanorum*, 7.

[132] *Passio sanctorum Scillitanorum*, 17.

[133] 'Who was the first to use the sword against us here'. *Ad Scapulam*, 3: 4.

Christians to death is triumphantly traced to the loss of his sight.[134] Tertullian names no other specifics, and restricts himself to the statement that Saturninus was the first persecutor of the Carthaginian Church. It is little more than a passing mention in his argument, and some prior knowledge of these historical events in the mind of Scapula, the successor of Saturninus, is intended to be understood. As accounts of any other Christians who suffered under the order of Saturninus are unobtainable, the story of the Scillitan martyrs has to stand out as the singular incident relating to Christians in his proconsulate, if only for its sole survival in documentary form.

Tertullian's language in *Apologeticum* 1: 12 is also reminiscent of the events of the *Passio.* Indeed, T. R. Glover's edition in the Loeb series inserts a footnoted reference to the *Passio* text, on the basis of Tertullian's apparently obvious dependence. Although this may seem to be a rather impulsive addition at first, there is evidence to justify its possible inclusion. Tertullian includes five major points in his summation of Christian trial and martyrdom; the lack of either shame or regret in holding Christian beliefs, a strong sense of glorification in the eventual denouncement, a deliberate restraint from all self-defence, the immediate confession of faith upon questioning, and the ultimate expression of resolve in the rendering of thanks for earthly punishment as a Christian believer. All five points are clearly represented in the *Passio sanctorum Scillitanorum*, and pose a potential physical embodiment of Tertullian's more general examples. Tertullian's line *si accusatur, non defendit; interrogatus uel ultro confitetur; damnatus gratias agit*,[135] is suggestive of both the narrated events and the abrupt style of the *Passio sanctorum Scillitanorum* text. Preceded by Speratus' rejection of the imperial oath, the otherwise unknown Vestia is the first to confess *Christiana sum*;[136] the very exemplar of Tertullian's *interrogatus uel ultro confitetur.* Speratus' refusal to swear *per genium domni nostri imperatoris*[137] is echoed by Tertullian's later exposition on the theological grounding for the Christians' attitude to swearing *per Genios Caesarum.*[138] The positive Christian attribute of unswerving obstinacy

---

[134] *Ad Scapulam*, 3: 4.

[135] 'If he is accused, he does not defend himself; he even confesses voluntarily as he is questioned. He gives thanks as he is condemned'. *Apologeticum*, 1: 12.

[136] *Passio sanctorum Scillitanorum*, 9.

[137] 'By the genius of our lord the emperor'. *Passio sanctorum Scillitanorum*, 5.

[138] *Apologeticum*, 32: 2. See also *Apologeticum*, 33; Tertullian's further expansion on the relationship between the Christians and the emperor.

in faith is also a recurring motif in the two works; it is prevalent in Saturninus' closing remarks,[139] and is answered by Tertullian in some of the final lines of the *Apologeticum*.[140] As the Scillitan Christians are led away to their beheading, they exclaim *Deo gratias* in unison, led by Speratus' initial *Deo gratias agimus*;[141] a central point in Tertullian's glorification of Christian martyrdom corresponding with his own *damnatus gratias agit*.[142] Based upon these textual possibilities, and added to the circumstantial evidence favouring his prior knowledge of the events, Tertullian's awareness of the *Passio sanctorum Scillitanorum* is certainly viable. That the text itself was utilised directly by Tertullian in his preparatory work for the *Apologeticum* could also be possible, although more anecdotal descriptions of the martyrdoms would likely have been a feature of the Christian community located in the environs of late second-century Carthage.

Minucius Felix

Tertullian's knowledge and usage of Minucius Felix is clear if the priority of the *Octauius* is accepted. The textual concurrences with the *Apologeticum* are numerous and lengthy, and an anterior dating location would place the *Octauius* as one of the key steps in the formulation of Tertullian's apologetic. In order to avoid the formulaic tabular comparison between the two works, this analysis will focus instead on two key facets in the apologetic arguments; the treatment of the reported accusations of immorality, and the assault on the futility of image-worship, following from its consideration above as a potentially shared feature with the *Ad Diognetum*.

The *Octauius* addresses the slurs of immorality against Christianity with Caecilius' original introduction to the topic in chapter 9, and Octavius' eventual response follows at chapters 30-31. The Christians are accused of enjoining in lurid orgies under the sanctified façade of holy meetings,[143] involving the adoration of both the head of an ass and the genitalia of the presiding priest.[144] The more colourful allegations

---

[139] *Passio sanctorum Scillitanorum*, 14.

[140] *Apologeticum*, 50: 15.

[141] *Passio sanctorum Scillitanorum*, 15.

[142] *Apologeticum*, 1: 12.

[143] *Octauius*, 9: 2.

[144] *Octauius*, 9: 3–4.

of cannibalistic infanticide and ritual blood-consumption are also mentioned,[145] before the recounting of the notorious image of the dog tied to the lampstand used in the initiation of incestuous embraces.[146] Minucius' Christian Octavius counters the most part of the accusations with the ever-present *tu quoque* of Latin apologetics.[147] All sexually immoral imputations are rejected, and the Christian aversion to blood is presented as so distinct as to forbid even the involvement of animal blood in food preparation.[148] Tertullian's treatment in the *Apologeticum* of the allegations in question is markedly similar, if more scattered. The crimes of infanticide and incest are alluded to,[149] the Christian abhorrence of blood is detailed,[150] and the alleged worship of an ass denied.[151] The *tu quoque* is again employed as the primary method of repudiation, particularly in reference to the accusations of ass-worship. Both Minucius and Tertullian employ the comparison to the cult of Epona,[152] and their arguments run along corresponding lines. Each comparison is also followed by a parallel rejection of cross-worship. That the similarities between the accusations could be explained by their common occurrences on the contemporary scene is not impossible, but the far more likely explanation would place the influence behind this aspect of the *Apologeticum* directly with the *Octauius.* The supporting argument would be that since it is probable that Minucius is engaging with Marcus Cornelius Fronto with chapter 9 of the *Octauius*,[153] then it becomes a more natural development for Tertullian to adapt Minucius' text to fit with his own more general defences of Christian practice. Minucius' address on the subject takes a much more concentrated form, providing a rejoinder to the accusations of Fronto in hand, while Tertullian's more scattered placement suggests a broader form of response that is more reminiscent of the copy rather than the primary source itself. The location of the particular accusations coupled with their analogous responses, squares best

---

[145] *Octauius*, 9: 5.

[146] *Octauius*, 9: 6–7.

[147] *Octauius*, 30–31.

[148] *Octauius*, 30: 6. See above, pp. 48–9.

[149] *Apologeticum*, 7: 1; 8: 2–3, 7–9.

[150] *Apologeticum*, 9: 9–15.

[151] *Apologeticum*, 16: 1, 12.

[152] *Octauius*, 28: 7; *Apologeticum*, 16: 5.

[153] See above, pp. 32–4.

with Minucius' original retort to Fronto, which is then picked up by Tertullian. If the *Apologeticum* is argued to come first in the textual tradition, then Tertullian's neglect in mentioning such a prominent source as Fronto is less likely in comparison with the opposing scenario. It is instead more plausible that Fronto's detailing of the popular slurs against the Christians came first, before Minucius' subsequent response in the *Octauius*, which is then ultimately followed by Tertullian's borrowing of Minucius' treatment of the subject in the course of his own textual argument.

The critique in the *Apologeticum* of the traditional forms of the veneration of statues, already broached under the possible relationship between Tertullian and *Ad Diognetum*, possesses its most shared features of argument with the *Octauius*. Minucius denounces the power of any idol created for the purpose of adoration as the manifestation of a god. What was once a collection of earthly substances cannot become the incarnation of a deity by nothing else than the desire of man; *tunc postremo deus est, cum homo illum uoluit et dedicauit.*[154] The statue in question can only be the icon of religious error, and is solely recognised for its true form by the *mures, hirundines, milui* and *araneae,*[155] who foul it with their marks and droppings. For Minucius, this is no incarnation of a deity, but only a personification of the folly of man. Tertullian's own address of the issue follows similar lines, and correspondingly pinpoints the witness of the *milui et mures et araneae.*[156] However, while Minucius goes on to lambast the attendant rites of image-worship, Tertullian expressly cites the example of the apparent sacrilege posed by the kites, mice and spiders to support the Christian defence of abstaining from all such rituals. In response to the issue of Christians angering the traditional gods by failing to adore their statues, Tertullian follows the defilement by animals with its logical conclusion; *quod non est, nihil ab ullo patitur, quia non est.*[157] All attendant rites are simply erroneous and therefore futile, and Christian dissent can be justified on the most discernable grounds; would only the worshippers recognise the unpunished

---

[154] 'Then finally he is a god, when man wants him to be and dedicates him'. *Octauius,* 24: 8.

[155] 'Mice, swallows, kites and spiders'. *Octauius,* 24: 9.

[156] *Apologeticum,* 12: 7.

[157] 'What does not exist, suffers nothing from anyone, because it does not exist'. *Apologeticum,* 12: 7.

blasphemy of creatures defiling the sacred icons. Both apologists have interpreted the actions of the *milui et mures et araneae* along unmistakeably similar lines as evidence in a deconstructionist argument. In this particular instance, questions of similar circumstances in the background to the works do not answer the problem of the degree of textual dependence, and can be effectively dismissed. With respect to these two texts, the earlier provides the clear and conclusive inspiration for the later. In the case of the *Octauius* predating the *Apologeticum*, Tertullian would have another confirmed source for his apologetic work in Minucius Felix.

Tertullian's Christian sources – Conclusion

Tertullian's deliberate refusal to cite from the Scriptures within his apologetic argument is a noted characteristic of the Latin apologists. Utilisation of the poets and philosophers serves the dual purpose of justifying some particular areas in the Christian systems of belief, while also providing ammunition for the attack on the irrationalities of traditional Roman worship. Tertullian's Christian sources, on the other hand, produce the influence behind other aspects within his apologetic concern. His usage of a variety of Christian texts has been established, but with varying degrees of probable dependence. An awareness of Justin Martyr's *Apologia*, Minucius' *Octauius*, and either the text or related events of the *Passio sanctorum Scillitanorum* can be identified from his own apologetic work, if not the *Epistula ad Diognetum* or Athenagoras' *Legatio*. Much of the immediate style of Tertullian's apologetic bears the influence of Justin Martyr, a close relationship with the *Octauius*, and a possible nod to the *Passio sanctorum Scillitanorum* for its embodiment of the archetype of Christian steadfastness in the face of persecution and martyrdom. This above analysis has been necessarily limited to strictly apologetic potential sources, and has aimed to introduce the prior textual steps existent in the background to the formation of Tertullian's apologetic work. But although sources can provide inspiration, Tertullian's apologetic is hardly the less creative, or hardly less meaningful. Even if Minucius' *Octauius* can be shown to carry the dating priority over the *Apologeticum*, the latter remains of far greater consequence, and the magnitude of its author arguably unsurpassed in Latin Christianity before Augustine of Hippo.

4. Conclusion – Tertullian the apologist

Several features of Tertullian's apologetic have been outlined and discussed. The above exploration into a potential few of his Christian sources is a contribution to the picture of Tertullian as if not the first Latin apologist, then at least one of the most prolific. Tertullian is also very much the most multifaceted of the early Latin apologists. His *Ad Scapulam* is a case in point; lifting the more general arguments off the pages of the *Apologeticum* and the *Ad nationes*, and reconstructing them in the format of its focused personal appeal. It is still a particularly insightful example of directed apologetic. Like Justin before him, Tertullian lives during a period of great fear and uncertainty for the safety of the Church, and takes on the responsibility of providing the outward voice of the misunderstood Christian believers. But even if Tertullian's apologetic does represent the defence of an embattled minority religion, the *Ad nationes* speaks to a confidence that is unafraid to enter into dialogue, and unashamed in responding to accusations with fiery polemic turning the Church into the sole guardian of true religion. The sense of theological self-assurance underlying the text can be felt. Like Minucius Felix and the Latin apologists following, Tertullian is prepared to join battle with the opponents of Christian belief on their own grounds, and testifies to a fluid versatility in the deployment of non-Christian textual authorities. Perhaps the greatest measure of the achievement of Tertullian's apologetic lies in the observation that although this is a theologian normally reliant on Scriptural interpretation and exegesis, he has nevertheless produced his most enduring pieces with barely any Scriptural citation. Within the pressing demands of an apologetic schema, the Scriptures have to be temporarily sidelined in favour of traditional precedent and philosophy, and then the Christian apology can develop out of a common sphere of understanding. But Tertullian also implicitly alludes to the Christian apologists who preceded him, and one of his greatest literary skills lies in the usage of multiple Christian and non-Christian sources, brought together and sharpened by his own inimitable and ferocious Latinity. The result is the production of one of the most significant texts in Christian apologetics; the masterful *Apologeticum.* Eusebius mentioned a Greek translation,[158] and it is not difficult to appreciate the great utility of this piece during such a turbulent era for the Church. The need for defence by elucidation of Christian practice

---

[158] *Historia ecclesiastica,* 2: 2.

stood at the forefront of the contemporary situation, and is borne out by the continual calls for varied articulations of Christian apologetic throughout the early centuries of the Church.

But in Tertullian's lifetime at least, hope for the substantial relaxation of harassment by the presiding Roman authorities was a distant one. One of his most characteristic forms of expression, the pithy rhetorical sentence, encapsulated the Christian position at the time of his writing:

> *Uictoria est autem, pro quo certaueris, obtinere. Ea uictoria habet et gloriam placendi Deo et praedam uiuendi in aeternum. Sed occidimur. – Certe, cum obtinuimus. Ergo uincimus, cum occidimur, denique euadimus, cum obducimur.*[159]

Christian apologetic in this form is concerned with explaining the actual truth behind the notorious public perception of Christians with a view to the reversal of attitudes, and the eventual softening of the criminal imputations of the Church. But as ever, there is a dichotomy between balancing the appeals for an end to punishment on the one hand, while simultaneously lauding the glory of martyrdom for the Christian name on the other. It is a concept that is ever present in the Christian apologists, but no more strongly felt than with Tertullian. The *Ad Scapulam* exemplifies his understanding of the theological quandary inherent in the deplorable suffering of the persecutions, which is yet the vehicle for a glorious Christian martyrdom. His appeal to curb the anti-Christian measures is couched throughout the text in the strongest terms of defiance, and the believer is portrayed as devoid of fear or alarm; confidently justified by the righteousness of Christian purity, and secure in the knowledge of eternal life in the aftermath.[160] Even though the cause of apologetic is to defend the innocent Christian believers from disproportionate acts of punitive violence, yet the judicial measures endow the Christian believer with the everlasting crown of martyrdom. The persecutors also unwittingly contribute to the appeal of the Church, as those attracted to Christianity by the witness of the martyrs often become the next generation to suffer in

---

[159] 'Victory lies in obtaining that for which you have fought. This victory has the glory of pleasing God, and the spoils of living in eternal life. We are overcome, but we have really prevailed. Therefore we conquer when we are killed; we finally escape when we are overcome'. *Apologeticum*, 50: 2–3.

[160] See, for example, *Ad Scapulam*, 1: 1, 4: 1, 5: 1.

public for the Christian name.[161] Tertullian voices a sarcastic criticism of the Christian obstinacy in undergoing suffering, with profound relevance for the purpose of apologetics; *cur querimini, quod uos insequamur, si pati uultis, cum diligere debeatis, per quos patimini quod uultis?*[162] In answer to this, the purpose of apologetic literature is to rationalise the truth behind the adversity, and vindicate Christianity as a consequence from the prominent smears of impurity and illegality.[163] The balance between appealing for an end to the suffering of the persecutions, which would then necessarily deprive the victorious Christian soldier of the *gloria placendi deo*, is maintained.

[161] *Apologeticum*, 50: 15. Also at *Ad Scapulam*, 5: 4.

[162] 'Why do you complain that we persecute you, if you wish to suffer? You ought to love those by whom you suffer as you wish'. *Apologeticum*, 50: 1.

[163] Outlined by Tertullian at *Apologeticum*, 4: 1.

CYPRIAN

1. Introduction

Thascius Caecilius Cyprianus, the celebrated martyr-bishop of Carthage, is the next great personality in the African Latin tradition.[1] His surviving body of work is extensive, and addresses a range of numerous ecclesiastical and theological topics. Although Cyprian lived during some of the most turbulent times in the Early Christian epoch, apologetics is only a minor part of his discourse. But nevertheless, his one major apologetic text, the *Ad Demetrianum*, is a valuable contribution to the developing Latin apologetic tradition after the original work of Minucius Felix and Tertullian. Cyprian's position in Latin apologetics is often diminished as a result of his far more substantial focus on questions of ecclesiastical office, baptism, and the controversy over the lapsed, but his apologetic concern should not be completely overlooked. The *Ad Demetrianum* may be only one comparatively brief text in the larger Cyprianic corpus, but in the wider sphere of Latin apologetics it is witness to a particular change in style and expression. The work is specifically marked by an employment of Scriptural interpretation under an apologetic format, couched with

[1] Cyprian's enduring prominence in Latin Christianity is reflected by the depth and accessibility of the modern scholarly literature. The collections of his *Opera omnia* in both the CSEL and CCSL can also be complemented by more detailed versions of individual texts. Such are the translations and commentaries of G. W. Clarke, Maurice Bévenot, and Jean-Claude Fredouille. Clarke's four-volume edition of *The Letters of St. Cyprian* has become an invaluable resource in the study of Cyprian's life and work. The Latin edition and apparatus for the *Ad Demetrianum* used within this study is that of Jean-Claude Fredouille, in his edition *A Démétrien* in the Sources Chrétiennes (2003). Clarke's edition of the *Epistulae* provides the basis for the numerical alignment of Cyprian's body of letters referred to within this work.

apologetic terminology, and directed in defence of the persecuted Christian brethren. The strong presence of Scripture distinguishes Cyprian's *Ad Demetrianum* as unique within African Latin apologetics.

Lactantius placed Cyprian on a higher level of distinction than Minucius Felix and Tertullian by virtue of his eloquent style, easy lucidity, and deserved renown.[2] But Lactantius is not so admiring of Cyprian's particular apologetic style, and criticises the *Ad Demetrianum* for its focus on Scriptural engagement when responding to one (Demetrianus) who is entirely ignorant of the solely Christian writings.[3] Within this, Lactantius specifically articulates the Latin Christian reluctance to utilise the Scriptures in apologetic work:

> *Qua materia non est usus, ut debuit; non enim Scripturae testimoniis, quam ille utique uanam, fictam, commentitiamque putabat, sed argumentis et ratione fuerat refellendus. Nam cum ageret contra hominem ueritatis ignarum, dilatis paulisper diuinis lectionibus, formare hunc a principio tanquam rudem debuit, eique paulatim lucis principia monstrare, ne toto lumine obiecto caligaret.*[4]

Cyprian is not an apologist after the template of Minucius Felix or Tertullian. Even though Jerome's *De uiris illustribus* presents a seemingly concrete picture of the significant influence of Tertullian over Cyprian,[5] it would be a mistake to ally the two Carthaginian writers too closely. It is a connection that is often drawn upon generalisations, and without much in the way of definitive textual support.[6]

---

[2] *Diuinae institutiones*, 5: 1; 24–25.

[3] *Diuinae institutiones*, 5: 4; 3–8.

[4] 'Cyprian did not use the material as he ought to; namely he [Demetrianus] should have been rebutted by argument and reasoning, and not by the testimonies of Scripture, which he believed to be untrustworthy, fictitious, and fabricated. For since he was arguing against a man ignorant of the truth, Cyprian should have held the divine writings back for a short time. He should have formed [the argument] from the beginning, just as if this man was completely ignorant; gradually revealing the light to him at first, in order that he would not blind him by throwing the whole light before him'. *Diuinae institutiones*, 5: 4; 4–5.

[5] *De uiris illustribus*, 53; regarding Cyprian's veneration for Tertullian as *magistrum* ('the master'), and *Epistula*, 84: 2; referring to Cyprian's apparently self-evident influence of Tertullian throughout his work. Jerome wrote: *beatus Cyprianus Tertulliano magistro utitur, ut eius scripta probant*. 'The blessed Cyprian makes use of Tertullian as [his] master, as his works demonstrate'.

[6] As, for example, with Hans von Campenhausen: 'Cyprian was bishop of Carthage and never mentioned the dissident Tertullian by name; all the same, his inner relationship to him can be noticed throughout his writings'. *The Fathers of the Latin Church*, p. 36.

Maurice Bévenot has drawn attention to this point, and cited some key examples of divergence between the two writers, with the conclusion that 'Cyprian was not the man to follow another blindly, least of all a Tertullian who had turned Montanist'.[7] Upon an inter-textual examination of Tertullian and Cyprian, Jerome's confident statements of influence and dependency certainly do appear to be over-emphasised, and perhaps even exaggerated. Also, Cyprian's vociferous condemnation of schismatic groups within the Church would make his confidence in Tertullian's later more overtly 'Montanistic' works (such as the *De pudicitia* and *De fuga* of Bévenot's comparative examples) suspect. Furthermore, in the *Ad Demetrianum*, although the direct format of the particular address to Demetrianus is reminiscent of the immediate style of Tertullian's *Ad Scapulam*, there are no textual allusions to the earlier work. The *Ad Demetrianum* is also very much a stand-alone text within the Cyprianic corpus itself. There is no mention of either the lapsed Christians or the intra-ecclesial controversies following the Decian persecution, and an equal level of silence relating to any background information or corroborating events.

The life of Cyprian

As is commonplace among Christians of his era, Cyprian divulges little of his pre-converted life. It is unnecessary for the edification of his people, and therefore almost completely absent from his biographical details.[8] Aside from a few hints within his own work, much of the information for Cyprian's life has to be taken from the *Uita Caecilii Cypriani* compiled by his deacon Pontius,[9] read with the necessary proviso that factual accuracy is subordinated to pious reflection throughout. The general observations that can be justified

---

[7] Bévenot, *De lapsis and De ecclesiae catholicae unitate*, p. xvii. The examples are *De lapsis*, 17–20, with *De pudicitia*, 2: 3, 11: 2, 18: 18, 22, regarding authority in the forgiveness of sins, *Epistula*, 64: 2–6, with *De baptismo*, 18: 4–5, regarding infant baptism, and *Epistula*, 14 and 20, with the positions of Tertullian's *De fuga in persecutione*, in contextualising the theological justification of Cyprian's retirement during the Decian persecution.

[8] An understanding encapsulated by Pontius; *fuerint licet studia et bonae artes deuotum pectus imbuerint, tamen illa praetereo: nondum enim ad utilitatem nisi saeculi pertinebant.* 'Although study of the liberal arts may have occupied his mind when devoted to them, I pass over these things. For they pertained to nothing but his secular advancement'. *Uita Caecilii Cypriani*, 2. Cyprian's own passing discussion of his pre-Christian life can be found at *Ad Donatum*, 3–4.

[9] Latin text in G. Hartel ed., *S. Thasci Caecili Cypriani Opera Omnia*, Vol. 3, pars 3.

are Cyprian's position of some degree of wealth and influence, his possible occupation as a teacher of rhetoric at Carthage,[10] and the location of his conversion at a relatively late point in life. His agnomen Caecilius is a touching reference to his spiritual mentor in the early days of his adoption of Christianity. Pontius defined Cyprian's regard for the otherwise unknown Caecilius as *non iam ut amicum animae*[11] *coaequalem, sed tamquam nouae uitae parentem.*[12] Beyond this, further information is difficult to elucidate. Cyprian seems to have been the popular choice for bishop at Carthage in 248-9,[13] and the rapid manner of his ascent to episcopal authority points towards a virtual celebrity status; at least in the eyes of the admiring Pontius, if nowhere else.[14] The African Church needed a strong, decisive leader; a position for which Cyprian possessed the required energy, character, and conviction, and his voluminous correspondence testifies to his key influence in wide-ranging ecclesiastical affairs in both Africa and further afield at Rome. The era of Cyprian's African Church is rife with both internal and external controversies, and his character remains indelibly imprinted upon them.

Cyprian's episcopal tenure witnessed two imperial-sponsored persecutions, becoming the key events around which his Christian life and legacy hinged. Under the effects of the Decian persecution at Carthage in 250, Cyprian's opting for a potentially ignominious form of retirement into exile had to be explained away by Pontius in a direct response to accusations of cowardice and unfaithfulness; *uultis scire secessum illum non fuisse formidinem?*[15] Although he continued to lead the Church *in absentia*, the decision not to face the persecution directly was a highly significant one which both Pontius and Cyprian himself felt the pressing

---

[10] Not mentioned by Pontius, but following Jerome, *De uiris illustribus*, 67.

[11] For example, like the relationship of Octavius and Minucius Felix. *Octauius*, I: 1–4.

[12] 'Not as an equal friend of the soul, but as the father of his new life'. *Uita Caecilii Cypriani*, 4.

[13] Following the dating of Michael M. Sage, *Cyprian*, p. 138.

[14] Although it is probably more a reflection of the appreciation of his social value (See Sage, p. 135), Pontius writes of Cyprian's great popularity amongst the Carthaginian believers. *Uita Caecilii Cypriani*, 5. So Clarke: 'It sounds as if Cyprian was an unusually well placed and educated convert for this Church; he was too competent and prominent a figure to pass by in filling the vacant *cathedra* of Carthage'. *The Letters of St. Cyprian*, Vol. I, p. 16.

[15] 'Do you wish to be assured that his withdrawal was not due to fear?'. *Uita Caecilii Cypriani*, 7.

need to justify.[16] The Decian persecution prompted the question of the treatment of Christians who had lapsed in fear of punishment, and a specific theological understanding of how to act under compulsion to sacrifice is enshrined in the *De lapsis*. The concern of the lapsed is one of the central issues in Cyprian's theological development. Upon his return to full episcopal control, the residual effects of persecution could be witnessed in such controversies as the re-baptism of heretics, the relationship between the Church and the confessors, and the administration of penance for those who stumbled under the threats of violence. Cyprian's directive was to call for absolute unity and solidarity in one community under its bishop, encapsulated in his tract *De ecclesiae catholicae unitate*; the heart of his theological legacy. In many ways, Cyprian's theological character is moulded by the events of the persecutions; the Decian compulsion to sacrifice precipitated the main subject-matter of his tracts and epistles, and Valerian's renewed anti-Christian onslaught eventually led to his trial and execution, exemplifying the actions of the steadfast believer under persecution.[17] His martyrdom for the Christian name under Valerian in September 258 at Carthage is elaborately described by Pontius,[18] and also exists in greater detail in the *Acta proconsularia*. Cyprian's conduct throughout his trial and martyrdom is seen as the very personification of the righteous Christian leader; appealing for unity and tranquillity to the utmost with his last epistle to the Carthaginian brethren,[19] and standing firm in his convictions under the direct accusations of the proconsul. His beheading gave the Carthaginian community its first heroic martyr-bishop, and the model figure essential for Christian unity in the face of persecution.

2. The *Quod idola dii non sint*

Conventionally, Cyprian's sole apologetic work is accepted to be the *Ad Demetrianum*, although there is dispute over the authorship of the obscure *Quod idola dii non sint*,[20] and its possible location amongst the

---

[16] *Epistula*, 14: 1, 20: 1, *Uita Caecilii Cypriani*, 7–8.

[17] Details of the Valerianic edict which outlined the terms of punishment for unrepentant Christians are given by Cyprian himself, at *Epistula*, 80: 1.

[18] *Uita Caecilii Cypriani*, 16–19.

[19] *Epistula*, 81.

[20] Also otherwise titled as the *De idolorum uanitate*. See *Clavis Patrum Latinorum* #57.

authentic Cyprianic corpus. Both Jerome[21] and Augustine[22] accept the work as genuine, but Pontius is completely silent on the issue.[23] Lactantius only refers to the *Ad Demetrianum* in discussing Cyprian's apologetic. Consequently, the modern debate is torn between acceptance and rejection. Considered on its own, the *Quod idola dii non sint* is an essentially unremarkable piece of work, except for the issues which arise from attempts at genre location. Although it is little more than a selective confluence of arguments from the *Octauius* and the *Apologeticum*, the *Quod idola dii non sint* is not strictly a piece of apologetic in itself. The compiler has utilised particular incidences from these prominent apologetic works in the service of his own agenda, which is a justification of Christian theological principles through the corresponding deconstruction of aspects of Roman religion. The tone is apologetic, but the primary audience could actually instead be Christian. The final chapters of the work, in detailing a basic Christology, also form an exhortation to the Christian believers to maintain their convictions in the face of pain and suffering.[24] It is not a piece of purely apologetic literature in the sense of the *Octauius* or the *Apologeticum*, even in view of the level of citation from the two works. Following is a brief consideration of the primary arguments on either side of the authenticity debate.

Against its authenticity, the text itself is a compilation of material borrowed from Minucius Felix's *Octauius* and Tertullian's *Apologeticum*, and as such bears almost no mark of independent thinking. Therefore, any personal stamp would be impossible to identify. The key textual influence is the *Octauius*, and large chunks of the *Quod idola dii non sint* are verbatim transcriptions. Incidentally, it has been

---

[21] *Cyprianus, quod idola dii non sint, qua breuitate, qua historiarum omnium scientia, quo uerborum et sensuum splendore perstrinxit?* 'With what conciseness, with what knowledge of all history, with what brilliance of words and reasoning did Cyprian touch upon in *That idols are not gods?*'. *Epistula*, 70: 5.

[22] *De baptismo*, 6: 44; 87. Augustine's allusion is to *Quod idola dii non sint*, 6.

[23] The allusion to Cyprian's apologetic would not seem to include the *Quod idola dii non sint*, if known by Pontius, due to the prominence of the *tu quoque* in his statement, which is entirely absent from the arguments of the compilation work. *Uita Caecilii Cypriani*, 7.

[24] *Dolor, qui ueritatis testis est, admouetur, ut Christus Dei filius, qui hominibus ad uitam datus creditur, non tantum praeconio uocis sed et passionis testimonio praedicaretur.* 'Pain, which is the witness of truth, is applied in order that Christ, the Son of God, who is believed to have been given to men for life, might be declared not only with the proclamation of the voice, but by the witness of suffering'. *Quod idola dii non sint*, 15. Latin text in G. Hartel ed., *S. Thasci Caecili Cypriani Opera Omnia*, Vol. 3, pars 1.

argued that this lack of originality 'militates against' the Cyprianic authorship.[25] Another argument is even to date the text post-Lactantius, on the basis of textual borrowings between the *Quod idola dii non sint* and the *Diuinae institutiones*.[26] Such varied dating ranges are supported by the lack of corroborating background evidence in the text, the absence of the work in the biography of Pontius, and its own less than conclusive position in the manuscript tradition.[27] Taken as a whole, the *Quod idola dii non sint* completely lacks an introduction, the style is markedly indirect throughout, and the unidentified author provides no level of detail that could be employed in any dating or contextualisation.

In favour of the Cyprianic authenticity of the *Quod idola dii non sint*, the testimonies of Jerome and Augustine are cited as the most ancient affirmative sources. Following this, it can be said that in spite of its later general condemnation as most likely spurious, it was once accepted as part of the Cyprianic canon. Any arguments based on the incongruity of the piece amongst Cyprian's accepted works due to questions of originality can also be discounted, as similar contentions to the advocacy of Tertullian's anteriority to the *Octauius* from the unsupportable interpretive evidence of an innovative personality alone. The *Quod idola dii non sint* is accepted by Claudio Moreschini and Enrico Norelli,[28] placing the text during the early period of Cyprian's Christian writing.[29] Quasten also favours its location within the authentic corpus.[30] In scholarly works where the authenticity of the text is favoured, there tends to be a general consensus in following the rationale of Manlio Simonetti's article on the subject.[31] But even in view of the nature of the *Quod idola dii non sint* as a compilation, there is nothing in it to definitively disprove the possibility of the Cyprianic authorship. Perhaps

[25] Sage, *Cyprian*, p. 373. It is also entirely absent from Luc Duquenne's *Chronologie des Lettres de S. Cyprien*.

[26] See H. Diller, 'In Sachen Tertullian-Minucius Felix', pp. 98–114, 216–239.

[27] It is noticeably missing from the 'Cheltenham List' of the Cyprianic corpus. For the details, see T. Mommsen, 'Zur Lateinischen Stichometrie', pp. 142-156, and also J. Chapman, 'The Order of the Treatises and Letters in the MSS of St. Cyprian', pp. 103–123.

[28] *Early Christian Greek and Latin Literature: A Literary History*, Vol. I, p. 366.

[29] Something previously held by Edward White Benson; ascribing the *Quod idola dii non sint* as 'his first labour'. *Cyprian: His Life, His Times, His Work*, p. 9.

[30] *Patrology*, Vol. 2, pp. 363–4.

[31] 'Sulla Paternità del *Quod idola dii non sint*', pp. 265–88.

it could have been compiled as something of an *aide-mémoire* – a selective composition in the conflict with Roman religion,[32] created by Cyprian for a specific purpose, and therefore retaining a place amongst his body of work without the particular format (for example, a formal introduction) which would be inserted for publication. Stylistically, the prominence of copied material makes textual comparison difficult, but the concluding remarks of the *Ad Demetrianum* and the *Quod idola dii non sint* bear certain similarities that reveal an insight into the underlying purpose of the individual works. Both endings are explicitly Christological, with studied fidelity to the Gospel accounts.[33] Each text also comes from an author who is unafraid to employ philosophy and Scripture side-by-side under the overriding concern of apologetics. While the purposes of the *Octauius* and the *Apologeticum* are the philosophical and legal justifications of Christianity respectively, the *Ad Demetrianum* and *Quod idola dii non sint* hinge around the importance of the evangelising role of apologetics, by concluding with exhortations to the Christian way of salvation. A shared understanding of the purpose of apologetics can thus be noted. Although this does not expressly point towards Cyprian's genuine authorship, it would help to locate the *Quod idola dii non sint* on a generically related plane with the *Ad Demetrianum*.

The consequence of the *Quod idola dii non sint* chiefly lies in the thematic structure of its selectively cited arguments, which in turn points toward the issues of greatest concern for the original compiler. The greatest part of the work is concerned with the question of the true status of deity; the Roman gods are deconstructed to an ultimately human provenance,[34] demons are identified as the true source of any non-Christian agency or prophecy,[35] and Christian monotheism is defended as the solely accurate portrayal of God.[36] In relation to the *Ad Demetrianum*, where the main reproach of Christianity stems from the blame for a supposed decline in worldly vitality, chapter five of the *Quod idola dii non sint* has particular significance. Within an understanding that ascribes the fortunes of the Roman empire to its

---

[32] In effect, along the same lines as the collection of Scriptural citations which form the *Ad Quirinium* and the *Ad Fortunatum*.

[33] *Ad Demetrianum*, 25–26, *Quod idola dii non sint*, 13–15.

[34] *Quod idola dii non sint*, 1–3.

[35] *Quod idola dii non sint*, 6–7.

[36] *Quod idola dii non sint*, 8–9.

conscientious piety in ensuring that all tutelary gods are propitiated, any ostensible worldly decay can be easily explained as the fault of those who refuse to sacrifice. The compiler of the *Quod idola dii non sint* employs material from the *Octauius*, and attacks the traditional confidence in the temporal benefits of the auspices and auguries.[37] But in a passage loaded with direct citations, one of the key lines of argument is not found in Minucius Felix; testifying to the need on the part of the compiler to further emphasise the point in question. In a work that is chiefly based upon the accumulation of second-hand arguments, this is one of the few original comments; here employed in the service of clarification and redirection of the point in hand. The contention is *non ergo de religionibus sanctis nec de auspiciis aut auguriis Romana regna creuerunt, sed acceptum tempus certo fine custodiunt.*[38] This would concur with the general position of the *Ad Demetrianum* regarding the *lex dei* and the issue of appointed time: *haec sententia mundo data est, haec Dei lex est ut omnia orta occidant et aucta senescant et infirmentur fortia et magna minuantur et cum infirmata et deminuta fuerint finiantur.*[39] The principal reasoning corresponds in its expression of the relationship between temporal fortune and the prescribed limitations of God. There is a thematic similarity between the two statements which could contribute towards a related identification, and would be conjecturally placed below the testimonies of Jerome and Augustine in favour of the authenticity of the *Quod idola dii non sint.* The proximity of style with Cyprian's two other compilatory works, the *Ad Quirinium* and *Ad Fortunatum*, is perhaps also too close to be completely ignored.

The question of authenticity remains unresolved, but the favour of Jerome and Augustine regarding its accepted place within the canon should be taken as the starting-point which needs to be conclusively disproved. Such is the conclusion of Simonetti,[40] and it seems to be the generally accepted, if not quite universal position. But that being stated, the value of the *Quod idola dii non sint* within an analysis of Cyprian's apologetic is still considerably below

[37] *Quod idola dii non sint*, 5. The citations are from *Octauius*, 25: 12–26: 4.

[38] 'The Romans have not attained domination by pious worship, auspices or auguries, but they hold their received time with a fixed limit'. *Quod idola dii non sint*, 5.

[39] 'This is the sentence pronounced upon the world, this is the law of God; all that is born will die, all that is abundant will decline, the strong will become weak, the mighty will be brought low, and when they are weakened and diminished they will be brought to an end'. *Ad Demetrianum*, 3: 3.

[40] 'Sulla Paternità del *Quod idola dii non sint*', pp. 287–8.

that of the *Ad Demetrianum*, primarily due to its nature as a document of compilation. The *Quod idola dii non sint* retains a position in the textual background of Cyprian's apologetic, but its actual value is second to the original literary platforms of the arguments in question.

3. Cyprian as Christian apologist – the *Ad Demetrianum*

We now come to an analysis of Cyprian's *Ad Demetrianum* and its place amongst the surrounding works of Latin apologetics. Cyprian's contribution to the developing tradition can be established through an examination of the text in its own right, in order to move away from the weight of his theological and ecclesiological impact and solely isolate his apologetic concern.

The *Ad Demetrianum* takes the form of a direct riposte to the anti-Christian railings of an otherwise unknown Demetrianus. Pontius is almost certainly referring to the *Ad Demetrianum* in his summing-up of Cyprian's apologetic undertaking; *per quem gentiles blasphemi repercussis in se quae nobis ingerunt uincerentur?*[41] The explicit hint at the *tu quoque* formula, already a marked feature in Latin apologetics after Minucius Felix and Tertullian, can indeed be strongly noted with Cyprian. The central argument of the text pivots on the question of the Christian role in a purported decline in worldly vitality and prosperity – the relatively common imputation of blame for natural disasters that is laid at the Christians' door. Another example of this can be found in Cyprian's *Epistulae*, in a letter from Firmilian, Bishop of Caesarea in Cappadocia, to Cyprian, in the aftermath of the baptismal controversy with Pope Stephen.[42] Firmilian recounts the incidence of a localised Christian persecution around Cappadocia and Pontus dated to 235 under the governor Serenianus.[43] Following a spate of devastating earthquakes, the Christians were targeted; *ut ex hoc persecutio*

---

[41] 'By whom would the blasphemous gentiles be overcome by retorting back on themselves the things they brandish against us?'. *Uita Caecilii Cypriani*, 7.

[42] *Epistula*, 75.

[43] Identified as the driving force behind the persecution itself; *Serenianus tunc fuit in nostra prouincia praeses, acerbus et dirus persecutor.* 'Serenianus was governor of our province at that time – a bitter and terrible persecutor'. *Epistula*, 75: 10; Latin text in G. Hartel ed., *S. Thasci Caecili Cypriani Opera Omnia*, Vol. 3, pars 2.

quoque grauis aduersum nos nominis fieret.[44] At least theoretically, the basis for persecution is an extension from the justification of Roman felicity from its celebrated piety in absorbing all deities under the umbrella of its polytheistic worship. At times when the Roman world seemed to be suffering, blame could relatively simply be apportioned to the publicly dissenting movement of Christians, particularly if they appeared to be growing in prominence. The theme of scapegoating the Christians can also be found in Tertullian[45] and Arnobius,[46] but Cyprian's *Ad Demetrianum* articulates the most extensive subject-specific response to the issue, in proportion to its text as a whole. The insight provided by Cyprian, and also by Arnobius of Sicca, points toward the denouncement of Christians due to their perceived nature as effectively being ritually unclean,[47] and offensive to the gods in consequence. Public discontent is manifested in outbursts of suspicion and ill-feeling, and the Christians become subject to accusations of bearing the moral culpability for the supposed acts of divine vengeance. The *Ad Demetrianum* is a rebuttal of these allegations, which also supports a platform for the apologetic establishment of Christian virtue in the face of legal harassment.

The structure of the *Ad Demetrianum* can be considered under six main thematic headings.[48] After the introductory remarks (chapters 1–2), and the outlining of the interpreted 'aging' of the world (3–4), the text moves on to its core arguments. The blame for divinely-influenced suffering is ascribed not to the lack of Christian reverence for the Roman gods, but instead to the immediate reverse: God's righteous anger upon the unbelief of the Roman world (5–9). Cyprian outlines the sin and hypocrisy of the non-Christian populace (10–16), followed by the Christian perspective on the issues of worldly suffering (17–21).

---

[44] 'As a result of this, a severe persecution arose against us because of the Name'. *Epistula*, 75: 10; 1.

[45] Hence Tertullian's well-known encapsulation of the subject: *si Tiberis ascendit in moenia, si Nilus non ascendit in rura, si caelum stetit, si terra mouit, si fames, si lues, statim Christianos ad leonem!* 'If the Tiber reaches up to the walls, if the Nile does not rise to the fields, if the heavens stand still, if the earth moves, if there is famine or plague, straightway it is cried "the Christians to the lion!"'. *Apologeticum*, 40: 2. See also *Ad nationes*, 1: 9.

[46] *Aduersus nationes*, 1: 1–13.

[47] For other examples of scapegoating the ritually unclean in the ancient world, see Brent D. Shaw, 'Rebels and Outsiders', in *The Cambridge Ancient History*, Vol. 11, pp. 391–2.

[48] Fredouille, at *A Démétrien*, p. 20, has defined three major parts plus an introduction, but it can be extended further for greater clarity.

A foretelling of judgment and a plea for the acceptance of Christianity form the concluding chapters (22–25).

Context

The person of Demetrianus himself is completely obscure outside of Cyprian's text. The historical record is devoid of any corroborating reference, and Cyprian's given details are insufficient for the construction of his profile. The scholarly estimates range from his unlikely position as the proconsul of Africa,[49] to the more plausible, if less specific, location as a local magistrate.[50] Little can be stated with certainty, but it is clear from the text that Cyprian regarded Demetrianus as connected with the fountain-head of localised anti-Christian feeling, and likely based around Carthage itself. It is likely that Demetrianus played a significant part in rousing a level of anti-Christian antagonism, if not actually during the recent Decian persecution then certainly in its aftermath. Cyprian suggests Demetrianus' influence, while also expressly describing the primarily apologetic nature of his text:

> *Respondeo igitur et tibi, Demetriane, pariter et ceteris quos tu forsitan concitasti et, aduersum nos odia tuis maledicis uocibus seminando, comites tibi plures radicis atque originis tuae pullulatione fecisti: quos tamen sermonis nostri admittere credo rationem. Nam qui ad malum motus est mendacio fallente, multo magis ad bonum mouebitur ueritate.*[51]

Coupled with a dating range of c. 251–3, with 252 as the strongest possibility,[52] a tentative contextualisation for the work can be achieved. Its location at Carthage in the post-Decian milieu can be justified. Cyprian's uncritical acceptance of the decline of worldly vitality is

---

[49] The inference of Robert Ernest Wallis, the translator of Cyprian's work for the Ante-Nicene Christian Library series. *The Writings of Cyprian, Bishop of Carthage*, Vol. I, p. 423.

[50] Sage, *Cyprian*, p. 276.

[51] 'Therefore I am responding to you, Demetrianus, together with all the rest whom you have perhaps inflamed. With your slanderous words you have sown hatred against us, and from the sprouting of your own root and origin you have made many companions; yet they are still those who I believe will admit the reason of my discourse. For whoever is moved to evil by the deception of a lie will so much the more be moved to good by the truth'. *Ad Demetrianum*, 2: 2.

[52] Although it bears no mention of the episcopal council assembled by Cyprian from May 252 to address the question of the lapsed, the text is singularly intended as a response to the criticism of Demetrianus, and has no purpose for the direct mention of division amongst the Carthaginian believers.

testament to its being a commonly-held conviction,[53] and one that is relatively free from the religious divide.[54] This particular outburst can perhaps be traced back to a resurgence with the empire-wide plague that reached Carthage around 252;[55] it also made no distinction between the religious communities, and touched its unfortunate victims regardless of their religious persuasion.[56] Cyprian's more direct treatment of the plague as a theological issue forms the ultimate purpose of the *De mortalitate*, in its provision of encouragement to remain steadfast in the faith despite the terrible effects of the ravaging disease. His exhortation even includes a detailed depiction of the bodily symptoms of the plague,[57] which are interpreted as another trial of Christian faith. The consolation is that as the plague is the instrument of mortal death, so it is therefore the release into sublime immortality.[58] Such death is not punishment or suffering, but liberation; *multi ex nostris in hac mortalitate moriuntur, hoc est multi ex nostris de saeculo liberantur.*[59] Even though direct discussion of the plague is more prominent in the *De mortalitate*, it is still present in the *Ad Demetrianum* in the textual undercurrent.[60] A response to Demetrianus' public blame of the Christians as being the source of the plague could be a key part of the motivation for the *Ad Demetrianum*, and therefore would be an

[53] The concept of the contemporary world and its associated generation existing in a perennial state of decline from a forerunning 'golden age' is a common motif. For another example within the Latin literary tradition, compare the imagery and description of humanity and the ages of the Earth of Ovid, *Metamorphoses*, I: 128ff.

[54] Excepting Cyprian's purely Christian eschatological interpretation of the unfortunate events as the deserved censure of an indignant God. *Ad Demetrianum*, 5: 1.

[55] An exact date for the plague is unattainable. However, following the reasoning of J. H. D. Scourfield, the starting-point of the summer of 252 seems a likely possibility. See 'The *De Mortalitate* of Cyprian: Consolation and Context', p. 23.

[56] Something which can be felt in Cyprian's justification of the indiscriminate nature of the public suffering: *intra unam domum boni et mali interim continemur. Quicquid intra domum uenerit pari sorte perpetimur.* 'In the meantime, we are, both good and evil, contained within one house. Whatever comes into the house, we endure with equal fate'. *Ad Demetrianum*, 19: 2. This concept of the communal experience of suffering can be found elsewhere in Latin apologetics with Tertullian, at *Apologeticum*, 41: 3. Cyprian himself deals with the issue again at *De mortalitate*, 8.

[57] *De mortalitate*, 14.

[58] 'From the perspective of the bishop instructing his flock, loss, and the grief resulting from it, are of minimal significance; sympathy and consolation are thus not called for'. J. H. D. Scourfield, 'The De Mortalitate of Cyprian: Consolation and Context', pp. 29–30.

[59] 'Many of us die in this mortality; that is, many of us are liberated from the world'. *De mortalitate*, 15. Latin text in G. Hartel ed., *S. Thasci Caecili Cypriani Opera Omnia*, Vol. 3, pars 1.

[60] With more explicit mentions occurring particularly at chapters 2, 5, 7, and 10.

important issue in the contextualisation. In its address to the Christian audience of the *De mortalitate*, the existence of the plague is interpreted in a purely eschatological sense, and understood throughout by the Lukan citation in Cyprian's words; *cum autem uideritis haec omnia fieri, scitote quoniam in proximo est regnum Dei.*[61] This is the crux of Cyprian's understanding of the plague: it is above all a prophetically foretold manifestation of the arrival of the end times.[62] The sentiment is replaced in the *Ad Demetrianum* by the metaphorical aging of the world towards a natural mortal end; used here as a means of articulating Christian eschatology to a non-believer. The explanation of the plague as a portent of the end times is stated,[63] but the Lukan citation itself is absent. For the purposes of the *Ad Demetrianum*, the plague is considered amongst the other natural catastrophes with which the contemporary world is blighted, and traced back to their fundamental origin with the wrath of the unpropitiated true God.

Cyprian's apologetic style

The *Ad Demetrianum* is a work occupied with one single issue; the question of culpability for the natural disasters that afflict the world and its people. Within this, Cyprian's defence of the Christian perspective is achieved using the pre-existent literary styles and constructions of apologetic. In many ways, an apologetic methodology is the best fit for his purpose – allowing for a concise, if not systematic, rebuttal of accusations of blame for any apparent divine displeasure. One immediately recognisable motif is the retortive *tu quoque.* In apologetic discourse it takes its place as an important means of expression, and a significant template for the construction of argument. The structure and terminology of the *tu quoque* is inescapably apologetic, and of most utility for Cyprian's concern. Its usage is prevalent throughout the work, but is most forcefully deployed in a catalogue of the multiple sinful and criminal acts committed by the persecutors, acting under the unequivocal instigation of Demetrianus:

> *Qui alios iudicas, aliquando esto et tui iudex, conscientiae tuae latebras intuere, immo, quia nullus iam delinquendi uel pudor est et sic peccatur*

---

[61] 'But when you see all these things happening, you will know that the kingdom of God is near'. Lk 21: 31, cited at *De mortalitate*, 2.

[62] See also Fredouille, *A Démétrien*, p. 41.

[63] *Ad Demetrianum*, 5.

quasi magis per ipsa peccata placeatur, qui perspicuus et nudus a cunctis uideris et ipse te respice.[64]

When it comes down to the specifics of usage, Cyprian's technique of retortion is unique. In Tertullian's *Ad nationes*, the *tu quoque* is used to throw back the slanders of immorality against the Christians upon their original accusers. If the Church is accused of practicing infanticide, for example, then Tertullian will point towards an incidence of historical precedent that testifies to its existence amongst the populace.[65] With Cyprian, however, his *tu quoque* follows the wider template of the *Ad Demetrianum*, and stays firmly rooted in the question of blame. Because the Christians are deemed to be culpable for the acts of contemporary misfortune, Cyprian turns the allegations back onto the non-Christian society.[66] In a theme that becomes a common feature of the *Ad Demetrianum*, Cyprian employs conventional apologetic techniques, but keeps them stamped with his own individual purposes. More specific arguments in his Christian defence are broached also with statements such as *dixisti per nos*,[67] or *Christianis imputas*;[68] characteristic components of an apologetic framework. Following such recognisably apologetic syntactic signposts, more implicit echoes of the apologies of Minucius Felix and Tertullian can be observed throughout the *Ad Demetrianum*, and Cyprian's text can be firmly placed within the African Latin apologetic tradition.

Minucius Felix

The inspiration of the *Octauius* can be observed in Cyprian's treatment of the origin of the gods of traditional Roman worship. Cyprian is not inventing theological principles in the *Ad Demetrianum*, and the influence of the *Octauius* behind the explanation of the actions of demons provides the necessary foundation for his statements of Christian belief. It is Minucius' postulation of the malevolent forces of the

---

[64] 'You who judge others, be also a judge of yourself; consider the hidden depths of your conscience. But indeed, there is no longer any wrongdoing or shame in sinning; it is rather that sinning itself is proper. You, who can be seen clearly and naked by all – look at yourself!'. *Ad Demetrianum*, 10: 1.

[65] See *Ad nationes*, 1: 15, also discussed at *Apologeticum*, 9: 2–8.

[66] *Ad Demetrianum*, 3.

[67] 'You have said that by us…'. *Ad Demetrianum*, 3: 1.

[68] 'You impute to the Christians…'. *Ad Demetrianum*, 4: 1.

daemones underlying the characters and heroes of Roman worship,[69] that is used as the influence for Cyprian's demonology.[70] The demons are presented as impotent and enfeebled spirits, who are so dependent on their followers as to negate all of the advantages of propitiation. They form the subject of an absurd image of worship, which Cyprian expresses with a cutting aphorism; *pudeat te eos colere quos ipse defendis, pudeat tutelam de eis sperare quos tu tueris.*[71] As with Minucius, the hierarchical significance of the demons being subject to the power of Christian adjuration is stressed;[72] they are nothing more than *captiui* under Christian hands.[73] Yet they remain the true source of all anti-Christian feeling, the instigators of the demonic possession which fires the persecutors themselves, and the offenders who restrain Demetrianus' soul within the dark night of ignorance.[74] In the final chapters of the *Ad Demetrianum*, Demetrianus is urged to emerge from this darkness and approach the light of the Church – a common Christian metaphor in itself, but expressed by Cyprian with terminology that is reminiscent of Minucius Felix's account of his own conversion to Christian belief: *hortamur ... Deo satisfacere et ad uerae religionis candidam lucem de profundo tenebrosae superstitionis emergere.*[75] Cyprian's usage of the *Octauius* is significant in placing the *Ad Demetrianum* within the developing Latin apologetic tradition, but Cyprian only utilises Minucius' construction of demonology within the requirements of his own argument, and always on his own terms. Although the influence of the *Octauius* is noted, it does not become a dependence. The similarities of expression and argument are effectively little more than passing allusions and borrowings from the earlier work, and the *Ad Demetrianum* remains directly focused on its own agenda

---

[69] *Octauius*, 27.

[70] Confidently articulated by Fredouille: '*Minucius Felix s'en inspirea, et ce passage de Cyprien est, précisément, tributaire d'Oct, 27, 5–7*'. *A Démétrien*, p. 168.

[71] 'It is shameful to worship those who you defend; it is shameful to hope for protection from those who you yourself protect'. *Ad Demetrianum*, 14: 2.

[72] *Ad Demetrianum*, 15. *Octauius*, 27: 7.

[73] *Ad Demetrianum*, 15: 2.

[74] *Qui nunc mentem tuam ignorantiae nocte caecauit.* 'Who now blinds your mind with the night of ignorance'. *Ad Demetrianum*, 15: 2.

[75] 'We exhort [you] to make satisfaction to God, and to emerge from the depths of dark superstition into the bright light of true religion'. *Ad Demetrianum*, 25: 1. See Minucius' own account: *et cum discussa caligine de tenebrarum profundo in lucem sapientiae et ueritatis emergerem.* 'And when, after the fog had been dissipated, I emerged out of the depths of darkness into the light of wisdom and truth'. *Octauius*, 1: 4.

throughout. The usage of Christian textual sources is selective in order to detract as little as possible from the overriding principle of Cyprian's own text. Cyprian moves on, and the *Ad Demetrianum* continues to be centred on its one core subject; the nature of the Christian relationship to the causes of suffering in the world.

Tertullian

The question that forms the most physically relevant issue of the *Ad Demetrianum* is the savage legal and moral hypocrisy with which the Christians are treated. It follows from the emphasis on the accusations of blame for temporal suffering, and underlies the numerous particular incidences of legalised maltreatment by the authorities. At one point, Cyprian condenses his entire treatise into a few candid lines, and provides the clearest window into the essence of his apologetic undertaking:

> *Ecce id ipsum quale est unde nobis cum maxime sermo est, quod nos infestatis innoxios, quod in contumeliam Dei impugnatis atque opprimitis Dei seruos. Parum est quod furentium uarietate uitiorum, quod iniquitate feralium criminum, quod cruentarum compendio rapinarum uita uestra maculatur, quod superstitionibus falsis religio uera subuertitur, quod Deus omnino non quaeritur nec timetur, adhuc insuper Dei seruos et maiestati ac numini eius dicatos iniustis persecutionibus fatigatis.*[76]

His motivation, just like Minucius Felix and Tertullian before him, is to justify his religious community in the face of the harsh treatment of the unjust persecutions that have forced his apologetic defence. The legal implications of the arrest and torture of Christians are at the forefront of Cyprian's argument. He addresses the judicial grounding for the Christian persecutions with a call for clarity in the declaration of the nature of the crime at hand, and betrays an extent of the Tertullianic influence behind the *Ad Demetrianum*. As with Tertullian's lengthier treatment of the subject in the opening chapters of the *Apologeticum*,[77] the specifics of the legal status of Christian belief

---

[76] 'Look at what is the very matter of the greatest part of our discourse; that you harass us, the innocent, and in an affront to God you attack and oppress the servants of God. It is insufficient that your life is polluted by the raging of multiple sins, the iniquity of deadly crimes, and the profit of bloodthirsty plunder. True religion is subverted by false superstitions, and God is altogether neither searched for nor feared. And still further, you weary the servants of God, and those consecrated to the divine majesty and will, by unjust persecutions'. *Ad Demetrianum*, 12: 1–2.

[77] *Apologeticum*, 2: 10ff.

are the key areas of concern. Tertullian's mode of expression is echoed in Cyprian's plea for the clarification of the law: *quin potius elige tibi alterum de duobus: christianum esse aut est crimen aut non est. Si crimen est, quid non interficis confitentem? Si crimen non est, quid persequeris innocentem?*[78] Within this, Cyprian also follows Tertullian in drawing attention to the justification of the use of torture in punishing the apprehended Christian believer.[79] The foundation for the exertion of violent torture is very much at the heart of the sense of injustice behind the persecutions,[80] and Cyprian calls instead for the official re-direction of anti-Christian feeling into the spheres of argument and religious discourse.[81] The influence of Tertullian in Cyprian's discussion of the legal injustice inherent in the persecutions can be noted, but is actually to be expected. One of the most enduring aspects of the *Apologeticum* is its legal emphasis; providing Cyprian with a source-text simply too valuable not to be utilised. The stress on the legal aspects of persecution broached within the *Apologeticum* is condensed by Cyprian into his argument, as with the usage of the *Octauius*, for a specific purpose. Tertullian's legal discussion provides Cyprian with the key textual influence for his own mention of the legal implications of anti-Christian persecution.

Scripture

Cyprian utilises these various characteristically apologetic incidences in the course of his appeal to Demetrianus to embrace the Christian religion and halt the unjust persecutions. In this sense, the *Ad Demetrianum* is apologetic in the service of evangelisation. Demetrianus is repeatedly urged to raise his posture into an upright stance, another common motif of Latin apologetics,[82] and elevate his countenance

---

[78] 'Why not rather make one of two choices: either it is a crime to be a Christian, or it is not. If it is a crime, why do you not kill those who confess to it? If it is not a crime, why do you persecute the innocent?'. *Ad Demetrianum*, 13: 1.

[79] *Ad Demetrianum*, 12: 5ff. See *Apologeticum*, 2: 10–17.

[80] *Innoxios, iustos, Deo caros domo priuas, patrimonio spolias, catenis premis, carcere includis, bestiis, gladio, ignibus punis.* 'The innocent, the just, the beloved of God; you deprive them of homes, you despoil their patrimony, you lock them in chains, shut them up in prison, and punish them with beasts, fire and the sword'. *Ad Demetrianum*, 12: 4.

[81] *Ad Demetrianum*, 13: 2.

[82] *Ad Demetrianum*, 16. See also *Octauius*, 17: 2, 11. This image is a common feature with Lactantius, and can be noted at *Diuinae institutiones*, 2: 1; 14–19, 2: 2; 23, and 2: 18.

alongside the worshippers of the true God. He is warned with the prospect of eternal recompense for his acts against the Christians, and faced with Cyprian's direct admonition; *laedere seruos Dei et Christi persecutionibus tuis desine.*[83] The closing chapters of the text strongly re-emphasise the ultimate goal of the conversion of the persecutors to Christian faith, acutely represented by the person of Demetrianus himself.[84] The conversion aim of the *Ad Demetrianum* is underlined by the usage of prophetic Scriptural citations, interpreted squarely in relation to the current climate. As a particular example, the tone of the Scriptural usage of the work as a whole can be encapsulated in a single citation:

> *Fieri enim ista uel ad disciplinam contumacium uel ad poenam malo-rum, declarat in scripturis sanctis idem Deus dicens: Sine causa percussi filios uestros, disciplinam non exceperunt. Et propheta deuotus ac dicatus Deo ad haec eadem respondet et dicit: Uerberasti eos nec doluerunt; flag-ellasti eos nec uoluerunt accipere disciplinam. Ecce irrogantur diuinitus plagae et nullus Dei metus est: ecce uerbera desuper et flagella non desunt et trepidatio nulla, nulla formido est.*[85]

This usage of Scripture is the most crucial instrument in Cyprian's expression of apologetic in the *Ad Demetrianum*. It is also the main difference in the apologetic character of the work when compared with Cyprian's predecessors in the Latin articulation of apologetics, Minucius Felix and Tertullian. The reluctance of the earlier Latin apologists to utilise Scriptural arguments in their apologetic con-structions is matched only by Cyprian's explicit recourse to them within the *Ad Demetrianum*. This important position of Scripture behind the arguments of the text can be noticed from some of the very opening words of the first chapter – Cyprian precedes his first direct Scriptural citation with the qualifier *nec hoc sine magisterii*

---

[83] 'Cease to hurt the servants of God and Christ with your persecutions'. *Ad Demetrianum*, 16: 2.

[84] *Ad Demetrianum*, 23–26.

[85] 'That these things come about either for the correction of the obstinate or the punishment of the evil, this same God declares in the Holy Scriptures, saying: "In vain I have struck your children; they have not received correction". And the prophet devoted and dedicated to God responds to these words, saying: "You have struck them, and they have not suffered; you have scourged them, and they have refused to receive correction". Behold, stripes of divine origin are inflicted, but there is no fear of God; whips and lashings from above are not lacking, and there is no trembling, no fear'. *Ad Demetrianum*, 7: 1–2.

diuini auctoritate faciebam, cum scipturum sit,[86] and it becomes clear that the work will be permeated by Scriptural interpretation and exegesis throughout. The particular statements employed to precede and introduce the Scriptural citations provide key insight into an understanding of Cyprian's purpose in utilising the Scriptures in a debate with Demetrianus; an individual unfamiliar with the texts in question, and certainly not bound by any need for fidelity to their religious and philosophical standpoints. Although Cyprian hints at a previous level of dialogue with Demetrianus personally,[87] he also measures his level of agreement with the Christian understanding without ambiguity; *ignarus diuinae cognitionis et ueritatis alienus es.*[88] This will not be Scripture utilised as a common source, but employed with force in the service of a single aim – the establishment of the truth of Scriptural prophecy in relation to the contemporary situation.[89] It is the plagues, disasters, and failings of the contemporary world that speak to the authenticity of the Scriptural prophecies; *hoc etiam nobis tacentibus et nulla de scripturis sanctis praedicationibusque diuinis documenta promentibus mundus ipse iam loquitur et occasum sui rerum labentium probatione testatur.*[90] A prophetic understanding of the cited Scriptural sentences is essential from Cyprian's perspective. His interpretation of the relationship between the Scriptures and the events under consideration is succinctly explained by Jean-Claude Fredouille:

---

[86] 'I am not doing this without the authority of the divine magisterium, as it is written…'. *Ad Demetrianum*, 1: 1.

[87] *Nam cum ad me saepe studio magis contradicendi quam uoto discendi uenires.* 'For often you came to me with the desire to contradict, rather than the wish to learn'. *Ad Demetrianum*, 1: 2.

[88] 'You are ignorant of the divine knowledge and a stranger to the truth'. *Ad Demetrianum*, 3: 1.

[89] Writing in defence of Cyprian, Edward White Benson argued that the hint of Demetrianus' prior conversations with Cyprian allows for the textual recourse to the Scriptures, in view of Demetrianus' previous level of engagement with Christianity. Furthermore, Benson observes that Cyprian does not once mention a particular book of Scripture when reproducing a citation; introducing them throughout with completely unspecific nomenclature. In short, Cyprian is using the Scriptures as ostensibly non-partisan prophetic statements supporting the innocence of Christianity. See Benson, *Cyprian: His Life, His Times, His Work*, pp. 255–6.

[90] 'Even if we are silent on this and bring forth nothing from the proclamations of the Holy Scriptures or the divine writings, the very world itself is already speaking, and testifying to its decline by the evidence of its deteriorating situation'. *Ad Demetrianum*, 3: 1.

Les Écritures, plus exactement les prophéties de l'Ancien Testament, val-orisées par leur haute antiquité, ne sont pas une preuve de la dégradation présente, mais la dégradation présente prouve la vérité des Écritures.[91]

The Scriptures are deployed by Cyprian as an effective form of Christian prophecy, almost in the sense of an equivalent to oracular portents and warnings. Demetrianus is urged to listen to the voice of God,[92] revealing his agency behind the calamitous worldly events through the ominous foretellings present in the sacred texts.[93] They are interpreted in an apologetic sense with direct bearing on explaining the current situation, and can therefore exonerate the Christians from blame by extension. Cyprian unites evangelisation and apologetics in his appeal to Demetrianus to *credite illi qui haec omnia futura praedixit.*[94] The final chapters of the text are punctuated with numerous Scriptural allusions, and an unmistakeable eschatological undercurrent which warns of dire eternal retribution under a plea for conversion to Christianity. The oracular tone behind the wider Scriptural usage of the *Ad Demetrianum* is re-emphasised in Cyprian's direct evangelical assault of the closing chapter.

Conclusion

The Scriptural citations that permeate the *Ad Demetrianum* are employed as defensive proofs of the Christian position amongst the worldly events; a conclusively apologetic position in itself, despite the Scriptural reticence of the other Latin apologists in the early African tradition. Lactantius is equally comfortable in the deployment of Scripture within apologetic discourse, although not quite to the same extent as Cyprian in the *Ad Demetrianum.* But even if Cyprian's Scriptural usage is the most marked feature of this particular piece, it would be inaccurate to pronounce the use of Scripture as the most defining characteristic of his own overall approach to apologetics. The *Ad Demetrianum* remains one comparatively brief text focused

---

[91] *A Démétrien*, pp. 39–40.

[92] *Ipsum denique audi loquentem, ipsum uoce diuina instruentem nos et monentum.* 'Finally, listen to him speaking; his divine voice instructing and warning us'. *Ad Demetrianum*, 6: 1.

[93] *Cum Dei ipsius praedicatione et prophetica contestatione ante praedictum sit.* 'By the proclamation of God himself and by the testimony of the prophets, it has previously been foretold'. *Ad Demetrianum*, 21.

[94] 'Believe in him who has foretold that all these things will come to pass'. *Ad Demetrianum*, 23: 2.

on one central issue; the degree of Christian blame for the ostensible decline in worldly vitality. The place of Scripture within Cyprian's defence of his community is fundamental in its bearing on a broader prophetic interpretation of events; as they are foretold by God, so they are inescapable, and the Christians are therefore vindicated. The true blame then lies with the impiety of the non-Christian world, which merits the righteous anger of the almost universally ignored true God. With the Scriptural reliance that underlies the work throughout, Cyprian's *Ad Demetrianum* is effectively apologetics, evangelisation, and prophetic exegesis brought together in defence of the post-Decian persecuted Church.

ARNOBIUS OF SICCA

1. Introduction

Approximately half a century after Cyprian's *Ad Demetrianum*, the *Aduersus nationes* of a newly-converted rhetor from the town of Sicca Veneria in Africa Proconsularis enters the scene of Latin apologetics.[1] Little is known of Arnobius himself, but his seven books of polemical apologetic[2] provide an invaluable collection of religious and philosophical argument from the period of one of Christianity's most serious open confrontations with the Roman state. The *Aduersus nationes* is a window into the intellectual debate by way of its engagement with the religious and philosophical standpoints that underpinned the outburst of anti-Christian feeling of the Diocletianic persecution, and ultimately preceded the imperial-sponsored toleration of the religion at the instigation of Constantine. It has been justifiably called

---

[1] The standard English edition of the *Aduersus nationes* is that of George E. McCracken (1949) in the Ancient Christian Writers series, while there is also a readily obtainable version in the Anti-Nicene Christian Library by Hamilton Bryce and Hugh Campbell (1871). The most utilised Latin editions are of August Reifferscheid in the CSEL series (1875), and Concetto Marchesi in the Corpus Scriptorum Latinorum Paravianum (1953). There are also editions of books one and three in Latin and French, by H. Le Bonniec (1982) and Jacqueline Champeaux (2007) respectively. The edition of Marchesi provides the base text used in this study, although Reifferscheid has also been consulted. The landmark work in Arnobian scholarship is Michael Bland Simmons' extensive study *Arnobius of Sicca: Religious Conflict and Competition in the Age of Diocletian* (henceforth *Arnobius of Sicca*). As Simmons notes, many of the principal works in the field of Patristics neglect to mention Arnobius at all; and as a result there are noticeably fewer modern voices than with the other writers of Latin apologetics.

[2] For a discussion on the particular genre location of the *Aduersus nationes*, see below, pp. 141–2.

'the most complete repertory of Christian criticism of mythology',[3] by virtue of its extensive treatment of the traditional rituals and ceremonies of Roman religion. The *Aduersus nationes* is a very unique piece of work within the wider Christian apologetic genre, not least for several of its controversial theological and doctrinal expressions. For posterity, Arnobius takes a place on the catalogue of apocryphal works named in the *Decretum Gelasianum*,[4] due to the serious questions of theological orthodoxy that accompany some of the central principles of the work.

Arnobius of Sicca as an historical individual is unfortunately obscured by a distinct lack of biographical information. The sole surviving ancient testimony regarding his personal details comes from the pen of Jerome, while even Lactantius, Arnobius' supposed student,[5] is silent on the subject of his master. Supplemented with a few passing references in his letters,[6] Jerome's key information can be found in his *Chronicon*:

> *Arnobius rhetor in Africa clarus habetur: qui cum in ciuitate Siccae ad declamandum iuuenes erudiret et adhuc ethnicus ad credulitatem somniis impelleretur, neque ab episcopo impetraret fidem quam semper impugnauerat, elucubrauit aduersum pristinam religionem luculentissimos libros: et tandem uelut quibusdam obsidibus pietatis foedus impetrauit.*[7]

And again in the *De uiris illustribus*:

> *Arnobius sub Diocletiano principe Siccae apud Africam florentissime rhetoricam docuit scripsitque aduersus gentes uolumina, quae uulgo exstant.*[8]

---

[3] Pierre de Labriolle, *History and Literature of Christianity*, p. 196.

[4] Ernst von Dobschütz ed., p. 57.

[5] According to Jerome; *Firmianus, qui et Lactantius, Arnobii discipulus.* 'Firmianus, also known as Lactantius, a disciple of Arnobius'. *De uiris illustribus*, 80.

[6] At *Epistula* 70: 5, 58: 10, and 62: 2.

[7] 'Arnobius is considered an illustrious rhetorician in Africa. While he was educating the youth in the city of Sicca in oratory, and still as yet a heathen, he was driven by dreams to [Christian] belief. But on not being able to procure acceptance from the bishop into the faith that he had always attacked, he devoted himself completely to compose the most splendid books against his former religion – and finally, with these pledges of loyalty, he procured his affiliation'. *Chronicon*, 326–7 AD. Latin text of the *Chronicon* in J. P. Migne ed., *Patrologia Latina*, Vol. 27.

[8] 'During the reign of Diocletian, Arnobius taught rhetoric most successfully at Sicca in Africa, and composed the books *Aduersus gentes*, which are commonly available'. *De uiris illustribus*, 79.

Arnobius' location at Sicca seems certain, as does his acknowl-edged occupation as a rhetor. But some of the other pieces inside the descriptions are not so straightforward. Jerome's information relating to his conversion by the experience of dreams is otherwise impossible to verify.[9] The depiction of the *Aduersus nationes* as works designed to impress the sincerity of Arnobius' newly-held belief onto his local bishop is acceptable, although again impossible to verify within the particular background. The identity of Arnobius' bishop is also unknown, not least perhaps to Jerome himself, who fails to specifically name him within his relation of the anecdote. Nothing else is known of Arnobius' particulars of life or death, and the *Aduer-sus nationes* contains virtually no hints at corroborating background information. At this point, there are immediate parallels in Latin apologetics with Minucius Felix. The two apologists are eternally con-nected due to their singular relationship in the manuscript tradition,[10] and there are intermittent echoes of the *Octauius* throughout the *Aduersus nationes*. But much like Minucius, Arnobius is difficult to adequately contextualise. As a result, the immediate background and direct audience of the *Aduersus nationes*, as with the *Octauius*, is the subject of recurring debate. In view of the problems of definitively dating the work, any attempt to define its historical and literary set-ting remains tentative by necessity. Nevertheless, Michael Simmons' argument of the ultimate purpose of Arnobius' work as a rebuttal of the anti-Christian writing of Porphyry seems highly probable,[11] despite the scarce and fragmentary nature of the extant Porphyrian anti-Christian texts.

The *Aduersus nationes* also contains precious little insight into the Christian belief and practice of its compiler; a point tradition-ally explained by Arnobius' recent conversion, and consequent

[9] Arnobius himself says nothing of the subject when personally describing his conversion, at *Aduersus nationes*, 1: 39.

[10] From the position of the *Octauius* as an addendum to the sole surviving man-uscript, the *Codex Parisinus* (1661) of the *Aduersus nationes* as *liber octauus*, and its attachment in the *editio princeps* of the *Aduersus nationes* by Faustus Sabaeus (1542/3), following the format of the *Codex Parisinus*.

[11] Also previously noted by Pierre Courcelle, in his chapter 'Anti-Christian Arguments and Christian Platonism: From Arnobius to St. Ambrose', in Arnaldo Momigliano's *The Conflict Between Paganism and Christianity in the Fourth Century*, p. 156. The relationship between the *Aduersus nationes* and the work of Porphyry forms the central thesis of Simmons' *Arnobius of Sicca*.

unfamiliarity with Christian practice.[12] Arnobius mentions no particulars as to the community of believers at Sicca, nothing regarding the details of Christian ceremony, and only the fewest hints at even some of the most important aspects of belief.[13] Christian worship is presented as the purest honouring of the *summus deus*; the unadulterated adoration of the Creator-God alone,[14] to be compared with the noxious rituals of Arnobius' opponents: *amare suspicere execrabilis religio est et infausta, impietatis et sacrilegii plena, caerimonias antiquitus institutas nouitatis suae superstitione contaminans?*[15] This contrast underlies Arnobius' reticence to give any detail of Christian ceremony. He is establishing the transcendent purity of Christian worship; rituals practiced by humanity would be distinctly beneath the purpose of the argument, and too liable to be included in his own criticism of human ceremony. God is the Supreme Being, the highest pinnacle of the universe, and as completely distinct from humanity as possible.[16] In this establishment of God as the Supreme Being, and therefore the essential antithesis of a tutelary deity, Arnobius employs a broad and unspecific terminology, and refrains from using overtly Christian language.[17] Even in a focused prayer to God within the text,[18] Arnobius uses no explicitly Christian expressions. It is only the primary motivation of the prayer itself,[19] added to the features of its prominent monotheism, that would otherwise identify it as likely Christian. Elsewhere in the work, Arnobius argues so forcefully against the anthropomorphisms of the gods that he

[12] As, for example, with Oliver Nicholson's description of the *Aduersus nationes* as 'The work of a Christian convert convinced but not yet instructed in the faith'. 'Arnobius and Lactantius', in *The Cambridge History of Early Christian Literature*, p. 260. The brief mentions of Arnobius' recent conversion in the *Aduersus nationes* are at 1: 39, and 3: 24.

[13] Somewhat romantically justified by Gustave Bardy in his *The Christian Latin Literature of the First Six Centuries*, p. 56: 'Nothing can be more curious than this work, written by a man who had not yet received baptism and who knew almost nothing of the religion to which he was henceforth to consecrate his life. For Arnobius had not time really to study the Bible or the Christian authors before writing... But what need had he of study to be convinced?'.

[14] *Aduersus nationes*, 1: 29.

[15] 'To love him [God] and to look up to him — is this the accursed and unholy religion full of sacrilege and impiety, defiling by the superstition of its novelty the ceremonies instituted from antiquity?'. *Aduersus nationes*, 1: 25.

[16] *Aduersus nationes*, 3: 19.

[17] See, for example, *Aduersus nationes*, 3: 2.

[18] *Aduersus nationes*, 1: 31.

[19] *Da ueniam, rex summe, tuos persequentibus famulos.* 'Grant pardon, King Most High, to those who persecute your servants'. *Aduersus nationes*, 1: 31.

even refuses to present God as being male,[20] or having any semblance of human form.[21] God is something utterly different, and essentially unknowable. Arnobius does describe the redemptive work of Jesus, but without any overt Scriptural allusions, and in characteristically general terms.[22] He is particularly puzzling when recounting a list of the various pieces of previously-hidden knowledge that the teachings of Jesus have made known to the believers.[23] It is one incidence among many in the *Aduersus nationes* where the source for Arnobius' information is questionable. Regarding the Church, Arnobius mentions nothing aside from its recent enjoyment of a period of great expansion,[24] and that the Christians are distinguished by an unwillingness to construct temples and images.[25] But Arnobius' purpose in the *Aduersus nationes* is not to present a picture of the life of the Church, but to validate Christian belief through a critique of the religion of its opponents. In this sense, Arnobius' lack of description of Christian practice can at least be understood, if perhaps not completely justified. He is often too vague to be convincing, and his refusal to explain or describe key things in higher levels of depth can read as a betrayal of his lack of detailed knowledge. Due to Arnobius' own extremely obscure place within the Church of his era, and added to the numerous theological and doctrinal inconsistencies throughout his text, evaluating the contribution of the *Aduersus nationes* to the study of the doctrine of the early fourth-century Church is problematic. Its more significant role lies in its situation within the religious conflict of the pre-Constantinian era, and for the scope of this study, Arnobius' position within early Latin apologetics. Yet it does provide a certain nuance in the development of Christian doctrine as an inescapably different perspective; perhaps as the contribution of a believer who is somehow outside the more recognisable currents of developing Christian theology. In view of his lack of awareness of the Scriptures, it is highly possible that Arnobius may have been one other variant in the formation of the Christian

---

[20] *Aduersus nationes*, 3: 8–12.

[21] *Aduersus nationes*, 3: 17. This would appear to be inconsistent with the teaching of Gen 1: 26–28, establishing the creation of humanity in the image of God, if Arnobius is aware of the Scriptural passage. However, perhaps it is more likely that Arnobius would categorise this belief with the so-called *Iudaeicas… fabulas* ('Jewish fables') he depicts so scathingly at *Aduersus nationes*, 3: 12.

[22] *Aduersus nationes*, 2: 64–5.

[23] *Aduersus nationes*, 1: 38.

[24] *Aduersus nationes*, 1: 55, 2: 5. Also present in Minucius Felix, *Octauius*, 9: 1, 31: 7.

[25] *Aduersus nationes*, 6: 1–3.

theological principles of the time; a feature that has incidentally left him open to a much later definition as doctrinally unorthodox.

The question of the date

The dating of the *Aduersus nationes* is continually an issue. Jerome's information in the *De uiris illustribus* ascribing Arnobius' *floruit* to the reign of Diocletian is conventionally coupled with a likely background hint at *Aduersus nationes* 4: 36 to produce a dating range of the general period of the Diocletianic persecution. But Jerome's more substantial mention of Arnobius in the *Chronicon* seems to contradict this, and instead would date the text to c. 327. Both of Jerome's dates seemingly cannot refer to the composition of one single work, so a line must be drawn somewhere. The few possible references within the *Aduersus nationes* to key historical events and traditional chronologies have been utilised to support an approximate dating period of the early fourth century.[26] However, the main weakness of the chronological argument is the often imprecise measurements of time, and the different dating possibilities raised by several conflicting templates in the ancient annalists.[27] The chronological method is too vague to be conclusively supportable. The detailed chapter of Michael Bland Simmons in establishment of the true dating range of the *Aduersus nationes* would identify Jerome's later date as inaccurate, and argues for the acceptance of the evidence of the *De uiris illustribus* as Jerome's solely reliable information. Therefore, Arnobius is placed within the early years of the Diocletianic persecution, and specifically at c. 302-5. After his formulation of a broadly systematic outline of the possible aspects of the text useful in its dating, with particular reference to the requirements of the persecuted Christians to perform sacrifices, Simmons writes:

> We conclude that Arnobius began to write the *Adversus nationes* no earlier than the last quarter of AD 302, and finished book 7 before the persecution had ended, and thus sacrifice was a contemporary issue, probably sometime during the first half of 305.[28]

[26] See *Aduersus nationes*, 1: 13; the allusion to the elapsed time since the establishment of the Christian faith, and 2: 71; the supposed age of the city of Rome.

[27] Both McCracken and Simmons list the different sources that could possibly have been used by Arnobius. In attempting to trace the foundation of Rome back 1050 years, they yield divergent resulting dates over the approximate twenty-year period from 297–322. The overall impression is that the arguments are too imprecise to be of significant value in pinpointing the date of the work. See McCracken, *The Case Against the Pagans*, Vol. 1, pp. 9-10, and Simmons, *Arnobius of Sicca*, pp. 55–62.

[28] Ibid., p. 93.

The majority in the field of study also follow the dating of the *Aduersus nationes* to the approximate period of the opening of the fourth century, and further located within the surrounding circumstances of the Diocletianic persecution.[29] But as Simmons notes, the majority of scholars dating the *Aduersus nationes* to the opening period of the persecution are guilty of placing too much credence on the supposed historical references within the text; a method which he dismisses as 'not sound'.[30] Even the very largest combination of possibilities and conjecture does not make for a conclusive argument. Also, even apparently sound features of argument concerning the dating of the *Aduersus nationes* can be called into question. Such is Simmons' attempt at referring the mention of *nouasque... poenas*[31] at *Aduersus nationes* 6: 11 to the punishments and tortures instituted by the Diocletianic edicts.[32] At first glance, Arnobius' attack on the sheer injustice of the penalties with which the Christians are plagued seems like a plausible allusion to the newly-introduced laws and punishments of the edicts of injunction to sacrifice. On this issue, Simmons concludes:

> The destruction of churches and scriptures, which were new proscriptions in themselves. Furthermore, he mentions in 5. 29. 13f., 'alio genere suppliciorum' in addition to flames, exiles, etc., perhaps implying penalties contained in a new edict. 'New punishments' of 6. 11. 24 may allude to any of the edicts issued after the First Edict.[33]

Both Simmons and McCracken[34] make the connection of the *nouasque... poenas* with the punishments of the Diocletianic persecution, most likely being unaware of the prior textual influence of Cyprian's *Ad Demetrianum* that actually underlies this statement of Arnobius. At this point of the text, Arnobius is reflecting his literary source behind a more general statement of frustration at the devices

---

[29] So Quasten, *Patrology*, Vol. 2, p. 384, and Claudio Moreschini and Enrico Norelli (following the arguments of Simmons), *Early Christian Greek and Latin Literature: A Literary History*, Vol. 1, p. 393. The imprecision of the *terminus ante quem* is characterised in a statement of Quasten; 'As for its date, it must have been completed before 311 AD., the end of the persecutions which are mentioned often but with no hint of the restoration of peace to the Church'.

[30] *Arnobius of Sicca*, p. 91.

[31] 'New punishments'.

[32] *Arnobius of Sicca*, pp. 83–4.

[33] Ibid., pp. 83–4.

[34] *The Case Against the Pagans*, Vol. 2, p. 462, n. 90.

of the Christian opponents, rather than directly referring to the penalties instituted under the Diocletianic edicts. At *Ad Demetrianum* 12: 5, after a catalogue of present tortures and punishments, Cyprian argued:

> *Nec saltem contentus es dolorum nostrorum compendio et simplici ac ueloci breuitate poenarum, admoues laniandis corporibus longa tormenta, multiplicas lacerandis uisceribus numerosa supplicia; nec feritas atque immanitas tua usitatis potest contenta esse tormentis, excogitat nouas poenas ingeniosa crudelitas.*[35]

Cyprian is here outlining the essence of his tract; the unfairness of the methods which are employed to condemn and punish the Christians, despite the embattled Church being the only guardian of true religion; *superstitionibus falsis religio uera subuertitur.*[36] Added to this, the Christians are considered to be so wrongful to merit the devising (*excogitare*; used by both Cyprian and Arnobius) of novel forms of torture and execution. The mention of *nouas poenas* is intended to convey the savage injustice present within the judicial penalties for the crime of refusing to recant adherence to Christianity. It is the climax of Cyprian's argument against the injustice, the gross disproportion, and even the absurdity, of the punishment in relation to the crime. The difference in treatment of the arraigned believers with other transgressors of the law is a prominent bone of contention amongst virtually every other early Christian apologist,[37] and Arnobius proves to be no exception. His own mention of the subject of *nouas poenas* occurs within a depiction of image-worship as an almost farcical misrepresentation of true divinity, and alongside an expression of the injustice with which the Christians are treated:

> *Utinam liceret introspicere sensus uestros recessusque ipsos mentis, quibus uarias uoluitis atque initis obscurissimas cogitationes: reperiremus et uos*

[35] 'You are not even satisfied with any brevity for our sufferings, and with a simple and quick method of punishment. You apply lengthy tortures, tearing bodies to pieces; you multiply numerous punishments by lacerating internal organs. And neither can your ferocity and savagery be satisfied with ordinary tortures; your ingenious cruelty contrives new punishments'. *Ad Demetrianum*, 12: 5.

[36] 'True religion is subverted by false superstitions'. *Ad Demetrianum*, 12: 2.

[37] The unjust trials and punishment of the Christians compared with other accused criminals is naturally a prevalent issue in both Latin and Greek apologies, being inseparable from their key motivations for writing. As other examples, see Minucius Felix, *Octauius*, 28: 3-4; Tertullian, *Apologeticum*, 2; Cyprian, *Ad Demetrianum*, 13; Justin, *Apologia prima*, 2-7; Athenagoras, *Legatio*, 2.

ipsos eadem sentire quae nos neque alias gerere super numinum figuratione sententias. Sed studiis facere quid peruicacibus possumus, quid intentantibus gladios nouasque excogitantibus poenas?[38]

Nouasque… poenas should not be taken as a direct hint at the punishments of the Diocletianic edicts, but instead as a more general allusion to the cruelly unjust methods of those who condemn and punish the Christians for their allegiance. Arnobius' statement is not in reference to any particular outburst of organized persecution, but rather a more unspecific expression encapsulating an abstract and generic form of Christian maltreatment by the Roman authorities. In view of the likely influence of Cyprian, *Aduersus nationes* 6: 11 cannot be utilised as a reliable factor in the dating of the text to the period of the Diocletianic persecution.

By far the most deployed passage of Arnobius in evidence of the textual dating to the period of the opening of the fourth century is *Aduersus nationes* 4: 36, where an allusion to the forms of punishment instituted by the first of the Diocletianic edicts[39] seems to be in operation. Within the course of an attack on the ludicrous depictions of the gods by both traditional literature and the public spectacles, Arnobius brings the subject around to the treatment of the Church; *nam nostra quidem scripta cur ignibus meruerunt dari? Cur immaniter conuenticula dirui?*[40] The question is intended as a dramatic contrast alongside the hypocrisies of the traditional forms of expression about the gods; if the poets write such blasphemies as they do, then why do the Christian writings merit the flames? If the plays and spectacles encourage so many ridiculous perceptions of the gods, then why are the Christian *conuenticula* razed to the ground instead of these? Arnobius is making a highly satirical observation on the injustice of his society; for

---

[38] 'If only we were allowed to look upon your feelings in the recesses of your mind, where you turn over and entertain various most secret thoughts; we should discover that you yourselves feel the same as us, and not otherwise, concerning the form of the gods. But what can we do against the obstinate zeal of those who are threatening us with swords and devising new punishments?'. *Aduersus nationes*, 6: 11.

[39] 23rd February 303. The context and promulgation of the edict is recorded by Eusebius, *Historia ecclesiastica*, 8: 2. For an overview of the Diocletianic persecution itself, see W. H. C. Frend, *Martyrdom and Persecution in the Early Church*, pp. 477–535, with details of the first edict at pp. 489–94. For the persecution from the perspective of the emperor Diocletian, see Stephen Williams, *Diocletian and the Roman Recovery*, pp. 173–85.

[40] 'For why indeed do our writings deserve to be given to the flames? Why our meeting places to be brutally razed to the ground?'. *Aduersus nationes*, 4: 36.

although the Christians alone profess the purest form of worship of true divinity,[41] and practice the virtues which benefit both man and society,[42] they are still so brutally punished. As unspecific as the allusion may be, Arnobius' statement at *Aduersus nationes* 4: 36 has to be taken to refer to effects of the first Diocletianic edict against Christian practice due to the key mention of burning the Scriptures and destroying the *conuenticula*. It does not follow that *Aduersus nationes* 4: 36 is contemporary with the Diocletianic edict by necessity, but it is at least a corroborative incidence that can be utilised in the general textual dating. If nothing else, the allusion forms an identifiable *terminus post quem* for the text.

Yet perhaps Jerome's two dates in the *Chronicon* are not necessarily in opposition, and he instead means to relate that although Arnobius enjoyed the height of his fame under Diocletian, the compilation of the *Aduersus nationes* was not undertaken until sometime later; specifically around 327. Mark Edwards has defended the possibility that there is no conclusive evidence to successfully disprove Jerome's later date, and only insufficient evidence extant to prove that Arnobius wrote during the persecution.[43] *Aduersus nationes* 4: 36 is therefore deconstructed as a contemporary hint at the background, and reduced to a more general statement regarding the former punishments attached to the Christian religion. Further to this, the lack of direct reference to anti-Christian statutes or major figures and events of the Diocletianic persecution can also be understood.[44] When writing of Christian times of trial, Arnobius would effectively be looking back into the past. Indeed, Edwards highlights the possibility that the polemic of the *Aduersus nationes*, and even the references to persecution, could originate from a justification of the recently-tolerated

---

[41] *In quibus summus oratur deus.* 'In which the Supreme God is prayed to'. *Aduersus nationes*, 4: 36.

[42] *In quibus aliud auditur nihil nisi quod humanos faciat, nisi quod mites uerecundos pudicos castos.* 'In which nothing else is heard than what makes men kind, nor nothing than what makes men gentle, modest, chaste, pure'. *Aduersus nationes*, 4: 36.

[43] 'The Flowering of Latin Apologetic: Lactantius and Arnobius', in *Apologetics in the Roman Empire*, pp. 198–9. See also his article 'Dating Arnobius: Why Discount the Evidence of Jerome?', pp. 263–71.

[44] '[Arnobius] names no pagan magistrate, and makes no appeal to laws in the manner of Justin or Tertullian; if he wrote when the persecution was abated, we can understand his silence'. Mark Edwards, 'The Flowering of Latin Apologetic: Lactantius and Arnobius', in *Apologetics in the Roman Empire*, p. 198.

Christian religion aimed at the advocates of the supplanted religion of the persecutors:

> Allusions to persecution in the treatise, even where the present tense is employed, prove only that Arnobius regarded this as a characteristic vice of paganism; the polemics of his seventh book suggest a living controversy, but one that is as likely to have resulted from a Christian project of suppressing sacrifice as from pagan legislation to enforce it.[45]

Edwards also draws attention to the chronographic argument, which can be redeployed in favour of the later date of 323.[46] The bottom line of Edwards' position on the dating of Arnobius' text is that 'the objections to Jerome's date of 327 for the writing of the treatise *Against the Nations* do not appear to be insuperable'.[47] This dating theory would also help to explain the infamous omission of any mention of Arnobius by Lactantius in his catalogue of the preceding Latin apologists by Lactantius in his *Diuinae institutiones*;[48] as quite simply, the *Aduersus nationes* would not yet have been produced. Edwards' contribution is highly welcome at this juncture in our understanding of the *Aduersus nationes*, as a counter-balance against the more general conviction of dating the work to the period of the Diocletianic persecution. Such opposition forces a refinement of the conventional arguments, and eventually contributes to a more critical establishment of the probable dating of Arnobius' text. For now, the main point against Edwards' argument for the later date of Arnobius remains its own weaknesses of textual support within the *Aduersus nationes* itself. It is to be hoped that further research, using the prospective 327 dating as a foundation, could throw up further corroborating possibilities as supporting evidence for the argument. Such a situation would only benefit the study of the date of Arnobius. In view of the current state of the evidence and the relevant informed debate, the *Aduersus nationes* must be dated to the general period of the Diocletianic persecution, but with at least

[45] 'Dating Arnobius: Why Discount the Evidence of Jerome?', p. 271.

[46] Ibid., pp. 270–1. However, in view of the divergent results, it must be stated that arguments from Arnobius' use of chronologies are too inconsistent to provide an impartial source of dating evidence.

[47] Ibid., p. 271.

[48] At *Diuinae institutiones*, 5: 4.

a provisional asterisk; a *terminus ante quem* of c. 311 is too vague to be accepted unreservedly. On the other hand, the distinct lack of any hints in the text to the era of the developing acceptance of Christianity following the patronage of Constantine is one of the strongest points against the c. 327 dating. Although such an argument centred around the lack of direct statements could equally be employed to disprove the dating to the opening of the fourth century, *Aduersus nationes* 4: 36 provides the strongest evidence in opposition for the moment. The reference to the destruction of the Scriptures and Christian buildings is of as contemporary a nature as can be observed from the work.

2. The *Aduersus nationes* within a tradition of Latin apologetics

Although Arnobius himself may seem to have emerged from complete obscurity, the *Aduersus nationes* stands within a well established tradition of Latin apologetic writing. In turn, the heartbeat of this tradition is inescapably African. Although Arnobius neglects to be specific, he acknowledges the Christian predecessors who have dealt with many of the same issues that form the subject matter of his own text. This is not to say that the cryptic allusion refers solely to Latin writers, but Arnobius does seem to be hinting at the work of Minucius Felix, Tertullian, and Cyprian at the opening of book three:

> *Iamdudum quidem criminibus his omnibus, maledictionibus potius ut uera dicamus, ab excellentibus parte in hac uiris et ueritatem istam commeritis nosse satis plene accurateque responsum est neque apex ullus ullius praetermissus est quaestionis qui non sit modis mille et rationibus ualidissimis refutatus. Non est igitur necessarium parte in hac causae diutius inmorari.*[49]

---

[49] 'Indeed, all these charges – or let us rather declare them as they really are – these diatribes, have long ago been answered sufficiently, completely, and accurately by men distinguished in this field and worthy to have learned the truth. And no single point of any question has been overlooked, without being refuted in a thousand ways with the strongest reasoning. Therefore, it is not necessary to linger further on this part of the case'. *Aduersus nationes*, 3: 1.

After a brief discussion of the genre of the *Aduersus nationes*, the focus of this section is to identify some of the echoes of these earlier apologists that occur over the course of Arnobius' work.

An apology?

Defining and classifying the particular genre of the *Aduersus nationes* is key to locating Arnobius within the literary surroundings of a Latin textual tradition. Although the *Aduersus nationes* is not an apology in the sense of Minucius Felix's *Octauius* or Tertullian's *Apologeticum*, its position alongside the other Latin apologetic works can be adequately justified. From the outset of the text, Arnobius explicitly states his motivation for producing the *Aduersus nationes* in a similar conceptual understanding as Cyprian's *Ad Demetrianum*. The recurring assertion of the opponents of Christianity is *postquam esse in mundo Christiana gens coepit, terrarum orbem perisse, multiformibus malis affectum esse genus humanum.*[50] Arnobius, with the characteristic self-deprecating remarks of the rhetor,[51] aims to defend the Church from the unjust charges of blame for any instances of human suffering. Hence the immediate conventional description of the *Aduersus nationes* as apologetic. But Arnobius' exoneration of the Christians takes the form of a highly polemical assault on the beliefs and customs of traditional Roman religion, with a particular emphasis on the worship of Roman North Africa. In this sense, apologetics and polemic are united in the justification of Christian belief through the deconstruction of the religion of its adversaries. Following this, questions about the status of Arnobius as a Christian apologist in the strictest sense of the term, have naturally been raised. Michael Bland Simmons advances one such perspective:

> The *Adv. nat.* should not be classified as a 'Christian Apology' in the traditional meaning; and for those who would still insist that Arnobius should be called a 'Christian Apologist', all would undoubtedly agree that he is much more successful in his attack upon paganism than he is in his 'defence' of Christianity.[52]

[50] 'After the Christian race began to exist in the world, the world has been ruined, the human race has been afflicted with many forms of misfortunes'. *Aduersus nationes*, I: 1.

[51] *Statui pro captu ac mediocritate sermonis contraire inuidiae et calumniosas dissoluere criminationes.* 'I have decided, according to my ability and the meanness of my discourse, to oppose the ill-feeling, and refute the false accusations'. *Aduersus nationes*, I: 1.

[52] *Arnobius of Sicca*, p. 22.

And although such is undoubtedly the case with the *Aduersus nationes*, Arnobius does still have a place within the Latin apologetic tradition. Christian belief is under fire from its intellectual adversaries, and the *Aduersus nationes* provides an extended response. It is polemic in the service of a defence of the Christian religion; the two formats may seem opposed, but a characterisation as 'polemical apologetic' for Arnobius' *Aduersus nationes* would not be oxymoronic. Indeed, this could also serve to describe Tertullian's own *Ad nationes* to some degree. As already discussed above,[53] apologetics and polemic need not be considered as two completely distinct formats, and the two are very closely linked in these textual defences of Christianity. This unity of apologetics and polemic is also present, if in a more restrained sense, in some of the other forerunning Latin apologetic works to Arnobius. There is no argument with the classification of Minucius Felix's *Octauius* or Tertullian's *Apologeticum* as apologetic, but both texts employ compartmentalised incidences of polemic within an overall apologetic argument.[54] The key difference with the *Aduersus nationes* is that apologetics is here the more minor part of the discourse, and the tone is throughout more of a direct attack rather than an embattled defence. Although the primary classification of the *Aduersus nationes* may not be 'apologetic' in its purest form, the definition as 'polemical apologetic' can be applied to refer to the character of the work. Very much in the sense of Tertullian's *Ad nationes*, Arnobius' *Aduersus nationes* embodies the attacking thrust essential within the broader scope of defence by means of offensive deconstruction.

Arnobius and his Latin predecessors

There are multiple textual incidences throughout the course of the *Aduersus nationes* that can be traced to the influence of preceding Latin apologetic works. Although it is a common (and highly pertinent) criticism of Arnobius that he seems to possess only a relatively

---

[53] p. 83.

[54] Much of Octavius' speech on behalf of the Christians utilises hostile polemics against differing aspects of Roman religion, but see especially *Octauius*, 21-26. With Tertullian, the bulk of his employment of polemical argument is reserved for the *Ad nationes*, but there are scattered incidences throughout the *Apologeticum*. See in particular *Apologeticum*, 12–15.

meagre knowledge of Scripture,[55] he nevertheless shows clear awareness of the compositions of some of the Christian writers who came
before him. Specific to these are Minucius Felix's *Octauius*, Tertullian's
Apologeticum and *Ad Nationes*, and Cyprian's *Ad Demetrianum*. Arnobius shares many features of style and focus with his Latin forbears;
some of which can be demonstrated to point towards the underlying
influence of these textual sources. It will be argued that the *Aduersus
nationes* is very comfortably at home within the early Latin apologetic
tradition.

However, it is important not to ascribe all parallels of focus and
argument to the prior influence of an earlier source. Arnobius' treatment of the criticism of the style of the Scriptures is one such example.
Although this particular subject had also been alluded to by earlier
apologists, and even dealt with at relative length,[56] the continuing prevalence of the issue betrays its importance in the intellectual
debate. For Arnobius the rhetorician, responsible for training others
in the recognised flourishes and nuances of high verbal skill, the style
and tone of the Scriptures would have been a significant issue requir-
ing explanation and defence. This is manifested in the two chapters of
the *Aduersus nationes* that are devoted to a response to common criticisms of the Scriptures. Arnobius relates three of the key contentions
from the critical perspective; [1] *Sed ab indoctis hominibus et rudibus*

---

[55] Following this comes the unavoidable observation of the implications of Arnobius' lack of recourse to the Scriptures throughout the *Aduersus nationes*. On the face
of it, there would appear to be no real problem; neither Minucius Felix nor Tertullian
cite from the Scriptures within their apologetic compositions, and Lactantius' well-
known criticism of Cyprian for doing so in the *Ad Demetrianum* makes the explicit
point of explaining the need to refute the opponents of the Church with their own
works. Yet Tertullian's Scriptural knowledge is unquestioned, and while it is generally
accepted that Minucius Felix has no purpose for Scripture within the *Octauius*, the
level of detail of Arnobius' knowledge of the Scriptures has been continually doubted.
Some knowledge is likely, as shown by his relation of a catalogue of Jesus' miracles
at *Aduersus nationes*, 1: 45–6, but other supposed reminiscences of the Scriptures in
Arnobius are generally vague. Also, several aspects of his theology can be shown to be
incompatible with Scriptural teachings, as with his expression of the character of God.
See above, p. 133, n. 21. Overall, it must be said that Arnobius seems to lack a detailed
awareness of the Scriptures. For an overview of the key points in the subject of Arnobius and the Scriptures, see McCracken, *The Case Against the Pagans*, Vol. 1, pp. 25–7.

[56] See, for example, Justin, *Apologia prima*, 60, regarding the barbarisms of
Christian language. Also the allusion by Caecilius in Minucius' *Octauius* to the
Christians as *indoctis inpolitis rudibus agrestibus*. 'Ignorant and uncultured, rude and
boorish'. *Octauius*, 12: 7. See also Clement of Alexandria, *Protrepticus*, 8, and Origen,
Contra Celsum, 1: 27, 1: 29, 3: 18, 3: 44, 3: 55, 6: 2.

scripta sunt et idcirco non sunt facili auditione credenda...[57] [2] *Triuialis et sordidus sermo est...*[58] [3] *Barbarismis, soloecismis obsitae sunt, inquit, res uestrae et uitiorum deformitate pollutae.*[59] Arnobius' concern is to draw attention to the broader picture, away from the grammatical and stylistic constraints of human origin; is the truth of an expression really subject to the skill with which it is articulated? Throughout his treatment of the topic, Arnobius never betrays the influence of a prior discussion from an earlier text, despite the undoubted existence of such possible sources. On this subject, his argument is his own, and his reasoning is studded throughout with the terminology of his art. Arnobius defends the beleaguered Christian Scriptures, arguing that truth needs no embellishment:

> *Quid enim officit, o quaeso, aut quam praestat intellectui tarditatem, utrumne quid glabre an hirsuta cum asperitate promatur, inflectatur quod acui an acuatur quod oportebat inflecti? Aut qui minus id quod dicitur uerum est, si in numero peccetur aut casu praepositione participio coniunctione? Pompa ista sermonis et oratio missa per regulas contionibus litibus foro iudiciisque seruetur deturque illis immo qui, uoluptatum delinimenta quaerentes, omne suum studium uerborum in lumina contulerunt.*[60]

It has been questioned whether Arnobius remained in his professional occupation after his conversion,[61] but nothing conclusive can be deduced from such statements where he seems to attack the achievements of rhetorical study. His intention is to subvert the place of rhetoric within religious expression, and thus defend the unrefined style of the Scriptures as an acceptable medium of religious testimony.

---

[57] 'But they were written by ignorant and uneducated men, and therefore ought not to be believed without hesitation'. *Aduersus nationes*, 1: 58.

[58] 'The language is commonplace and vulgar'. *Aduersus nationes*, 1: 58.

[59] 'Your narratives are overrun with barbarisms and grammatical mistakes (one says), and soiled with ugly faults'. *Aduersus nationes*, 1: 59.

[60] 'For how, I ask you, does it impede or retard comprehension, whether something is put forth smoothly or with unpolished roughness? Whether something is accented with the acute that ought to be accented with the grave? (*inflectatur quod acui an acuatur quod oportebat inflecti?*) Or how is the truth of something that is said lessened if there is a mistake in number, or case, preposition, participle, or conjunction? Let that ostentation of diction and oratory, according to the rules [of rhetorical speech], be reserved for public assemblies, lawsuits, for the forum and the courts of justice, and for those who, seeking after soothing pleasures, devote all their enthusiasm to the brilliance of words'. *Aduersus nationes*, 1: 59.

[61] As with McCracken, p. 104, n. 282. See also Hans von Campenhausen, *The Fathers of the Latin Church*, pp. 61–2, asking the same question of Lactantius.

The treatment of the issue stems only from a direct need to personally address it within the scope of the *Aduersus nationes*.

Minucius Felix

There are a number of clear allusions to the *Octauius* in the *Aduersus nationes*. Although Arnobius never specifically names his Christian textual sources, it does become evident that the *Octauius* provided one such influence. For the purpose of this following comparative study, three textual incidences will be analysed in order to assess the extent of Arnobius' borrowings from Minucius Felix. They are *Aduersus nationes* 3: 9-10 with *Octauius* 24: 3-4, *Aduersus nationes* 6: 14-20 with *Octauius* 24: 5-10, and *Aduersus nationes* 6: 5 with *Octauius* 10: 5.

With numerous recurrences throughout the text, one of the most prevalent techniques of argument employed by Arnobius is the *reductio ad absurdum*. His style is to drag the particular argument in hand beyond the limits of its acceptable boundaries, and into a generally farcical extension where it can be ridiculed within its own original parameters. Its deployment is the characteristic feature of the argument of the *Aduersus nationes*, and is at a height in the assault on the anthropomorphic deities of traditional Roman belief.[62] Arnobius paints a lurid depiction of the life of the gods, resplendent in an all-too-human vulgarity despite their heavenly station. The heavens are full of gods with bodies that are nothing more than human, but have been spared the release of death. Female deities are subjected to nauseous pregnancies, miscarriages, premature births and birth-pains. Their sexual organs allow them to continually procreate, free from the effects of the *frigoribus... senectutis*.[63] But if this is not the case, then the presence of genitalia is more akin to a terrible practical joke,[64] whereby nature has provided the gods with body parts for which they have no use. Arnobius addresses his argument with biting sarcasm; *quid dicitis, o sancti atque inpolluti antistites religionum?*[65] The absurd depiction culminates in a sordid image of rampant sexual intercourse that should be far removed from the true characters of the gods; *quid ergo iam superest, nisi ut eos credamus inmundorum quadripedum ritu in libidinum furias gestire, cupiditatibus rabidis ire in mutuas complexiones et ad postremum fractis*

---

[62] *Aduersus nationes*, 3: 9–15.

[63] 'The frigidity of old age'. *Aduersus nationes*, 3: 9.

[64] The *lusus* ('trick') played by nature.

[65] 'What do you say, o holy and undefiled priests of the religions?'. *Aduersus nationes*, 3: 10.

dissolutisque corporibus uoluptatis eneruatione languescere?[66] The essence of the ridiculous situation is the *humanity* of the gods; the anthropomorphic characters to which Arnobius' understanding of divinity is strictly opposed. The description may be theatrical and excessive, but it serves a clear purpose. The core of Arnobius' argument is that the Christians cannot be said to insult the gods by their unbelief, when such grossly impious fables are promulgated as matters of faith.[67] The use of the *reductio ad absurdum* is fundamental in compiling this sordid picture of heavenly life, excessively developed by Arnobius from a prior point of argument. It is also likely that the original basis for this facet of Arnobius' attack on the anthropomorphisms of the gods is *Octauius* 24: 3–4; the initial inspiration which Arnobius has then extended to its furthest point of interpretation.

Minucius' address of the subject also occurs within an assault on the perceived divinity of the gods; they are argued instead to be nothing more than mere mortals, deified after death in spite of their own intentions.[68] Minucius intends to identify every god as being of human origin, which can then be utilised as the foundation for his central point; *quoniam moritur omne quod nascitur; diuinum autem id est, quod nec ortum habet nec occasum.*[69] The anthropomorphisms of the gods are attacked in the service of this position; if they can be shown to be human-born, and are believed to retain their human characteristics even into their heavenly existences, then their status as truly divine can be doubted with good reason. On the subject of the continuation of pregnancy amongst the gods, Minucius argues:

> *Ceterum si dii creare possent, interire non possent, plures totis hominibus deos haberemus, ut iam eos nec caelum contineret nec aer caperet nec terra*

---

[66] 'What then remains, except for us to believe that after the manner of filthy quadrupeds they are transported into raging lusts, enter into mutual embraces with frenzied desires, and finally, with broken and dissolute bodies, are made weak by their pleasure?'. *Aduersus nationes*, 3: 10.

[67] *Nonne multo est rectius maledicere, conuiciari atque alia ingerere diis probra, quam sub obtentu pio talia de his monstra opinionum indignitate praesumere?* 'Surely it is more proper to abuse, to revile and to heap other insults on the gods, than under the pretence of piety to presume with indignity such monstrous beliefs about them?'. *Aduersus nationes*, 3: 10.

[68] *Octauius*, 24: 2.

[69] 'Everything that is born dies, but that is divine which has neither beginning nor ending'. *Octauius*, 24: 3.

gestaret. Unde manifestum est homines illos fuisse, quos et natos legimus et mortuos scimus.[70]

The core idea is that new gods are no longer born only because people have generally ceased to believe in such fables, as otherwise there would be an innumerable multitude of divine characters thronging both heavenly and earthly locations. This is particularly reminiscent in Arnobius' address of the same issue:

Ergo si haec ita sunt, id est si dii procreant superi et supter[71] *has leges experiuntur se sexus, suntque inmortales nec frigoribus fiunt senectutis effeti, sequitur ut debeant plena esse diis omnia neque innumeros caelos eorum capere multitudinem posse, siquidem et ipsi perpetuo generant et per suboles subolum multiplicata semper innumerabilitas ampliatur.*[72]

While it is the summit of Minucius' argument on the humanity of the gods, it is another step in Arnobius' employment of the *reductio ad absurdum* on the topic, reaching a crescendo in an intense depiction of pregnancy and childbirth amongst the female deities. It is highly probable that Arnobius has taken Minucius' treatment of the implications of the human qualities of the gods in the support of his own argument, and extended it using his characteristic mode of interpretation to its most extreme level.

Arnobius' usage of the *reductio* technique is again in operation throughout his focus on the subject of the veneration of images and statues,[73] and the influence of Minucius Felix is clearly evident.[74] There are a great number of possible allusions to the *Octauius* within Arnobius' text, with some being naturally more obvious than others,

---

[70] 'Besides, if the gods were capable of procreating but incapable of perishing, we should have more gods than all of humanity; and by now heaven could not sustain them, nor the air contain them, nor the earth bear them. From this it is obvious that of those whose births we read, and whose deaths we know, they were men'. *Octauius*, 24: 4.

[71] Reading *supter*, following McCracken, p. 198, n. 34.

[72] 'Therefore, if these are so – that is, if the gods above procreate and are themselves subject to these laws of sex, and are immortal and not made impotent by the frigidity of old age – it follows that the whole universe ought to be full of gods, and innumerable heavens incapable of containing their multitude, since they are themselves continually procreating, and through the offspring of offspring their innumerability is always being increased'. *Aduersus nationes*, 3: 9.

[73] *Aduersus nationes*, 6: 14–20.

[74] See also McCracken, *The Case Against the Pagans*, Vol. 1, p. 45.

but they are nowhere more direct and emphatic than on this subject. Regarding religious images, Arnobius mentions the raw materials, the workmanship, the defilement by roving vermin and birds, and the subsequent care and protection by the same people who prostrate themselves in fear before them. All issues are present in the *Octauius*,[75] and its influence is highly likely. Indeed, Arnobius' treatment of the numerous insects and small animals whose lack of compunction allows them to crawl over and even soil these sacred objects of veneration, is so close to the corresponding depiction in the *Octauius* as to be explicit. Arnobius follows Minucius in advising his opponents to learn the true nature of the sacred images from such humble creatures:

> *Quanta uero de diis uestris animalia muta naturaliter iudicant! Mures hirundines milui non sentire eos sciunt.*[76]

> *Erubescite ergo uel sero atque ab animantibus mutis uias, rationes accipite doceantque uos eadem nihil numinis inesse simulacris, in quae obscena deicere neque metuunt neque uitant leges suas sequentia et instincta ueritate naturae.*[77]

The connections are too strong to ignore, and it can be stated with some confidence that the textual source behind this particular argument of the *Aduersus nationes* should be traced to its prior occurrence in Minucius Felix.

Another possible allusion to the *Octauius*, albeit in an altogether different sense, concerns Arnobius' criticism of the abilities of the gods to providentially interfere in the lives of their followers. He articulates a depiction of a somewhat frenetic god of Roman religion beseeched to help his people, yet unable to fulfil such a number of requests to the satisfaction of all. Arnobius' intention is to establish the failings of the gods to achieve any kind of omniscience or

---

[75] See *Octauius*, 24: 5–10. See also *Apologeticum*, 12: 7, for a briefer variant of the same essential argument.

[76] 'How much truer is the judgment that the dumb animals instinctively pass on your gods? Mice, swallows and kites understand that they have no feeling'. *Octauius*, 24: 9.

[77] 'Blush, then, however late, and take your paths and reasoning from the dumb animals, and let them likewise teach you that there is nothing of the divine in images on which they do not fear or avoid to defecate, following their own laws and led by their natural instinct'. *Aduersus nationes*, 6: 16.

omnipresence, bound as they are by human-like weaknesses. A reminiscence of *Octauius* 10: 5 results:

> *Molestum illum uolunt, inquietum, inpudenter etiam curiosum, siquidem adstat factis omnibus, locis omnibus intererrat, cum nec singulis inseruire possit per uniuersa districtus nec uniuersis sufficere in singulis occupatus.*[78]

> *Aut enim nullis erit in partibus praesens, si uspiam poterit aliquando non esse, aut aderit unis tantum, quoniam praebere communiter suum non potest atque indiscretus auditum. Atque ita perficitur, ut aut nullis deus opituletur omnino, si occupatus re aliqua ad audiendas uoces non quiuerit aduolare, aut exauditi tantummodo uni abeant soli, nihil egerint ceteri.*[79]

The style and tone of the descriptions are concurrent, and the Minucian influence is certainly plausible. If this is the case, it follows that Arnobius has redirected the nature of the utilised argument, turning it from a criticism of monotheistic Christian providence into a Christian attack on the providential abilities of the gods. From the force of this text in particular, but also from a wider reading of the *Aduersus nationes* as whole, it is clear that there is little room for providence in Arnobius' theology. At this point, continuity with the *Octauius* ends. Providence is a theological tenet held and defended by Minucius as a critical part of his theological understanding.[80] Arnobius' attack, even though on a non-Christian providence, is testament to his departure from a key theological principle within Latin Christian belief, so strongly emphasised in the *Octauius*. This criticism of providence provides an important insight into Arnobius' own theological expression of the relationship between God and humanity.

Throughout the *Aduersus nationes*, Arnobius is deliberately reticent in discussing the character of the Christian God in detail. He explicitly pleads his ignorance at being able to answer such a question

---

[78] 'They are willing for him to be troublesome, restless, to pry shamelessly and assist in everything that is done, wandering through every place. He can neither take care of particulars because he is distracted by universal things, and is not capable of managing these because he is occupied by the particulars'. *Octauius*, 10: 5.

[79] 'For either he will be present nowhere, if it is possible for him not to be present somewhere at any time, or he will be present at one place only, since he is not able to indiscriminately offer a hearing to all. And so it comes about that either the god brings help to none at all, if being busy with something he was unable to hasten to hear the cries, or only some go away with their cries heard, while the rest accomplish nothing'. *Aduersus nationes*, 6: 5.

[80] See above, pp. 50–54.

with implications so remote from human conception: *respondeamus necesse est, nescire nos ista nec quae nullis possent facultatibus comprehendi expetisse aliquando aut studuisse cognoscere.*[81] He would seemingly be content to leave the matter rest unresolved, in deference to the incomprehensible nature of the *summus deus.*[82] However, observations can be made from other mentions of God in the *Aduersus nationes.* God is most predominantly defined as the 'first cause'[83] and the ultimate precursor of the created universe. There is no degree of allowance made for his continuing interference in the affairs of humanity. Arnobius' God is a distinctly remote personality; he is unquestionably omnipotent without being a benevolent overseer, and firmly omniscient without ever altering the course of the planet. This is emphasised in his relationship with the Christians; although they are the few who are truly faithful to him, and even though they suffer the very harshest torments in his service, God does not interfere to help them. The explanation is not that he is powerless or uncaring, but instead that he is only the observer of worldly events: *sed et nobis in huiusmodi casibus minime auxiliatur deus. Prompta et manifesta causa est. Nihil est enim nobis promissum ad hanc uitam nec in carunculae huius folliculo constitutis opis aliquid sponsum est auxiliique decretum.*[84] The Christians will go to him when they leave this life, and God will remain throughout as the ultimate mover, creator, and therefore ruler, of all.[85] Arnobius' God is not ruler in the sense of the decisions and responsibilities attached to personal kingship, but ruler as the sovereign, if remote, *rex summus.*[86] Arnobius refuses to trace the problem of evil to the instigation of God, and affirms that God is only capable of being behind the good things in life.[87] Questions of misfortunes, occurrences of evil, and other harmful

---

[81] 'We must answer that we do not know those things, and have never striven for or desired to get to know that which could not be comprehended by any of our abilities'. *Aduersus nationes*, 2: 55.

[82] 'Supreme God'. *Aduersus nationes*, 4: 36.

[83] Directly addressed as such in the prayer of *Aduersus nationes*, 1: 31. *Prima enim tu causa es.* 'For you are the first cause'.

[84] 'But God grants us no help at all in such calamitous events. The reason is clear and manifest. For nothing has been promised to us with respect to this life, nor has any help been pledged, nor aid decreed to those established in the husk of this flesh'. *Aduersus nationes*, 2: 76.

[85] Perhaps an analogous modern theological understanding on this issue would be more proximate to Deism.

[86] 'Supreme King'. *Aduersus nationes*, 2: 75.

[87] *Aduersus nationes*, 2: 55.

incidents in the world are tacitly assigned to the innate instability of the planetary elements,[88] before being evaded by a refusal to answer in real theological detail. Perhaps a lack of confidence in theological articulation and interpretation could be alleged from this failure to explain controversial issues about the character of God.[89] But in view of his resorting to apophatic terminology elsewhere,[90] it is equally likely that for Arnobius such an incredibly high consideration of God as all-powerful and unknowable prohibits any vulgar discussion of his abilities, or more pertinently, his limitations. This style of discussion is far removed from the *Octauius*, where God is instead presented as being closely intermingled within the Christian believer; *ubique non tantum nobis proximus, sed infusus est.*[91] Minucius also makes allowance for God's possible intervention in the world through the bestowal of blessings, should the supplicating Christian ever require such earthly goods.[92] There is a significant contrast in the two theological positions, and although Arnobius has testified to his reading of Minucius Felix throughout the *Aduersus nationes*, he shows no such influence in his own presentation of the nature of God. Arnobius has borrowed Minucius' criticism of God, but not his defence. What is included by Minucius as a characteristically mistaken belief about the character of the Christian God is actually held by Arnobius to be a valid retort to

---

[88] *Aduersus nationes*, 1: 8, 2: 55.

[89] Arnobius' refusal to explain particular subjects is evident throughout the *Aduersus nationes* and is something of a prominent strain of thought. It is particularly in operation at this point in his discussion of God and the human soul. His intention is to redefine ignorance or lack of knowledge as a positive state, and one that is to be preferred over ungrounded conjecture. See, for example, 2: 47, 2: 51, 2: 56, 2: 74, 2: 78.

[90] In the prayer of book one, a greater employment of apophatic statements would be difficult to achieve: *infinitus ingenitus inmortalis perpetuus solus, quem nulla deliniat forma corporalis, nulla determinat circumscriptio, qualitatis expers, quantitatis, sine situ motu et habitu, de quo nihil dici et exprimi mortalium potis est significatione uerborum, qui ut intellegaris tacendum est atque, ut per umbram te possit errans inuestigare suspicio, nihil est omnino muttiendum.* 'Infinite, unbegotten, immortal, everlasting alone, whom no bodily shape may represent, no boundary determine, unlimited in nature and magnitude, without location, motion, and condition; of whom nothing with significance can be said or expressed in the words of mortals. That you may be understood, we must be silent; and so that erring conjecture may seek after you even vaguely, nothing must be muttered at all'. *Aduersus nationes*, 1: 31.

[91] 'Not only is he near to us everywhere, but he is infused within us'. *Octauius*, 32: 7.

[92] *Et tamen facultates, si utiles putaremus, a deo posceremus; utique indulgere posset aliquantum cuius est totum.* 'And yet, we would ask God for material goods, if we thought them to be useful; certainly he to whom everything belongs would be able to grant us a portion'. *Octauius*, 36: 7.

belief in the providential abilities of the statues and images of Roman religion. A similar situation can also be shown to recur on the subject of the relationship between Arnobius and Cyprian.

Tertullian

McCracken provides a list of numerous parallels with Tertullian, with some being more likely than others, suggesting Arnobius' borrowings from the *Apologeticum* and the *Ad nationes*.[93] But there are also strong points of divergence between Arnobius and Tertullian. After an establishment of a positive parallel between the *Aduersus nationes* and the *Apologeticum*, the issue of Arnobius' depiction of the soul will be discussed, with specific relation to Tertullian's *De testimonio animae* and *De anima*.

There is a noticeable reminiscence of the *Apologeticum*, and its corresponding passage in the *Ad nationes*,[94] in the second book of the *Aduersus nationes*. Arnobius aims to disprove the common argument from antiquity, by establishing both the novelty of Roman religion and its recurrent failure to maintain a faithful line of tradition. The charge of Christianity as novel is prominent throughout the apologists, and it is no different with Arnobius. He is here defending Christianity against a dismissive description as merely days old in comparison to the long history of Roman religion.[95] His response is to point towards several antiquated laws, customs, and rites which common neglect has rendered obsolete. Alongside this, the introduction of Egyptian deities into the pantheon is cited as an example of infidelity to ancient religious tradition; an argument with resonance on the subject of the novelty of Christianity. Arnobius can identify the hypocrisy inherent in such condemnation of Christian belief with a direct *tu quoque*:

> *Nam si mutare sententiam culpa est ulla uel crimen et a ueteribus institutis in alias res nouas uoluntatesque migrare, criminatio ista et uos spectat, qui*

---

[93] *The Case Against the Pagans*, Vol. 1, pp. 45–7.

[94] Firstly, on the issue of the title format *Aduersus nationes*, as McCracken comments, 'Arnobius may have been influenced in his choice of title by the *Ad nationes*'. Ibid., Vol. 1, p. 45. Whether this is the case or not, the precedent in Latin apologetics was certainly set by Tertullian.

[95] *Nouellam esse religionem nostram et ante dies natam propemodum paucos.* 'Our religion is new, and arose just as a few days ago'. *Aduersus nationes*, 2: 66.

totiens uitam consuetudinemque mutastis, qui in mores alios atque alios ritus priorum condemnatione transistis.[96]

Apparently forgotten ancient practices are named, and formulated into blunt and forthright questions. Arnobius is explicitly taking the intellectual high ground in the debate. Although the details on the list of neglected religious practices given by Arnobius are different to that of Tertullian,[97] it should be noted that Arnobius is primarily dealing with a religious issue, while Tertullian is focusing more on its legal aspects. Arnobius is concerned with establishing a sense of novelty regarding contemporary religious practice, and Tertullian is working to prove contemporary infidelity to ancient law. Nevertheless, the inclusion of the treatment of women in order to ascertain their sobriety is common to both.[98] Although the reference itself also occurs in Aulus Gellius,[99] it is likely that Arnobius is betraying the influence of Tertullian's treatment of the subject. Aside from this brief crossover, the distinction between Arnobius' focus on ritual customs and Tertullian's on legal and moral practice applies. But both arguments have the same intention; to draw attention to the gross double-standard in the condemnation and subsequent persecution of Christianity.

Tertullian immediately follows his detailing of the legal aspects of the neglected tradition by turning to an example of newly-introduced gods. He relates the story of the banishment of the Egyptian deities Serapis, Isis, Harpocrates, and Anubis from the *curia deorum*[100] at the instigation of the consuls Piso and Gabinius.[101] By overturning their altars, the actions of the consuls were to symbolically refuse them a place within the canonical Roman pantheon; Tertullian incisively hints that although the consuls were not Christian, they have effectively acted as such. That is not to go so far as to appropriate them as proto-Christian, but only to recall a period of a greater religious and moral conscience than exists amongst Tertullian's contemporaries. Its purpose

---

[96] 'For if it is any fault or crime to change an opinion, and to depart from ancient customs for other things and new inclinations, this charge also includes you. You, who have many times changed your manner of living and practice, and have gone over to other customs and ceremonies, with the condemnation of the past'. *Aduersus nationes*, 2: 67.

[97] *Apologeticum*, 6: 1–6.

[98] *Aduersus nationes*, 2: 67, and *Apologeticum*, 6: 5.

[99] *Noctes Atticae*, 1: 10.

[100] 'Assembly of the gods'. *Apologeticum*, 6: 8.

[101] *Apologeticum*, 6: 8, and also at *Ad nationes*, 1: 10.

is to pinpoint a failure to honour received religious tradition by a specific example, and to underline the accompanying decline in common morality. Characteristically, Tertullian has a pithy maxim to adorn his argument; *laudatis semper antiquos, sed noue de die uiuitis.*[102] Arnobius picks up this argument in the course of his own treatment of the gradual public adoption of foreign deities, and the influence of Tertullian is manifest.[103] Arnobius relates the same story, albeit in a shortened version, in the service of an argument aimed at pinpointing the novelty of Roman worship of Egyptian deities, brought back around to the treatment of the Christians by the question *sed causa in [nos] huiusmodi uertitur sola?*[104] Arnobius' key intention in the argument is to extend the popular acceptance of such religious innovation towards the Christian movement also. If nothing else, Christianity could at least be tolerated along with the inclusion of these other comparatively new foreign cults. The general purpose and flow of the argument, added to the two shared fragments, contributes to the highly probable identification of the *Apologeticum* as the textual influence behind this section of the *Aduersus nationes.* But demonstration of influence on one point does not mean that Tertullian blanketly influences Arnobius as a matter of course. Some aspects of Arnobius' expression of the Christian belief in the soul could hardly be further removed from Tertullian's own treatment of the subject. The following discussion serves to express first an incidence of general agreement, followed by a significant degree of difference between the two Latin writers on the issue of the human soul. That is not to condemn Arnobius for deliberately diverging from Tertullian, as it appears to be a likely prospect that he has not read Tertullian's *De anima.* The purpose of this analysis of the treatment of the nature of the soul is to identify the extent of Arnobius' variance with earlier Latin theology through a relevant example.

Both apologists concur on arguing against the degree of the soul's innate knowledge – the Platonic idea of *reminiscentia.*[105] As

---

[102] 'You are always praising the ancients, but living in a new manner day by day'. *Apologeticum,* 6: 9.

[103] Although as McCracken notes, Tertullian's mention of Varro as his textual source (*Ad nationes,* 1: 10) could implicate Arnobius' independent reading of Varro, the Tertullianic influence remains a likely prospect due to the location of the cited arguments.

[104] 'But is a charge of this sort turned against us alone?'. *Aduersus nationes,* 2: 73.

[105] 'Recollections'. Developed in Plato, *Meno,* 81b-d, and *Phaedo,* 72e-74d. On the subject of anamnesis/*reminiscentia* in Plato, see R. E. Allen, 'Anamnesis in Plato's "Meno and Phaedo"', and Dominic Scott, 'Platonic Anamnesis Revisited'.

McCracken follows J. H. Waszink in noting, the actual employment of the term *reminiscentia* seems only to occur with Tertullian and Arnobius.[106] But this is used to provide the Latin equivalent of the original *anamnesis*, and needs not be taken as evidence of the textual dependence of Arnobius on Tertullian. Both apologists are heavily critical of the doctrine that souls are forgetful of the once-great depths of their learning; Tertullian directly attacking Plato for providing arguments since taken up by Gnostic exponents,[107] and Arnobius deconstructing the theory of *reminiscentia* by the lengthy analogy of an uncorrupted man as a *tabula rasa*.[108] Arnobius corresponds with Tertullian in arguing that belief in the soul's forgetfulness of its previous life with God is thoroughly redundant.[109] Learning comes from the schools, and not from the soul. But neither apologist will take the criticism further than the subject of recollected knowledge regarding human activities – it is essential for both Tertullian and Arnobius that the soul can provide a witness to its Lord and Creator. For Tertullian, the soul naturally recognises and fears God,[110] but the combination of its own fallen nature added to the sinful desires of man prevent it from fully worshipping its maker in the adoption of Christian faith.[111] Arnobius articulates a similar expression of the soul's natural awareness of its creator, as a testimony implanted from the moment of conception.[112] The purpose of the argument is to exhibit the soul as a personified witness to the power of God in the act of its creation. The key distinction between Tertullian and Arnobius in their usage of the *reminiscentia* argument and criticism is that Arnobius would carry it to invalidate belief in the soul as immortal,[113] while Tertullian confines it to disproving the theory of recollection alone.[114] So far, Tertullian and Arnobius are at least broadly concurrent, but the differences between the two apologists on the subject of the human soul become heightened in the explanation of its nature.

[106] Tertullian, *De anima*, 23: 6, and *Aduersus nationes*, 2: 19. See McCracken, p. 133, n. 134.

[107] *De anima*, 23–4.

[108] *Aduersus nationes*, 2: 20–25.

[109] *Aduersus nationes*, 2: 26-8, and *De anima*, 24.

[110] *De testimonio animae*, 2: 4–6, also briefly mentioned at *De anima*, 41.

[111] *De testimonio animae*, 6: 5–6.

[112] *Aduersus nationes*, 1: 33.

[113] *Aduersus nationes*, 2: 25.

[114] *De anima*, 24.

Much of book two of the *Aduersus nationes* is devoted to an inter-mittent discussion on the origin and meaning of the soul, forming a lengthy digression to address the philosophical doctrines of the so-called *uiri noui*. Arnobius holds that the soul is neither strictly mortal nor immortal, and instead of *mediae qualitatis*.[115] Immortality is only bestowed by God on the righteous,[116] and is thus not inherent in the soul's natural character. This principle of the soul as neither human nor divine underpins Arnobius' argument, and the soul's intermediate character allows for an explanation of the problem of evil by ensuring that morally bankrupt humanity has not been endowed with a gift from the divine. The immoral actions of man preclude their intimate bond with a divinely-created soul, otherwise it must follow that God has sent souls in spite of the eventual likelihood that they may become evil. All manner of crimes and blasphemies are cited by Arnobius as incidences of human evil which a divinely-created soul should be incapable of committing.[117] Even the ascetic qualities of morally upright men prove the natural tendency of humanity to sin, and thus disprove the immor-tal and virtuous character of an innate soul by extension.[118] Immortal-ity can only be a gift from God,[119] and true salvation is therefore from the eternal destruction of the soul.[120] It is blasphemous impiety to sug-gest that humanity has anything to do with future immortality:

> *Uos uestrarum animarum salutem in ipsis uobis reponitis fierique uos deos uestro fiditis intestinoque conatu; at uero nos nobis nihil de nostra infirmi-tate promittimus naturam intuentes nostram uirium esse nullarum et ab suis adfectibus in omni rerum contentione superari.*[121]

The crux is the intermediate nature of the soul throughout; it is somewhere above the level of humanity, but below the position of an

---

[115] 'Intermediate character'. *Aduersus nationes*, 2: 14.

[116] *Aduersus nationes*, 2: 14, 2: 33, 2: 62.

[117] *Aduersus nationes*, 2: 39–42.

[118] *Aduersus nationes*, 2: 50.

[119] *Aduersus nationes*, 2: 53.

[120] *Mortis nobis cum proponatur metus id est animarum interitus.* 'Since the fear of death is before us, that is, the destruction of our souls'. *Aduersus nationes*, 2: 33.

[121] 'You rest the salvation of your souls on your own selves, and are confident that by your own personal exertions you become gods; but we, on the other hand, promise nothing to ourselves on account of our weakness, considering that our nature has no strength and is overcome by its own passions in every struggle for anything'. *Aduersus nationes*, 2: 33.

immediate creation of God: *non esse animas regis maximi filias... Sed alterum quempiam genitorem his esse, dignitatis et potentiae gradibus satis plurimis ab imperatore diiunctum, eius tamen ex aula et eminentium nobilem sublimitate natalium.*[122] This *alterum genitorem*, firmly of lesser divinity, is employed in the creation of souls in order to prevent the tracing of any evil back to the instigation of God himself. There can be no connection of evil with the *summus deus*. For Arnobius, this would be a blot on the divine character that is utterly insupportable.[123] The association of this position with the conception of a demiurge has undoubtedly contributed to Arnobius' tentative classification as a 'Gnostic' of some degree.[124] But Arnobius refuses to be drawn on details in identifying this lesser creator divinity, and characteristically pleads ignorance as more proper than ungrounded conjecture.[125] The inherent weakness of Arnobius' understanding of the soul is its imprecision; both the *alterum genitorem* itself and the *mediae qualitatis* of the soul are unspecified, leading to a critically unconvincing argument. In this particular discussion, Arnobius' pleading of ignorance as more fitting in discourse concerning God reads as an attempt to avoid further elaboration. It is a technique that here serves little purpose other than to cap his failure to adequately express the character of the human soul.

Tertullian's own understanding of the soul can be read in his *De testimonio animae* and *De anima*, and is described within fundamentally different parameters to Arnobius. Indeed, Arnobius' encapsulation of the 'Christian' position regarding the soul is so radically divergent from Tertullian's as to be incompatible. For instance, in relating the various perspectives on the character of the soul, Tertullian allows only for it to be either divine, or else created. Arnobius' *mediae qualitatis* fits into neither category.[126] For Tertullian, the soul is a gift from God to humanity, and therefore of divine origin.[127] In characteristically blunt style, Tertullian provides a brief summary of his position:

---

[122] 'Souls are not children of the Supreme King... But they have some other creator, separated very greatly in rank and power from their ruler, yet nevertheless of his court, and are distinguished by the sublimity of their highborn positions'. *Aduersus nationes*, 2: 36.

[123] *Aduersus nationes*, 2: 46.

[124] See Simmons, *Arnobius of Sicca*, pp. 1–2.

[125] *Aduersus nationes*, 2: 47–8. *Si infucata uultis audire nec ab aliqua uocis ostentatione deducta, item confitemur nos istud ignorare.* 'If you want to hear the unembellished truth, not drawn out in vain ostentation of expression, we likewise confess that we do not know this'. *Aduersus nationes*, 2: 47.

[126] *De testimonio animae*, 1: 5.

[127] *De testimonio animae*, 5: 2.

Definimus animam dei flatu natam, immortalem, corporalem, effigiatam, substantia simplicem, de suo sapientem, uarie procedentem, liberam arbitrii, accidentis obnoxiam, per ingenia mutabilem, rationalem, dominatricem, diuinatricem, ex una redundantem.[128]

There is no possibility of an *alterum genitorem* of lesser divinity. The Scriptural definition of the soul as the breath of God that animates each created individual is utilised prominently by Tertullian in explanation of its origin in the personal instigation of God.[129] The soul is united to its conjoined human body at the moment of conception,[130] and is inseparable until the moment of earthly demise.[131] Although the body is susceptible to its corporeal end in death, the soul possesses immortality, and flies to Hades to await the future judgement of God.[132] Its immortality is a continual feature in the argument, and the distinct opposite of Arnobius' refusal to allow for anything more than *mediae qualitatis* in the nature of the soul. Whereas Arnobius describes salvation as deliverance from the eternal destruction of the soul in the afterlife, Tertullian understands immortality as being bestowed on both the saved and the damned alike; salvation is thus deliverance from eternal punishment in Hades. The corporeal essence of the soul makes such suffering possible,[133] and reprobate souls are condemned to everlasting torments for their failure to serve God in their human existence. This, in turn, can be traced to the machinations of Satan, and his destructive agency in contriving the fall of man.[134] The once-supreme virtue of the soul, a product of its divine birthright, has been forever tainted by original sin.[135] But furthermore, Tertullian enforces a duality within the question of the impact of the fall onto the nature of the soul; its

---

[128] 'We define the soul as born of the breath of God; immortal, corporeal, possessing form, of simple substance, of its own understanding, advancing in various ways, of free will, subject to changes of circumstance, changeable in character, rational, dominant [over body and mind], evolved from one [archetype]'. *De anima*, 22: 2.

[129] *De anima*, 3–4, see Gen 2: 7.

[130] *De anima*, 27.

[131] *De anima*, 51–53.

[132] *De anima*, 58. On this issue, Tertullian includes the possibility of minor purgatorial punishments, even if the soul in question will eventually be destined for eternal bliss.

[133] *De anima*, 5–9.

[134] *De testimonio animae*, 5: 2, *De anima*, 39. For Tertullian, the perverting influence of the devil is present within the individual from the moment of birth, and lies behind the tarnishing of each human soul by sin.

[135] *De anima*, 41.

divine origin has been obscured, but not extinguished.[136] Because it is not entirely divine, it can be affected by the consequences of sin, but since it enjoys such an elevated status due to its divine origin, its innate character can never be completely lost to evil. Even the souls of the very worst of men are not completely bad, as some degree of goodness will always remain.[137] This can be contrasted with the position of Arnobius, which pinpoints the evils committed by humanity as basis for an argument against the innately virtuous character of the soul.[138]

It is evident that Arnobius and Tertullian differ significantly in their understanding of the nature of the human soul. Although they generally concur in critiquing the doctrine of *reminiscentia*, the gulf between Arnobius' *mediae qualitatis* and Tertullian's immortal creation of the divine cannot be bridged. If Arnobius' treatment of Minucius Felix's address on providence is taken as a precedent, then it becomes quite possible that Arnobius could also have disregarded Tertullian's description of the soul due to its level of conflict with his own. Such an argument would undoubtedly be likely, if Arnobius' reading of the *De anima* could be proven. But instead it seems probable that Arnobius was unaware of the *De anima*,[139] and there is also no concrete reason to assume that he read the *De testimonio*. Certainly the *Apologeticum*, and perhaps the *Ad Nationes*, can be defined as textual influences for Arnobius' *Aduersus nationes*; but as it has been demonstrated, aspects of the theology of Tertullian and Arnobius are mutually incompatible, and even irreconcilable. Tertullian and Arnobius on the soul is one of the most significant theological differences of its kind within the broader picture of the African Latin Christian writers.

Cyprian

Arnobius' declaration of the primary motives of the *Aduersus nationes* is immediately reminiscent of Cyprian's *Ad Demetrianum*. They both write with the explicit intention of responding to accusations of Christian blame for worldly misfortunes. According to the reasoning of Arnobius' opponents, Christian failure to sacrifice to the ancient gods brings about a just and deserved punishment – taking the form of such

---

[136] *De anima*, 41.

[137] *Propterea nulla anima sine crimine, quia nulla sine boni semine.* 'Just as no soul is without sin, so no soul is without the seed of good'. *De anima*, 41: 3.

[138] *Aduersus nationes*, 2: 39–42.

[139] McCracken, Vol. 1, p. 41, n. 322. See also McCracken, 'Review: Tertullian on the Soul', p. 349.

terrible events as plagues of insects, pestilence, famine, natural disasters, military defeats, crop failures, and other similar outbreaks of public suffering.[140] Culpability is placed firmly with the Christians, which contributes to a heightened level of public ill-feeling, and ultimately intensifies the grounding for persecution. Arnobius' stated rationale at the opening of the *Aduersus nationes* is to defend the Christians from such imputations, and to firmly exonerate the Church from any impiety or wrongdoing.[141] Similar attacks blaming the Christians for calamitous events occur intermittently during the early Christian epoch; Arnobius, like Cyprian before him, writes to counteract the unjust condemnation of the Church. But Arnobius is also conscious of the recurrence of maltreatment of the innocent Christian believers; public condemnation at times of civic, economic, or military insecurity is a widespread situation, and Arnobius has heard it all before. He derides the significance of the arguments of his opponents as merely repetition of vulgar rumour.[142] Reminiscences of the motives of the *Ad Demetrianum* are inescapable, but although many features of Cyprian's dialogue are also shared by Arnobius, the two apologists understand the subject of blame for worldly misfortune in intrinsically different ways.

Cyprian recounts the numerous events that are traced to the fault of the Christians,[143] but with the added rejoinder of his own; *hoc scias esse praedictum.*[144] The various calamities with which humanity is assailed are jointly presented as due to the natural aging of the world,[145] and as the deserved products of an angry God. Far from the Christians being impious, it is the failure of the non-Christian establishment to propitiate the true God that merits the plagues, famines, and natural disasters. Cyprian retorts the blame against his opponents, and threatens the continuation of such impiety towards the only true God with portents of the end times.[146] He is unequivocal in assigning culpability to the rivals of Christianity; *non enim, sicut tua falsa querimonia et*

---

[140] *Aduersus nationes*, I: 3.

[141] *Aduersus nationes*, I: I.

[142] *Aduersus nationes*, I: I.

[143] *Ad Demetrianum*, 5: I.

[144] 'Know that this has been predicted'. *Ad Demetrianum*, 5: I.

[145] The *lex dei*, by which all living things, and even the world itself, must eventually come to an end. *Ad Demetrianum*, 3–4.

[146] *Appropinquante iam iudicii die*. 'The day of judgment is now approaching'. *Ad Demetrianum*, 5: I.

imperitia ueritatis ignara iactat et clamitat, ista accidunt, quod dii uestri a nobis non colantur, sed quod a uobis non colatur Deus.[147] The actions are of a justly angry God laying waste to the land of the unbelievers; *ad disciplinam contumacium uel ad poenam malorum.*[148] Unfortunately for the Christians, they are fated to suffer alike with the worst of the enemies of God,[149] but they do so with a reassured air of dignified acceptance.[150] Fiery prophecies of judgment and retribution from the Old Testament Prophets are deployed to give force to the argument, reading as a lengthy castigation in the very strongest language.[151] If the opponents and persecutors of Christianity will not learn from such temporal punishment, then eternal punishment awaits.[152] In Cyprian's world-view, it is clear that the disasters and calamities which intermittently blight human society are the actions of an unpropitiated sovereign ruler. The blame then lies with the impiety of the world towards God.

Cyprian's reasoning can be contrasted with Arnobius' own explanation of the issue of human culpability for worldly suffering. Instead of working within the situation of an increased level of suffering, as Cyprian does, Arnobius opens by refuting it – there has been no increase in public calamities, and therefore no reason to accuse the Christians of angering the gods.[153] He loudly dismisses any fear of an outburst of divine anger at the impiety of the Christians. As long as there has been human civilisation, there have been plagues and famines,[154] and natural disasters have existed since the formation of the very elements themselves.[155] Perhaps the world is not solely intended to serve the needs of man; something which would take the personal tragedy out of such unfortunate events, and reduce them to the instigation of an

---

[147] 'For these things happen, not as your mistaken complaints and ignorant inexperience of the truth assert and repeat, because your gods are not worshipped by us; but because God is not worshipped by you'. *Ad Demetrianum*, 5: 1.

[148] 'For the correction of the obstinate or the punishment of the evil'. *Ad Demetrianum*, 7: 1.

[149] *Ad Demetrianum*, 19.

[150] *Inter ipsas saeculi labentis ruinas erecta mens est.* 'Among these ruins of a fallen age, our spirit stands tall'. *Ad Demetrianum*, 20: 1.

[151] *Ad Demetrianum*, 6–9.

[152] *Ad Demetrianum*, 9: 1.

[153] *Aduersus nationes*, 1: 2–5.

[154] *Aduersus nationes*, 1: 3.

[155] *Aduersus nationes*, 1: 8.

inorganic and impassible force.[156] For Arnobius, this mode of thinking is far better than to assign the origin of all calamities to the agency of the gods: *et tamen, o magni cultores atque antistites numinum, cur irasci populis Christianis augustissimos illos adseueratis deos? Ita non aduertitis non uidetis, adfectus quam turpes, quam indecoras numinibus attribuatis insanias?*[157] Arnobius cannot believe that even the gods would be so moved against the Christians as to unjustly cause the world to suffer on their behalf.[158] Since humanity suffers together, regardless of religious persuasion,[159] this surely must prove that the gods are not the cause of public disasters.[160] It equally cannot be stated that the proper veneration of the gods leads to blessings in public life, otherwise the favour of the gods would be markedly inconstant.[161] With this, the focus of Arnobius' condemnation switches to the self-serving priests who promote such nonsense fables; it is their vested interest in the financial condition of the temples that engenders fear in the anger of the gods, and empowers the anti-Christian treatment by extension.[162]

After an early emphasis on this subject at the opening of the *Aduersus nationes*, the text shifts to various other subjects in the religious controversy. But Arnobius ends his work by returning to his original motivation; asking whether the gods can truly be said to punish humanity in anger at being neglected.[163] For Arnobius, divinity can betray no semblance of emotion, and anger is far too human a trait to be shared by God.[164] Tracing the roots of the calamitous events to their true source would be a real step forward in establishing the theological authenticity of the gods: *utrumne hi dii sint quos saeuire adseueratis offensos reddique sacrificiis mites an sint longe aliud et ab*

---

[156] *Aduersus nationes*, I: 8–11.

[157] 'And yet, o great worshippers and priests of the gods, on what account do you assert that these most august gods are angry with the Christian people? Do you not notice, do you not see how indecent are the feelings, how disgraceful the insanities that you attribute to the gods?'. *Aduersus nationes*, I: 17.

[158] *Aduersus nationes*, I: 19–20.

[159] *Aduersus nationes*, I: 21-2. A theme also addressed by Cyprian, at *Ad Demetrianum*, 19.

[160] *Aduersus nationes*, I: 22.

[161] *Aduersus nationes*, I: 15.

[162] *Aduersus nationes*, I: 24.

[163] *Aduersus nationes*, 7: 38–42.

[164] The doctrine of the impassibility of God occurs throughout the *Aduersus nationes*. For a good discussion, see McCracken, *The Case Against the Pagans*, Vol. I, p. 71, n. 82.

huius ui debeant et nominis et potentiae segregari.[165] He cites the example of Jupiter and the games, providing a case in point to underline his key assertion; *nihil esse repperies diis dignum.*[166] Arnobius does not blame the gods for the public misfortunes, because there is no personal force acting in their provocation. The observation of sacrifices can achieve nothing in halting the course of worldly events, so the worship of the gods holds no purpose.[167] Compared with Cyprian, Arnobius' understanding of the issue of natural disasters and public calamities is fundamentally different; something that would amount to a major divergence if Arnobius elsewhere shows evidence of his awareness of the *Ad Demetrianum*. In support of this can be added Arnobius' otherwise unnoticed borrowing of the incidence of *nouas poenas* from Cyprian's text. The conclusion must be that Arnobius had read the *Ad Demetrianum*, but the aspects of Cyprian's thought that are so different to his own – exhibited here by the understanding of the source of public calamities – have again been disregarded in favour of his own argument.

Conclusion

Arnobius is often condemned as doctrinally unorthodox on the basis of numerous theological constructions of the *Aduersus nationes*.[168] But this definition could also be employed to express his relationship to the other writers in early Latin apologetics. It is in this sense that Arnobius' orthodoxy can be acutely questioned, without recourse to any sweeping identifications with heretical movements. Although he explicitly mentions the work of his apologetic forbears, he neglects to state the areas where he has directly gone against their positions. A comparative study with his predecessors in Latin apologetics, such as the above, can help to pinpoint the character of the *Aduersus nationes* within the African tradition. From this, his consistency with the positions of his forbears can be observed. Perhaps Arnobius never read the *De testimonio animae* or the *De anima*, so he cannot definitively be said

---

[165] 'Whether these really are gods who, as you assert, rage when offended, but are restored to calm by sacrifices; or are something completely different, and should be removed from the meaning of this title and power'. *Aduersus nationes*, 7: 39.

[166] 'You will find nothing worthy of the gods'. *Aduersus nationes*, 7: 41.

[167] *Aduersus nationes*, 7: 11.

[168] As with Arthur Cushman McGiffert, *A History of Christian Thought*, Vol. 2, p. 43; 'Whether because of ignorance or indifference he gave expression to many beliefs quite out of line with the orthodox theology of the day'.

to have knowingly diverged so radically from Tertullian's expression of the nature of the human soul. However, it is significantly more likely that Arnobius shows evidence of having read Minucius' *Octauius* and Cyprian's *Ad Demetrianum*, yet he is poles apart from Minucius' theory of providence, and equally removed from Cyprian's perspective on the issue of worldly suffering. Arnobius is aware of the theological positions of his predecessors, but has only selectively borrowed the arguments which fit with his own personal standpoints. Conflicting theological and doctrinal principles are ignored, and his own understanding is put forward as the general Christian position.[169] Because of this, the theology of the *Aduersus nationes* is not consistent with either Minucius Felix, Tertullian, or Cyprian. If Arnobius is to be to be defined as theologically unorthodox on any level, his place within Latin apologetics can form one such basis.

---

[169] As, for example, in his definition of the soul. *Aduersus nationes*, 2: 33–5.

LACTANTIUS

1. Introduction

Lucius Caecilius Firmianus Lactantius is the final Latin Christian apologist before the end of the era of intermittent persecutions with the eventual imperial-sponsored toleration of Christianity. His *Diuinae institutiones*,[1] originating from the period of the Diocletianic persecution,[2] is thus the final Latin apologetic witness to the Church as a beleaguered minority in need of a presentation of faith. That is not to say that apologetics can solely originate from the perspective of an embattled subgroup, but in the sense of a defensive encapsulation of belief in the service of an appeal to end the injustice of the persecutions, Lactantius provides the last such voice before the Constantinian period of acceptance of the Christian faith. His work is, therefore, highly valued; and is of key significance within the apologetic tradition. Due to his location at this highly important juncture in the history of the early Church, Lactantius has been the subject of an extensive level of scholarship. In turn, much of this is focused on aspects of his most substantial work; the *Diuinae institutiones*.[3]

[1] Otherwise titled *Diuinarum institutionum libri uii*, but also with various other similar renderings. The form *Diuinae institutiones* is here preferred, being the title format used at the *Clavis Patrum Latinorum*, #86.

[2] Following the arguments of T. D. Barnes, *Constantine and Eusebius*, p. 13, n. 96, for a completion date of the text as most likely in Africa in 308/9.

[3] Numerous critical editions of the text exist, although the same cannot be said for Lactantius' other writings. His *Opera omnia*, edited by S. Brandt and G. Laubmann in the CSEL series (1890–3) continues to be utilised, and retains a central place of reference. These volumes can be supplemented by more up-to-date versions of the *Diuinae institutiones* in the Sources Chrétiennes (1973–2007) although this series lacks renderings of books three and seven. The most modern editions are in the Bibliotheca

Comparatively little information concerning Lactantius' biographical details is available, and originates almost completely from the pen of Jerome. According to the *De uiris illustribus*, here as elsewhere one of the few sources for early Christian biographical information, Lactantius was a native of Africa, and perhaps a student of Arnobius at Sicca Veneria.[4] Lactantius himself does provide a small number of autobiographical hints, which can be used as separate pieces of evidence to substantiate the more general outline of Jerome. One such is the detail of his employment as teacher of rhetoric in Bithynia[5] at the time of the onset of the Diocletianic persecution. Lactantius recounts these circumstances as forming part of the context behind the motivation for compiling the *Diuinae institutiones*. Apologetics essentially originates, at least ostensibly, from a present need, and Lactantius allies the production of the *Diuinae institutiones* to the actions of two men in particular: *ego cum in Bithynia oratorias litteras accitus docerem contigissetque ut eodem tempore dei templum euerteretur, duo extiterunt ibidem, qui iacenti atque abiectae ueritati nescio utrum superbius an importunius insultarent.*[6] Much argument has been compiled on the subject of these two characters.[7] It is now generally accepted that the second is Sossianus Hierocles, governor of Bithynia,[8] but the identity of the first, the so-called *antistes philosophiae*,[9] is rather more controversial.

Teubneriana, edited by Eberhard Heck and Antonie Wlosok. These latter editions have been used for the citations within this work, but pending the planned 2011 publication of the final volume in the series containing book seven and the indices, Brandt's version of book seven remains in use. The recent translation of the *Diuinae institutiones* by Anthony Bowen and Peter Garnsey (henceforth 'Bowen and Garnsey') has provided a major contribution to the modern English study of the text, and its introduction is an invaluable starting-point in a reading of Lactantius' most significant work.

[4] *De uiris illustribus*, 80.

[5] Most likely at Nicomedia; the principal seat of Diocletian.

[6] 'I point out [my experiences] when I was summoned to teach rhetoric at Bithynia; it happened at this same time that a temple of God was overturned, which caused a pair of people to stand forth and jeer at the abject prostration of truth; though whether more from disdain or insolence I do not know'. *Diuinae institutiones*, 5: 2; 2. This mention of a Christian building being razed to the ground is likely to represent the destruction of the church of Nicomedia; one of the major opening acts of the persecution. It is detailed more fully at *De mortibus persecutorum*, 12. The beginning of the persecution at Nicomedia is also recorded by Eusebius, at *Historia ecclesiastica*, 8: 2, 5–6.

[7] Fully detailed by Lactantius at *Diuinae institutiones*, 5: 2–3.

[8] *Diuinae institutiones*, 5: 2; 2–17. See T. D. Barnes, 'Sossianus Hierocles and the Antecedents of the "Great Persecution"', pp. 242–3, and Elizabeth DePalma Digeser, *The Making of a Christian Empire: Lactantius and Rome*, pp. 5–8. Regarding Sossianus Hierocles, see also *The Prosopography of the Later Roman Empire*, Vol. 1, p. 432.

[9] *Diuinae institutiones*, 5: 2; 3.

It is argued to refer to none other than the Neoplatonist philosopher Porphyry of Tyre, author of numerous works against Christianity, and one of its most prominent early critics.[10] But while Arnobius' engagement with Porphyry in the *Aduersus nationes* seems conclusive, Lactantius' in the *Diuinae institutiones* is somehow less so. T. D. Barnes has argued against the identification of Porphyry with Lactantius' depicted philosophical opponent; highlighting the far from certain connection between the two men.[11] Perhaps Porphyry is one of the express targets of the *Diuinae institutiones*, but in view of the problematic nature of the evidence, conclusions are necessarily restricted. If nothing else, Porphyry can be considered as representative of one particular area within Lactantius' broader ambition of the probable audience of his apologetic text. Lactantius is not solely defending his Church against contemporary smears of either immorality or impiety, and neither is he only reinforcing Christian belief in the minds of its prior adherents; the *Diuinae institutiones* is an attempt at explaining Christianity to all levels of society,[12] and Porphyry would take his place among Lactantius' other opponents of high intellectual standing. There is no solid reason to dismiss the possibility that Lactantius addresses standpoints of Porphyry within the *Diuinae institutiones* – whether Porphyry is to be identified with the *antistes philosophiae* or not – but there is equally no real foundation as yet upon which to argue for Lactantius' text as a substantial rejoinder to Porphyry's own anti-Christian writing.

From his perspective located in the very heartland of the persecution, Lactantius is a first-hand witness, and an invaluable source of evidence. In particular, his *De mortibus persecutorum* rises above its extroverted one-sidedness on behalf of the Christian cause to provide at least a broadly verifiable account of the circumstances of the Great Persecution. It is the perspective of an informed, if highly partial, observer. Lactantius' works overflow with continual praise for Constantine, the

[10] In the original support of this identification with Porphyry, see Henry Chadwick, *The Sentences of Sextus*, pp. 142–3, although he is highly aware of the uncertainties in operation. More comprehensive support of the connection with Porphyry can be found in Robert L. Wilken, *The Christians as the Romans Saw Them*, pp. 135–6 and 155, Digeser, 'Lactantius, Porphyry, and the Debate over Religious Toleration', and *The Making of a Christian Empire: Lactantius and Rome*, pp. 93–107, also Robert M. Berchman, *Porphyry Against the Christians*, p. 4.

[11] Barnes, 'Porphyry Against the Christians: Date and the Attribution of Fragments', pp. 437–9, and 'Scholarship or Propaganda? Porphyry *Against the Christians* and its Historical Setting', pp. 58–9.

[12] In the words of Oliver Nicholson, 'a final answer to all critics of Christianity'. '*Caelum potius intuemini*: Lactantius and a Statue of Constantine', p. 185.

divinely-appointed saviour of the Church, and the gracious leader of a glorious new time of Christian security. His actual proximity to Constantine is embodied in the appointment as teacher of Latin literature to Crispus, Constantine's eldest son and natural heir.[13] Jerome's *Chronicon* relates a rare insight into Lactantius' personal situation at this time: *quorum Crispum Lactantius Latinis litteris erudiuit, uir omnium suo tempore eloquentissimus; sed adeo in hac uita pauper, ut plerumque etiam necessariis indiguerit.*[14] It is a highly privileged appointment, and one for which Jerome is certain of Lactantius' merit. Yet Jerome is also concerned with drawing a contrast between Lactantius' worldly fame and renown for his linguistic abilities, which is all combined with an exemplary degree of individual poverty. Lactantius is thus depicted as an exceptional archetype of the Christian character faced with earthly distinction; although he is the most eloquent man of his era, his lifestyle is modest and uncorrupted by personal fortune. The level of truth in Jerome's anecdote is unverifiable, but is an interesting point in Lactantius' personal characterisation even so. His personal fame carried him from North Africa to Nicomedia, and from Nicomedia to Gaul;[15] a truly ecumenical recognition of his academic talents. Christian or not, Lactantius never lost his high regard for the style and thought of Cicero; his works are marked by continual imitation, and intermittently studded with direct citations and engagement. Lactantius' association as something of a Christian manifestation of the great classical rhetor and philosopher can be traced to this high personal admiration.[16] It seems likely that Lactantius died in Gaul at c. 325, although it cannot be corroborated with certainty. By virtue of such fame and public recognition, on top of the achievements and continued popularity of the *Diuinae institutiones*,[17] Lactantius remains one of the foremost intellectual Christian characters of his generation. The

---

[13] Crispus would have been the natural imperial successor at this point, before his execution in 326 on the orders of his father. Sozomen glosses over Constantine's moral culpability for the event, at *Historia ecclesiastica*, 1: 5. The non-Christian Zosimus, on the other hand, is scathing of Constantine's act of filicide. *Historia noua*, 2: 29.

[14] 'Lactantius, the most eloquent man of his time, educated Crispus in Latin literature; but was actually in this life a pauper, as he frequently lacked even the necessities'. *Chronicon*, 317–8.

[15] Most likely at Augusta Treverorum (Trier).

[16] This connection of Lactantius and Cicero is also mentioned by Jerome, at *Epistula*, 58: 10, and 70: 5.

[17] The work has been the subject of continued attention over the centuries since its very first appearance, and also holds the honour of being the first book printed in Italy, at Salerno in 1465.

depth of his theology far surpasses that of Arnobius of Sicca, and the *Diuinae institutiones* stands as perhaps the most extensive single piece of Latin apologetics prior to the important *De ciuitate dei* of Augustine of Hippo. Although Lactantius is certainly not without fault,[18] his *Diuinae institutiones* nevertheless becomes the major work of early Latin apologetics after the *Apologeticum* of Tertullian.

His writings

The *De opificio dei*, dated to c. 303, and addressed to a certain Demetrianus,[19] articulates a systematic description of the human body in its place as the creation of God. Although officially aimed as a response to those who would classify humanity amongst the animals,[20] the *De opificio dei* does not immediately bear an outwardly apologetic character. That is, until the concluding remarks of the text make its apologetic purpose evident. For Lactantius, the trademark feature of humanity is reason and the soul, which are immortal gifts from God himself.[21] It is the relationship between the mortal body and the immortal soul that forms the real core of the work.[22] The nature of the soul as a gift from God is also accompanied by the wisdom of God; a circumstance which underlies the ability to truly define the human character.[23] Theological duality, itself a substantial recurring

---

[18] As lamented by Jerome; *utinam tam nostra affirmare potuisset, quam facile aliena destruxit.* 'If only he could have affirmed our doctrines as readily as he tore down those of others'. *Epistula,* 58: 10. Jerome's other criticism of Lactantius concerns the question of his orthodoxy on the subject of the Holy Spirit, with Lactantius apparently denying its substance as an individual member of the godhead. He is accused of mistakenly following the *error Iudaicus* ('Jewish error') on this matter, but not to the overall detriment of the benefits of the *Diuinae institutiones* – their clarity and utility ensures that they retain great merit. Jerome, *Epistula,* 84: 7.

[19] Also the recipient of two books of letters, now lost. See Jerome, *De uiris illustribus,* 80.

[20] *De opificio dei,* 2–3.

[21] *De opificio dei,* 19: 4.

[22] As it seems most likely that Arnobius of Sicca and Lactantius were unaware of each other's Christian literary work, there is no reason to attribute the difference in their understandings of the soul as anything of a divergence. Indeed, Arnobius' own arguments have no major foundation within early Christian theology, and Lactantius is in accord with the far more acceptable doctrine of the immortality of the soul.

[23] *Errat enim quisquis hominem carne metitur: nam hoc corpusculum quo induti sumus, hominis receptaculum est. Nam ipse homo neque tangi neque aspici neque comprehendi potest, quia latet intra hoc quod uidetur.* 'He errs who measures man by the body. For this worthless body, with which we are clothed, is the receptacle of man. Man himself cannot be touched, nor seen, nor grasped, because he lies hidden inside

theme throughout Lactantius' work, is employed as the central mode of explaining the nature of man as combined mortality and immortality; earthly body and heavenly soul. In a direct address to Demetrianus, the *De opificio dei* closes with Lactantius' personal notes on his motivation for compiling his Christian work; he writes for the benefit of those who may read and embark on the journey to Christian salvation,[24] and directs them against those who would corrupt the presentation of truth. Such overtly apologetic motives have become the defining characteristics of Lactantius' literary corpus as a whole.

The *De ira dei* (c. 316) can be understood in a similar methodological sense to the *De opificio dei*; although it may not seem explicitly apologetic, it carries an apologetic purpose that transcends its primary address to a Christian audience. The *De ira dei* provides an engagement with Lactantius' theological adversaries on the subject of God's capacity to the apparently human emotion of anger. Epicureans,[25] Stoics,[26] and others who would construct an image of the impassability of God are refuted in the service of an argument of God's susceptibility to the very opposite. Lactantius maintains the crucial purpose of the doctrine of the anger of God; *in eo enim summa omnis et cardo religionis pietatisque uersatur.*[27] If God cannot anger, then piety and religion are worthless. It is the fear of God that motivates the believer to remain constant in true worship.[28] Within this, Lactantius broaches the widely significant issue of the purpose of true religion as the means for keeping human society with a moral compass. Throughout the text there is a continual emphasis on the theme that both human and divine anger can be just, and that this concept of perfectly just anger has a fundamental place in God's

---

that which is seen'. *De opificio dei*, 19: 9. Latin text in Michel Perrin ed., *Lactance: L'Ouvrage du Dieu Créateur*.

[24] *Si labor meus aliquos homines ab erroribus liberatos ad iter caeleste direxerit.* 'If my labour has directed some men, freed from error, onto the path to heaven'. *De opificio dei*, 20: 9.

[25] *De ira dei*, 4.

[26] *De ira dei*, 5.

[27] 'For everything, and the essential nature of religion and piety depend upon this'. *De ira dei*, 6: 2. Latin text in Christiane Ingremeau ed., *Lactance: La Colère de Dieu*.

[28] *Nam neque honor ullus deberi potest deo, si nihil praestat colenti, nec ullus metus, si non irascitur non colenti.* 'For no honour can be due to God, if he furnishes nothing to his worshippers; and no fear, if he does not anger with those who do not worship him'. *De ira dei*, 6: 2.

punishment of the unrighteous.[29] God's anger is not human, as it is perfect and incorruptible, and although immortal it is perpetually open to forgiveness.[30] Lactantius' recourse to theological duality again marks his explanation of the relationship of good and evil,[31] personified as soul and body.[32] The apologetic character of the work comes through in the mode of expression of the subject in hand; the philosophers, though many, are in error – Lactantius' text provides an appeal to embrace the true wisdom solely held within Christian doctrine.[33]

If the *Diuinae institutiones* is Lactantius' most iconic work, then it is closely followed by the *De mortibus persecutorum*.[34] Its convenience for historians recounting the events of the Diocletianic persecution tends to outweigh the thorough bias that is prevalent throughout, and it retains an ubiquitous presence in every study of the early-fourth century Church. But it is no work of history; the *De mortibus persecutorum* is a fiery and graphic diatribe, and therefore not of much objective reliability for its portrayal of the Caesar Maximian Galerius, for example. The style of the text is markedly different from Lactantius' other work;[35] but the *De mortibus persecutorum* is also markedly more pertinent to contemporary events than his other work. If authentic, it is Lactantius detailing episodes from an era of his own experience, and is as emotionally-charged and prejudiced as can be expected. Whether or not Lactantius actually witnessed the terrible events of the persecution himself, he is still recording the sufferings and misfortunes of his contemporary religious compatriots.

---

[29] *Haec est ira iusta; quae sicut in homine necessaria est ad prauitatis correctionem, sic utique in deo, a quo ad hominem peruenit exemplum.* 'This is just anger, and just as it is necessary in man for the correction of depravity, so it is with God, from whom comes the example to man'. *De ira dei*, 17: 18.

[30] Because God's anger remains completely controlled. *In potestate habere iram suam nec ab ea regi, sed ipsum illam quemadmodum uelit moderari.* 'He has his anger in control; he is not ruled by it, but regulates it according to his will'. *De ira dei*, 21: 8.

[31] *De ira dei*, 15.

[32] *De ira dei*, 19.

[33] *De ira dei*, 1, 23.

[34] Of uncertain date, but the reasoning of T. D. Barnes in favour of a 313–15 dating estimate seems valid, and is conventionally followed. See 'Lactantius and Constantine', pp. 29–46. See also Arne Søby Christensen, *Lactantius the Historian*, pp. 21–3.

[35] Despite this, the Lactantian authenticity is generally accepted. For a discussion of arguments on both sides surrounding the authorship of the text, see J. L. Creed ed., *De mortibus persecutorum*, pp. xxix–xxxiii.

His bias against the instigators of the persecution can be excused. Lactantius' faith in the long-awaited triumph of Christianity, even if its future is still not assured, is vindicated by the terrible ends of the prime movers in the anti-Christian assault. One-by-one, their tragic and gruesome deaths prove that the vigilance of God is unfailing, and the avenging hand of the divine accompanies all those who would attack God's own worshippers.[36] Yet although its historical utility is often marked with an asterisk, its apologetic value is high indeed. The primary interpretation of historical events within an apologetic framework highlights its status as a distinct anomaly within the Latin apologetic tradition. The *De mortibus persecutorum* is Lactantius glorifying in situations deemed to be products of the just anger of God; for once, the Christians cannot be accused of blame for such terrible circumstances of death or suffering.[37] From this perspective, the tables have turned in favour of the Christians, and Lactantius calls upon the Roman world to give thanks to the one true God who is so obviously manifested by his actions.[38] The tokens of these emperors who emerged successfully from the imperial conflict are the marks of a Christian emblem,[39] and a monotheistic prayer for victory.[40] Perhaps, so Lactantius argues, Rome has been given a chance at this moment to accept God and reform its impious ways, for the ultimate benefit of both Christian Church and Roman State. The closing words of the text, in the final commission to the addressee Donatus to be grateful for God for the Christian victory,[41]

---

[36] *De mortibus persecutorum*, 1: 6.

[37] As with the accusations of Christian culpability for public suffering, in the motivation behind Cyprian's *Ad Demetrianum*.

[38] *Sic omnes impii uero et iusto iudicio dei eadem quae fecerunt, receperunt.* 'Thus all the wicked received by the true and just judgment of God, the very same that they had done'. *De mortibus persecutorum*, 50: 7. The Latin edition and apparatus used for citation from the *De mortibus persecutorum* is that of J. L. Creed (1984).

[39] The Chi-Rho, supposedly given to Constantine in a dream. *De mortibus persecutorum*, 44: 5.

[40] According to Lactantius, this prayer was given to Licinius by a mysterious *angelus dei*: *Summe deus, te rogamus; sancte deus, te rogamus. Omnem iustitiam tibi commendamus, salutem nostram tibi commendamus, imperium nostrum tibi commendamus. Per te uiuimus, per te uictores et felices existimus. Summe, sancte Deus, preces nostras exaudi; brachia nostra ad te tendimus; exaudi sancte, summe Deus.* 'Supreme God, we beseech you. Holy God, we beseech you. To you we commend all justice, to you we commend our health, to you we commend our empire. By you we live; by you we are victorious and happy. Supreme Holy God, hear our prayers. We extend our arms to you. Hear, Holy Supreme God'. *De mortibus persecutorum*, 46: 6.

[41] *Diurnis nocturnisque precibus celebremus, celebremus, ut pacem post annos decem*

articulate a confidence in the flourishing Church that earlier apologists could only dream of. Lactantius is opening up about his hope for an assured future of the Church, built on the judgment of God against the persecutors.[42] In this sense, and due to its location at this point in the relationship between Christianity and Rome, the *De mortibus persecutorum* is a text like no other in Latin Christian writing. In the wider field of apologetic literature, it is also unique for its focus on action rather than argument; the interpretation of current events within an apologetic plea for tolerance, underlined by a warning of the ever-present judgement of God.

At c. 320, Lactantius produced his *Epitome diuinarum institutionum* in response to a call, ostensibly ascribed to *Pentadius frater*, for a shortened version of the *Diuinae institutiones*. What results is a loosely systematic, and far briefer summary of the key points of Lactantius' major work, particularly underpinned by a recourse to the matter of Providence. Although some time has passed since the composition of the *Diuinae institutiones*,[43] bringing the Constantinian acceptance of Christianity along with it, Lactantius is still aware of the need for his apologetic contribution. The rites and ceremonies of Roman religion remain active, and the old gods continue to be venerated. The patronage of Constantine may have brought the imperial acceptance of the Christian religion, but centuries of traditional belief on a private level are not so radically changed by one official movement of toleration.

2. The *Diuinae institutiones*

One of Lactantius' cited motives for compiling his greatest contribution to Latin apologetics is to redress the deficiencies within the earlier works of the tradition, and so to formulate the quintessential Latin apology – the literary work to stand at the very apex of the field. His intentions are outlined through the metaphor of the path to true religion, where his work acts as both guide and teacher. The primary apologetic nature of the *Diuinae institutiones* is unmistakeable, but the utility of the text itself is not solely confined to periods of

---

plebi suae datam confirmet in saeculum. 'Let us celebrate it [the *triumphum dei* = 'the triumph of God'] with prayers by day and night, let us celebrate it so that he may confirm forever the peace which he has given to his people after ten years'. *De mortibus persecutorum*, 52: 4.

[42] *De mortibus persecutorum*, 52: 5.

[43] *Epitome diuinarum institutionum*, 1.

persecution. The *Diuinae institutiones* is more than a defensive encapsulation of Christian belief fostered by the situation of a public assault on Christian practice. Lactantius' work is also highly relevant for the post-Diocletianic persecution milieu as a justification of the practices of the newly-tolerated religion, with particular reference to philosophy, oracular prophecy, and the works of highly esteemed poets and secular authors. It is intended as a manual of Christian instruction, by way of an engagement with its religious and philosophical opponents. Lactantius himself is aware of the significance of his undertaking, and acknowledges the meaning of the subjects detailed within the text in reference to his own personal circumstances:

> *Succurrendum esse his erroribus credidi, ut et docti ad ueram sapientiam dirigantur et indocti ad ueram religionem. Quae professio multo melior utilior gloriosior putanda est quam illa oratoria, in qua diu uersati non ad uirtutem, sed plane ad argutam malitiam iuuenes erudiebamus, multoque nunc rectius de praeceptis caelestibus disseremus, quibus ad cultum uerae maiestatis mentes hominum instituere possimus, nec tam de rebus humanis bene meretur qui scientiam bene dicendi adfert quam qui pie atque innocenter docet uiuere.*[44]

He alludes to the benefit of his rhetorical training, in sharpening his reasoning for the task at hand.[45] It is made clear that the text will develop along the forensic lines of a courtroom defence, with Lactantius taking on the role of the pleader for truth. The title format of the *Diuinae institutiones* is also a reference to manuals of civil law;[46] carrying the legal implications of the *apologia* style one step further into a larger, more in-depth work: *et si quidam prudentes et arbitri aequitatis institutiones ciuilis iuris compositas ediderunt, quibus ciuium dissidentium lites contentionesque sopirent, quanto melius nos et rectius diuinas institutiones litteris persequemur.*[47] The *Institutiones*

---

[44] 'I have believed that help from these errors is needed, in order that the learned are directed to true wisdom, and the ignorant to true religion. This profession is to be thought much better, more useful and glorious than that of oratory – in which being long engaged, we instructed young men not in virtue, but in clever wickedness. Now it is far more proper to discuss the precepts of heaven, that we may educate the minds of men to the worship of true majesty. He does not deserve as well of humanity who conveys the knowledge of speaking well, than he who teaches how to live piously and innocently'. *Diuinae institutiones*, 1: 1; 7–9.

[45] *Diuinae institutiones*, 1: 1; 10.

[46] See Bowen and Garnsey, p. 13, n. 32.

[47] 'And if certain skilled arbiters of justice have published *Institutes of civil law*, which settle the quarrels and contentions of disputing citizens, how much better and

terminology regarding civil law is well established,[48] and is utilised as the immediate outlining structure for Lactantius' presentation of the text. The work is thus allied with the main characteristics of a civil *Institutiones*; thorough, systematic, and detailed.

However, the essential nature of the *Diuinae institutiones* does not lie in the implications of legal imitation. It is, above all, a religious text that serves a religious purpose. In Lactantius' theological understanding, true religion has been almost entirely forsaken by humanity, and gradually corrupted since the days of a forerunning 'golden age' of piety and worship. The purpose of this manual of religious instruction is to refute error in the forms of traditional religion and philosophy, and to endow Christian belief with a worthy and fitting textual defence. The work is also a response to the present situation, addressing a need on the Christian side of the religious divide felt by Lactantius after an appraisal of his Latin predecessors. In this sense, the *Diuinae institutiones* is a classic piece of apologetics for its central motive of response to the literary assaults on Christian practice. This is achieved throughout the text by both a deconstruction of philosophy and Roman religion, and an accompanying justification of Christian belief as a counterpoint to the criticism in hand. Lactantius is aware of the secondary benefit of his apology for Christianity in its reception by those already convinced in the faith, yet perhaps needing further strengthening of key principles. It is the most overt definition of such a standpoint throughout early Latin apologetics, and emphasises a very salient point in the nature of apologetic work. Apologetics is not solely of relevance to those on the external side of the religious divide. As the *Diuinae institutiones* does not formulate its Christian positions on the unique basis of Christian texts, a confidence in the usage of classical Greek and Roman literature instead of the often-criticised books of the Scriptures,[49] would certainly contribute to a further confidence in the evidence for Christian belief. In answer to a rhetorical question

---

more proper is it that we follow this with books of the *Institutes of the divine'*. *Diuinae institutiones*, 1: 1; 12.

[48] See, for example, the *Institutiones* of Gaius, the 'main source' for the later *Institutes* of the *Corpus Iuris Ciuilis* of Justinian. W. M. Gordon and O. F. Robinson eds., *The Institutes of Gaius*, p. 8. The jurist Ulpian, himself a compiler of an *Institutiones*, is referred to by Lactantius under the name of 'Domitius' at *Diuinae institutiones*, 5: 11; 19. On Lactantius' use of this form of his name, see Tony Honoré, *Ulpian*, p. 8.

[49] Something which is a feature with Lactantius, as with the other Latin apologists. It is directly referred to at *Diuinae institutiones*, 5: 1; 15–18, and *Epitome diuinarum institutionum*, 62.

as to the possible failure of his text to impact the standpoints of his adversaries, Lactantius argues:

> *Quid igitur? Operamne perdemus? Minime. Nam si lucrari hos a morte, ad quam concitatissime tendunt, non potuerimus, si ab illo itinere deuio ad uitam lucemque reuocare, quoniam ipsi saluti suae repugnant, nostros tamen confirmabimus, quorum non est stabilis ac solidis radicibus fundata et fixa sententia.*[50]

The dual purpose of apologetics, being the outward engagement with non-believers while also serving to inwardly empower the Church, is succinctly demonstrated. The particular timing of the *Diuinae institutiones* around the Diocletianic persecution gives the last clause of this citation special relevance; Lactantius is expressly referring to those fellow believers who may be liable to wavering belief at this most difficult of periods. If Lactantius' arguments can convince either of the dual audience of his text, then the number of opponents would be lessened, and the faith of the persecuted strengthened. These tenets lie beneath the subject matter of the work in itself, and can be utilised to locate the *Diuinae institutiones* within the religious conflict of the early fourth century.

Lactantius' relationship with his Latin apologetic predecessors can also be explored to contribute to a picture of the literary context of the work. He is little more than dismissive of the three central forerunning Latin apologists, and unambiguously identifies the major faults that prevented their own compositions from achieving prominence as acceptable Christian defences. Although they each possess their own merits, they are broadly condemned in one consummate stroke with a charge of inadequacy.[51] Lactantius' own work can therefore be brought under fair scrutiny on the terms of his criticism of Minucius Felix, Tertullian, and Cyprian. Minucius is spared the full brunt of Lactantius' critique, probably due to the stylistic Ciceronian imitation of the

---

[50] 'What, then – will we be wasting our labour? Not at all. For if we cannot win them back from the death which they are speeding so rapidly towards, nor recall them from their erroneous path back to life and light – for they are fighting against their own salvation – yet we will strengthen our own, whose opinion is not steadfast, and not grounded with a stable and solid foundation'. *Diuinae institutiones*, 5: 1; 9.

[51] *Eo fit, ut sapientia et ueritas idoneis praeconibus indigeat. Et si qui forte litteratorum se ad eam contulerunt, defensioni eius non suffecerunt.* 'Consequently, it has come to pass that wisdom and truth lack adequate heralds. And if, by chance, scholars have come to their aid, their defence has not sufficed'. *Diuinae institutiones*, 5: 1; 21.

Octauius. In view of Lactantius' own esteem for Cicero, his refusal to pass further judgement on the *Octauius* can be understood.[52] Lactantius only regrets that Minucius could have been a better defender of Christian truth had he laboured to add more to his single work.[53] The best evidence for Lactantius' assessment of Minucius' contribution to Latin apologetics is the multiple reminiscences of the *Octauius* that occur throughout the *Diuinae institutiones*, betraying its prior influence behind varying aspects of Lactantius' thought and argument. Tertullian comes in for stylistic criticism above all else; something hardly unexpected given Lactantius' express attention to stylistic detail throughout his text. Tertullian's skill is acknowledged, but his eloquence in the elucidation of his subjects lamented.[54] Lactantius is also critical of Tertullian's methodology in the *Apologeticum*, in failing to assemble a positive argument after responding to each separate point against Christian belief. This is to be contrasted with Lactantius' own defence of Christianity, which is motivated by an attempt to construct an argument in response to the case in progression, rather than simply moving onto the next scenario after each defensive explanation.[55] Lactantius is most complimentary of Cyprian, mindful of his enjoyment of greater distinction than the previous two apologists. His fame, eloquence, lucidity, and persuasive talents are all appreciated.[56] However, Lactantius cannot refrain from including the puerile smear of the nickname '*Coprianus*',[57] and castigating Cyprian directly for committing a core error in the methodological construction of the *Ad Demetrianum*.[58] Cyprian should have restrained his usage of Scriptural citation, and refuted Demetrianus using common philosophical and logical sources; the evidence of man before the evidence of God.[59] The fault for this is traced to Cyprian's absorption in heavenly matters, leading to a consequent estrangement from mere human understanding.

---

[52] Excepting some brief negative comments on Minucius' version of a legend of Saturn, at *Diuinae institutiones*, I: II; 55–62.

[53] *Diuinae institutiones*, 5: I; 22.

[54] *Diuinae institutiones*, 5: I; 23.

[55] *Diuinae institutiones*, 5: 4; 3.

[56] *Diuinae institutiones*, 5: I; 25.

[57] *Diuinae institutiones*, 5: I; 27.

[58] *Diuinae institutiones*, 5: 4; 3–7.

[59] *Diuinae institutiones*, 5: 4; 6.

Lactantius' evaluation of his forerunners provides a telling insight into his estimation of his own contribution to the field; the *Diuinae institutiones* is designed to be the ultimate apology standing at the pinnacle of Latin apologetics. The inclusion of criticism of Minucius Felix, Tertullian, and Cyprian ensures that he has firmly established the pressing need for such a creation. Lactantius intends to rise above the mistakes and pitfalls of his predecessors, and produce a piece of apologetic that is both responsive and constructive in argument, systematic in its subject matter, but also accessible to the reader unaware of Christian Scriptural texts. Furthermore, the *Diuinae institutiones* is also proposed as a landmark work for other educated Christians to build upon and follow, fired by Lactantius' encouragement.[60] He is unequivocally detailing the requirements of the work designed to be the cornerstone of Latin apologetic writing; more constructive than Tertullian, longer than Minucius Felix, and more accessible to the non-Christian reader than Cyprian. Such is Lactantius' own understanding of the meaning and location of his key apologetic text.

Lactantius' apologetic style

The apologetic works in the early Latin tradition can be distinguished by a reticence of Scriptural engagement, and a consequent focus on the appropriation of non-Christian textual sources in the service of the Christian argument. Lactantius is no different, but the *Diuinae institutiones* is expressly marked by an attempt at a more sophisticated synthesis of sources in the course of its own theological advancements. Non-Christian sources are still generally employed as the primary foundation of argument, but there is also room for a Scriptural engagement that is proportionally only surpassed in early Latin apologetics by Cyprian's *Ad Demetrianum*. In addition, Lactantius both dispenses with philosophy, and accepts it as at least a partial witness to a more transcendent form of truth. This section will focus on Lactantius' own format of dealing with 'Christian' theological principles[61] through philosophical sources, and reinterpreting the Scriptures in order to deploy them in support of more specifically Christian articles of faith. The areas of theological establishment within the *Diuinae institutiones* are more ambitious than elsewhere in early Latin apologetics; hence

---

[60] *Diuinae institutiones*, 5: 4; 8.

[61] The single inverted commas denote a standpoint such as monotheism; not, strictly speaking, Christian in itself, but considered by Lactantius as a fundamentally important belief that should be shared by all – if not solely allied to Christianity.

the implications of the text becoming something of a hybrid between various modes of expression.[62] The way in which these motivations are reconciled forms the heart of Lactantius' apologetic methodology, and defines the work as unique within the early Latin apologetic tradition. If Lactantius considers his text to be at the very peak of the discussion, it is due to this multifaceted use of sources within an overall apologetic concept. This discussion is then followed by a focus on Lactantius' apologetic establishment of true religion, as another issue contributing to the intended monumental nature of the *Diuinae institutiones*. An address of these subjects presents a suitable window of insight into the singular nature of Lactantius' central apologetic contribution.

In the opening book of the *Diuinae institutiones*, Lactantius offers a brief explanation of his reasoning behind the usage of non-Christian authorities in the citations from the poets and philosophers:

> *Sed omittamus sane testimonia prophetarum, ne minus idonea probatio uideatur esse de his quibus omnino non creditur. Ueniamus ad auctores et eos ipsos ad ueri probationem testes citemus, quibus contra nos uti solent, poetas dico ac philosophos.*[63]

Such a position is fairly characteristic of the early Latin apologists. But Lactantius is not so rigorous in refusing to handle the Scriptures in apologetic argument as Minucius Felix, Tertullian or Arnobius, yet he is still aware of the need to minimise Scriptural engagement unless it is of necessity, unlike Cyprian. Lactantius is also at ease in using the writings attributed to Hermes Trismegistus and the Sibylline oracles,[64] as appropriated textual sources in the Christian argument.[65] The poets and philosophers are first utilised in the *Diuinae institutiones* in support of the Christian tenet of monotheism, in opposition to the traditional Roman pantheon.[66] Lactantius endeavours to prove the monotheistic argument without direct reference to specifically Christian texts; it must be first established without

---

[62] See Bowen and Garnsey, p. 14.

[63] 'But let us lay aside the testimony of the prophets, lest evidence from those who are not trusted by all should appear unacceptable. Let us come to the writers, and in proving the truth, let us cite as witnesses those who are accustomed to being used against us; I mean the poets and philosophers'. *Diuinae institutiones*, 1: 5; 1–2.

[64] Lactantius' usage of Sibylline testimonies is referred to by Augustine at *De ciuitate dei*, 18: 23.

[65] On this subject, see R. M. Ogilvie, *The Library of Lactantius*, pp. 28–36.

[66] *Diuinae institutiones*, 1: 3.

doubt that God is one, or else the further particulars of Christian theology cannot be constructed. The prophets of the Old Testament are referred to as *praecones* of the true knowledge of God,[67] and although Lactantius argues in favour of their personal impeachability on moral grounds, their testimony must be disregarded in an appeal for commonly respected sources. Yet this seems to be no loss to Lactantius' argument, and his explanation of the recourse to the poets and philosophers overflows with confident assertions of God's innate truth coming forth. He stops short of ascribing any personal knowledge of God to the writers themselves,[68] for to do so would necessarily tarnish the unique nature of Christian wisdom. Lactantius is concerned with tracing monotheistic terminology throughout the poets, of whom Virgil and Ovid stand out as being the closest to true formulations of the divine character. Indeed, if only they could have persisted in so expressing the nature of God, *eandem quam nos sequimur doctrinam comprehensa ueritate tenuissent.*[69] Lactantius' outline of some monotheistic elements in the cited philosophers betrays his reading of Minucius Felix,[70] and the substantial influence of Cicero's *De natura deorum.*[71] He also follows the conclusion of Minucius on the question of the relationship of the philosophical standpoints to those of the Christians:

> *Siue enim natura siue aether siue ratio siue mens siue fatalis necessitas siue diuina lex siue quid aliud dixeris, idem est quod a nobis dicitur deus. Nec obstat appellationum diuersitas, cum ipsa significatione ad unum omnia reuoluantur.*[72]

---

[67] 'Heralds'. *Diuinae institutiones*, 1: 4; 4.

[68] *Ex his unum deum probemus necesse est, non quod illi habuerint cognitam ueritatem, sed quod ueritatis ipsius tanta uis est, ut nemo possit esse tam caecus, quin uideat ingerentem se oculis diuinam claritatem.* 'From these we must demonstrate the oneness of God, not because they themselves hold knowledge of the truth, but because the strength of the truth is so great that no one can be so blind as not to see the divine brightness when it forces itself upon their eyes'. *Diuinae institutiones*, 1: 5; 2.

[69] 'They would have comprehended the truth, and grasped the very same doctrine which we follow'. *Diuinae institutiones*, 1: 5; 14.

[70] *Octauius*, 19.

[71] *De natura deorum*, 1: 25ff.

[72] 'For whether you call it nature, ether, reason, mind, the necessity of fate, or the divine law, or anything else, it is the same that is by us called God. The difference of terms does not hinder anything, since in their meaning they all return to one thing'. *Diuinae institutiones*, 1: 5: 21.

Quid aliud et a nobis deus quam mens et ratio et spiritus praedicatur? Recenseamus, si placet, disciplinam philosophorum: deprehendes eos, etsi sermonibus uariis, ipsis tamen rebus in hanc unam coire et conspirare sententiam.[73]

The establishment of monotheism is fundamental to the development of the theological principles of the *Diuinae institutiones*. It also sets the tone for the methodology behind Lactantius' style of argument – theological or philosophical commonplaces in the non-Christian texts are appropriated for the Christian cause, while conflicting positions are disregarded as merely fables and errors. Lactantius can firmly be located alongside Minucius Felix, Tertullian, and Arnobius in the continual recourse to non-Christian sources as the primary foundation in the apologetic establishment of the validity of Christian belief. His own definition of this methodological approach stands with equal pertinence for the apologetic genre as a whole; *sed cum defendamus causam ueritatis apud eos qui aberrantes a ueritate falsis religionibus seruiunt, quod genus probationis aduersus eos magis adhibere debemus quam ut eos deorum suorum testimoniis reuincamus?*[74] However, Lactantius' apologetic framework also possesses a facet that is not found in the *Octauius*, Tertullian's *Apologeticum* and *Ad nationes*, or Arnobius' *Aduersus nationes*. That is, although not to the same extent as Cyprian, Lactantius is comfortable with Scriptural interpretation in the course of his more specifically Christian theological points. Philosophical sources still form the basic core of Lactantius' argument, and therefore greatly outnumber the Scriptural citations, but Lactantius can only outline some of the key particulars of Christian belief on the support of Scriptural evidence. The ultimate reasoning behind this lies in the dual purpose of the *Diuinae institutiones* when compared with the other apologetic works in the early African Latin tradition. Lactantius is conscious of a need for the construction of theological and doctrinal principles as a counterpoint to the usual deconstruction of traditional Roman belief and practice. Such a construction would be impossible for certain questions without even the most passing reference to Scripture as the necessary prophetic or historical evidence

[73] 'What else is God proclaimed to be by us, than mind, reason and spirit? If you like, let us review the teaching of the philosophers: you will discover that although with different words, they all agree and concur on this one opinion'. *Octauius*, 19: 2–3.

[74] 'But since we are defending the cause of the truth from those who wander astray and serve false religions, what kind of proof could we better use against them, than to disprove them by the testimonies of their own gods?'. *Diuinae institutiones*, I: 6; 17.

behind the argument. In order to justify the employment of these controversial sources, Lactantius provides a list of the Old Testament prophets in chronological alignment with key historical events around the Mediterranean. Moses is (unspecifically and erroneously) predated to approximately 900 years before the Trojan war, and the reigns of Cyrus the Great and Tarquin the Proud are dated to concurrent periods.[75] Lactantius is eager to disprove accusations of the Scriptures as novel, and to instead force a reconsideration of the potential historical validity of the Old Testament works.[76] The meaning of the Old Testament is understood and explained entirely by reason of its predictive relationship to Jesus,[77] and the New Testament is the corresponding fulfilment of the prophetic religion of the Jews.[78] Accurately foretold prophecy forms the most reliable vindication of the Scriptural writings, and explains Lactantius' recourse to the Old Testament prophets in detailing the related Christological principles. This is prophecy utilised in the manner of evidence; something made explicit in Lactantius' lengthy quotation from the apocryphal *Preaching of Peter and Paul*, intended to impart a foretelling of the destruction of the Jerusalem temple and the decimation of the Jewish people at the hands of the armies of Vespasian and Titus.[79] The authenticity of the Scriptures, once adequately justified on both an historical and prophetical basis, allows Lactantius to deal with more specifically Christian points of theology, which Hermes Trismegistus and the Sibylline oracles would otherwise be unable to address in the required detail. Lactantius demonstrates an outward confidence that the Scriptures could provide the sole foundation for every facet of argument, but affectedly condescends to rely primarily on non-Christian sources in the establishment of particularly Christian tenets.[80] Nevertheless, Scriptural engagement has an accepted place within the *Diuinae institutiones*, even if it is not the overt form of textual support primarily underlying the majority of the points of argument. Scholarly accusations of Lactantius' unfamiliarity

---

[75] *Diuinae institutiones*, 4: 5; 5–8. For further information on the subject of Biblical chronology alongside Greco-Roman historical events, see Ben Zion Wacholder, 'Biblical Chronology in the Hellenistic World Chronicles'.

[76] *Diuinae institutiones*, 4: 5; 9.

[77] *Diuinae institutiones*, 4: 15; 30.

[78] *Diuinae institutiones*, 4: 20; 4–5.

[79] Israel is punished for its rejection of Jesus in a similar compensatory manner as the persecutors of the *De mortibus persecutorum*. *Diuinae institutiones*, 4: 21; 2–5.

[80] *Diuinae institutiones*, 4: 22; 1–2.

with the Scriptures are unfounded, and only reveal a misunderstanding of the apologetic methodology utilised within the text.[81] Where there is a call for the usage of the Scriptures, they are engaged with, but Lactantius' overall purpose behind the *Diuinae institutiones* is to compile a significant manual of Christian agreement with the classical sources. This issue is adeptly expressed by Peter Garnsey:

> His strategy was to draw to the full on the Roman philosophical and literary tradition, with which his addressees were familiar. His aim was to show self-consciously that a Christian could handle these topics with scholarly dignity and style. If he could establish that the Christians were true philosophers, there was a better chance that his audience would accept that they were *the* true philosophers, possessing the *uera sapientia*.[82]

Scriptural citation has little immediate place within such argument, and only comes into its own importance in the more specific theological details, such as in Lactantius' Christological focus.

The main recourse to Scripture in the *Diuinae institutiones* is focused on the theological presentation of Jesus. Lactantius' theological exploration into the character of the Son of God is based on a mixture of sentences attributed to Hermes Trismegistus, the Sibylline oracular utterances, and then the interpretation of Old Testament prophecy. Hermes and the Sibylline verses are used to trace Jesus' divine birthright,[83] along with a direct Scriptural citation referring to the creation of wisdom, which is then united with the Son of God.[84] Lactantius affirms Jesus' dual birth[85] and origin as the *uerbum dei*;[86] supported and clarified by a rare citation from the New Testament.[87] Lactantius speaks highly of Hermes, who has almost arrived at the truth on even this subject.[88] The earthly life of Jesus is

---

[81] As with G. W. Trompf, *Early Christian Historiography*, p. 119. 'A recent convert, Lactantius had barely absorbed any knowledge of the Bible, and these works accordingly contain (perhaps surprisingly) few allusions to Scripture'. The further statement of Trompf, allying Arnobius with 'the old method of quoting the Bible at pagans', also at p. 119, is equally inexplicable.

[82] Peter Garnsey, 'Lactantius and Augustine', p. 158.

[83] *Diuinae institutiones*, 4: 6; 4–5.

[84] *Diuinae institutiones*, 4: 6; 6–8.

[85] *Diuinae institutiones*, 4: 8; 1–2.

[86] 'Word of God'. *Diuinae institutiones*, 4: 8; 9.

[87] *Diuinae institutiones*, 4: 8; 16. The citation is from Jn 1: 1–3.

[88] *Qui ueritatem paene uniuersam nescio quo modo inuestigauit*. 'Who by some unknown means tracked down almost all of the truth'. *Diuinae institutiones*, 4: 9; 3.

contextualised by a brief overview of the history of the Israelites, and their rejection of successive prophets which culminates in the human manifestation of the Son of God.[89] Lactantius defends the Christian doctrines of the Incarnation, the Virgin Birth, and the humanity of Jesus with lengthy prophetic quotations from the Old Testament.[90] Jesus is high priest, teacher, healer and miracle-worker, and the support of the Sibylline texts is temporarily demoted to the priority of the Scriptures in relating the great works of Jesus' human life.[91] The subjects of the Passion, Resurrection and Ascension are treated with a similar recourse to Old Testament prophecy.[92] Lactantius also takes the opportunity at this point to turn his Scriptural exegesis against the Jews, and to unfold the meaning of the Mosaic law in light of its fulfilment with the advent of Jesus.[93] After this brief Christological discussion, Lactantius returns to his conventional methodology, and the Scriptures are again placed to one side in favour of the philosophical and oracular sources.

Book six of the *Diuinae institutiones*, although focusing on true worship, only contains a handful of allusions to the Scriptures, and even though much of book seven has evidently been compiled with continual reference to the book of Revelation, direct citation is rare. Lactantius is again expressly concerned with utilising the testimony of the Sibylline verses on top of such philosophical conjecture as has bearing on the subject at hand. Even in view of his readiness to engage with Old Testament prophecy in the course of his argument, the commonplace criticism of the Scriptures still hangs over his treatment of the subject. Their obscurity of style, marked lack of elegance,[94] and total remoteness from more acceptable literary works ground a series of obstacles that Lactantius cannot overcome. But he does still defend the lack of stylistic eloquence in the Scriptures as owing both to the lofty proclamation of God, uncaring of the rhetorical formulae of humanity,[95] and the uneducated nature of the prophets who served as the means of describing the sentences of divine

---

[89] *Diuinae institutiones*, 4: 11.

[90] *Diuinae institutiones*, 4: 12–13.

[91] *Diuinae institutiones*, 4: 14–15.

[92] *Diuinae institutiones*, 4: 18–21; 1.

[93] *Diuinae institutiones*, 4: 17.

[94] *Diuinae institutiones*, 5: 1; 16–17.

[95] *Diuinae institutiones*, 3: 1; 11.

inspiration.[96] Indeed, the simpler the language, the greater ease with which it can be understood.[97] Lactantius recounts the problems with the literary style of the Scriptures in terms that point towards a deep personal involvement in the matter. It is a teacher railing against the trivialities of his profession:

> Non credunt ergo diuinis, quia fuco carent, sed ne illis quidem qui ea interpretantur, quia sunt et ipsi aut omnino rudes aut certe parum docti. Nam ut plane sint eloquentes, perraro contingit; cuius rei causa in aperto est. Eloquentia enim saeculo seruit, populo se iactare et in rebus malis placere gestit, siquidem ueritatem saepius expugnare conatur, ut uim suam monstret; opes expetit, honores concupiscit, summum denique gradum dignitatis exposcit.[98]

Even such a derisory painting of the superficial nature of rhetorical style cannot allow Lactantius to rely on the stark purity of the Scriptures within the *Diuinae institutiones*. His engagement with the Old Testament is certainly notable within early Latin apologetics, but is equalled by his consistent refusal to utilise the New. For Lactantius, the Old Testament prophecies can be naturally aligned with the discourse of Hermes Trismegistus and the Sibylline oracles. Neither are particularly Christian authorities,[99] but both can be employed within a wider argument to prove the validity of Christian standpoints, thereby countering the critics of Christian belief on their own grounds. The writings of the New Testament, as well as lacking the antiquity that would undoubtedly contribute towards a greater sense of historical respectability, are too expressly partisan to provide much real force as the necessary theological or philosophical evidence in the argument. If Lactantius devoted more of his subject matter to expounding the Scriptures, then the *Diuinae institutiones* could be

---

[96] *Diuinae institutiones*, 5: 1; 15.

[97] *Diuinae institutiones*, 6: 21; 4–6.

[98] 'They do not believe the divine writings, which are free from embellishment, but also those who interpret them, because they themselves are either completely ignorant or else of very little learning. It happens that they are very rarely entirely eloquent; but the reason for this is clear. Eloquence serves the world; it desires to flaunt itself to the people, and to please in its mischief. Accordingly, it frequently attempts to subdue the truth, so that it may show its own power; it seeks out wealth, desires honours, and demands the highest position of esteem'. *Diuinae institutiones*, 5: 1; 18–19.

[99] Lactantius forcefully dismisses the charge that any of the Sibylline oracles bear the marks of Christian manipulation. *Diuinae institutiones*, 4: 15; 26–30.

marred by Cyprian's over-reliance upon them within the apologetic argument. Lactantius' criticism of Cyprian's methodology, coupled with his evident frustration at the lack of intellectual appreciation of the Scriptures, exemplifies one of the key dilemmas shared by the early Latin apologists. Although the Scriptures compose the vehicle for God's related truth, yet they reek of barbarisms, harsh turns of phrase, and other equally poor stylistic qualities. Thus almost paradoxically, the words of God are articulated by the most meagre speech of man. A Christian intellectual response to this state of affairs is demonstrated effectively by the early Latin apologies, of which Lactantius considers his *Diuinae institutiones* to be the pick of the genre. Lactantius' methodological approach to handling the Scriptures within an apologetic argument incorporates a more sophisticated awareness of the utility of the Scriptures than that of Minucius Felix and Arnobius. He is also capable of appealing to the historical validity of the Scriptures, in a similar manner as Tertullian before him,[100] but he is able to restrain their deployment in order to primarily emphasise the non-Christian sources used throughout the text. The Scriptures must be called upon to verify some of the key theological points in the nature of Jesus as Son of God,[101] but can always again be thrust into the background of the evidence when necessary. The result is a more nuanced deployment of the textual authorities, leading to a wider range of evidentiary support for the theological and doctrinal principles outlined in Lactantius' argument.

The apologetic establishment of true religion

As one of the key elements of the *Diuinae institutiones* is its constructive ambition, Lactantius is expressly aware of the need for a positive aspect in the standard apologetic format, in order to serve as a progressive balance to the more deconstructive elements of polemical critique. That is not to say that he displays any real restraint in citing and lambasting aspects of traditional Roman religion, but rather to draw attention instead to the corresponding focus of the *Diuinae institutiones* in presenting Christianity as a philosophically and morally viable alternative religion. Lactantius is specifically engaging with the polemic of Tertullian's central apologetic work, the *libro cui Apologetico*

---

[100] *Apologeticum*, 19.

[101] As with his identification as the logos of God. *Diuinae institutiones*, 6: 8; 12–16.

nomen est,[102] even if an immediate inference of Lactantius' response to the almost entirely polemical *Ad nationes* is perhaps unavoidable. However, much of the polemical argument of the *Ad nationes* is also present in the *Apologeticum*, which retains its character as Tertullian's most influential work, and it is to this text that Lactantius refers. In so doing, he outlines the constructive aims of the *Diuinae institutiones*: *tamen quoniam aliud est accusantibus respondere, quod in defensione aut negatione sola positum est, aliud instituere, quod nos facimus, in quo necesse est doctrinae totius substantiam contineri.*[103] This ambition will be considered through a discussion of the outline of the *uera religio* within an apologetic setting, and its possible situation as an alternative to the religion of Lactantius' opponents. It is of primary importance to locate Lactantius' discussion of the *uera religio* within its original location; the apologetic foundation that defines its principles, and underlies its meaning.

Lactantius differentiates between false religion and false wisdom, but the two are united as part of a larger critique in the polemical areas of the *Diuinae institutiones*. This sets up a duality in Lactantius' presentation of contemporary religion: the ignorant masses of the populace follow the rites and customs of religious ceremony without questioning, while a select few intellectuals benefit from an exclusive form of philosophical exploration. Even though the philosophers are endowed with reason, understanding, and the ability to identify mistakes in belief and practice, yet they persist in following the same erroneous rituals as the uneducated rabble.[104] Public Roman religion has fallen into a state of intellectual neglect, and those who supposedly possess the theological and philosophical knowledge to combat it are to blame. Lactantius does not quite follow the cynicism of Tertullian in ascribing this stagnation of religious practice to the personal greed of the priests,[105] but instead traces culpability to the continuing apathy of the philosophers.[106] As a result, a multitude of varied and deep-seated impieties have developed. The unchecked process of deification has added to the already substantial number of the gods, to the extent

---

[102] 'The book which is named *Apologeticum*'. *Diuinae institutiones*, 5: 4; 3.

[103] 'It is one thing to answer those who attack, in which defence and denial is the sole format, but another thing to institute, as we are doing, where the full doctrinal substance must be contained'. *Diuinae institutiones*, 5: 4; 3.

[104] *Diuinae institutiones*, 2: 3; 1.

[105] *Apologeticum*, 13: 6.

[106] *Diuinae institutiones*, 2: 3; 22.

where even people unable to remain virtuous in life are elevated to divine status in death.[107] Lactantius confidently strikes names from the pantheon; gods of but recent creation can surely be no gods at all.[108] In direct consequence, if the objects of worship can be shown to be fraudulent, then antique belief can be quashed. The attendant rites and ceremonies are attacked on the grounds of unbecoming violence and suffering, and their thirst for blood that must necessarily count against any power for good.[109] Lactantius' dismissal of the validity of such religious practice[110] is remarkably scathing within the otherwise generally less ferocious style of the *Diuinae institutiones*. Idol worship is also confronted on the grounds of intrinsic theological inconsistency and inadequate rational foundation; *quae igitur amentia est aut ea fingere quae ipsi postmodum timeant aut timere quae finxerint!*[111] The key feature of Lactantius' argument on this issue concerns the distinction between heaven and earth; God and man. Human veneration of created objects, themselves devoid of life, ensures that they remain theologically tied to the material world which ultimately leads to death. In this understanding, humanity has rejected its special status at the height of creation,[112] and must therefore suffer eternal rejection by God.[113] Continuing in the worship of created idols and deities only contributes to man's further alienation from the only acceptable mode of true worship. Ritual offerings of perishable earthly items cannot appease the universally transcendent God.[114] Lactantius heightens the contrast between true and false worship in the most dramatic terms; *etiamne haec sacra sunt? Non satius est pecudum modo uiuere quam deos*

---

[107] The given example of the goddess Faula, identified as a prostitute. *Diuinae institutiones*, I: 20; 5.

[108] *Diuinae institutiones*, I: 23; 1–5.

[109] *Diuinae institutiones*, I: 21; 4.

[110] *Diuinae institutiones*, I: 21; 44–49.

[111] 'What madness is it to create the very things that they should afterwards fear, or to fear what they have created?'. *Diuinae institutiones*, 2: 2; 1.

[112] In Lactantius' theological rationale, to demean humanity by an association with the beasts of the earth is an acutely heinous blasphemy; *cum id ipsum maximi sit erroris, uitam pecudum sub figura hominis imitari*. 'Since this is the greatest error, to copy the life of animals in the form of man'. *Diuinae institutiones*, 2: 3; 22.

[113] *Diuinae institutiones*, 2: 2; 22.

[114] *Mactant igitur opimas ac pingues hostias deo quasi esurienti, profundunt uina tamquam sitienti, accendunt lumina uelut in tenebris agenti.* 'Therefore they sacrifice plump and juicy victims to God as if he is hungry, they pour him wine as if he thirsts, they light lamps as if he is in the dark'. *Diuinae institutiones*, 6: 2; 1.

tam impios, tam profanos, tam sanguinarios colere?[115] The purpose of his polemical critique is to appeal for an end to such religious ceremonies, by a sweeping attack on inherited forms of worship.[116] He employs a particularly favourite metaphor, and urges his audience to raise their posture from the animalistic stoop characteristic of the created order, and rise into a more befitting upright stance facing the true God in the heavens.[117] Throughout his attack on the beliefs and practices of contemporary religion, Lactantius highlights his perspective on the issue of culpability; the uneducated masses are being effectively misled to immortal punishment by their social and intellectual superiors. They are left alone to continue in error, and therefore must suffer the eternal consequences of the reactionary attitudes of Roman religion.

Although the poets can be blamed for inventing the fabrications concerning the gods, and the *pontifices* of the cultic systems have continued to promulgate them,[118] the full brunt of the blame is reserved for the philosophers. They are attacked on several grounds; for failing to desist in their own adherence to blatant religious falsehood, for failing to recognise true religion despite their supposed awareness of knowledge and truth, and for their own individual issues of unbridled immorality. Lactantius cites Cicero and Lucretius as examples of men who have comprehended the errors of popular religion, yet neglected to realize the full potential of their more developed theological awareness.[119] Even if the scepticism of certain philosophers has rightly led towards a rejection of any truth inherent in Roman religion, they have either continued in such worship regardless of their own conclusions, or drifted towards a state of no personal religion at all.[120] Such apathy is deplored by Lactantius, and judged to be far worse than the unthinking persistence in error of the ill-informed populace.[121] The philosophers themselves are continually reminded

---

[115] 'Are these things really sacrifices? Is it not better to live like animals than to worship gods so impious, so profane, so bloodthirsty?'. *Diuinae institutiones*, 1: 21; 18.

[116] *Diuinae institutiones*, 2: 6.

[117] Occurring at *Diuinae institutiones*, 2: 1; 14–19, 2: 2; 23, and 2: 18.

[118] 'High-priests'. *Diuinae institutiones*, 1: 21; 44.

[119] *Diuinae institutiones*, 2: 3; 1–17.

[120] *Diuinae institutiones*, 2: 3; 22.

[121] *Uenia concedi potest imperitis et qui se sapientes non esse fateantur, his uero non potest, qui sapientiam professi stultitiam potius exhibent.* 'Forgiveness can be given to those who are ignorant and do not admit to being wise, but not to those who profess wisdom while displaying stupidity'. *Diuinae institutiones*, 2: 3; 18.

of the actual etymological breakdown of the term *philosophus*,[122] and
faced with the argument that if they had achieved knowledge of the
truth, then there would be no basis for the existent factional disa-
greements.[123] In addition to this, the most basic awareness of true
wisdom should certainly preclude aspects of personal behaviour that
would be considered shameful in even the most uncivilised of people.[124] Lactantius, the eloquent rhetor, is not above recounting the
basest of accusations against his opponents.[125] The purpose of this
assault on the philosophers is to directly confront the intellectual
drive behind the opposition to Christianity, and thus to join battle
with the highest authorities in the debate; *quis autem nesciat plus esse
momenti in paucioribus doctis quam in pluribus imperitis?*[126] Lactantius' deconstruction of the benefits of philosophy takes varied theoretical forms,[127] but on a more personal level, as philosophy does not
teach how to live a virtuous life, so it must be discarded.[128] He pleads
for philosophy to be rejected, and replaced by the search for true
wisdom; life is far too short for such continuance in error.[129] The
elitism of the philosophers[130] is not compatible with the true wisdom
that should be available to all.[131] It is the case made for Christians
to fully assume the role of the philosophers, and to inherit the *uera
sapientia* with conviction.[132] Lactantius closes book three with a summary of his arguments against the philosophers, re-encapsulating the
central points of his critique; they have either maintained a plainly

[122] *Diuinae institutiones*, 3: 2; 3–10.

[123] *Diuinae institutiones*, 3: 4; 3. Lactantius later attempts to undercut the potential deployment of this assertion against the Christians by claiming the knowledge of
truth for the *catholica ecclesia* alone; thus identifying any splinter groups as *haeretici*.
Diuinae institutiones, 4: 30; 11–13.

[124] Even if the soundness of an argument that judges a religion by the morality of
its people can be questioned, it serves Lactantius' immediate concern.

[125] *Diuinae institutiones*, 3: 15.

[126] 'Everybody knows that there is more importance in a few learned men than in
a greater amount of the ignorant'. *Diuinae institutiones*, 2: 19; 4.

[127] *Diuinae institutiones*, 3: 4–23.

[128] *Diuinae institutiones*, 3: 14; 12–21.

[129] *Cito inueniri debet, ut cito suscipi possit, ne quid pereat ex uita, cuius finis incertus
est.* 'The finding [of wisdom] must be quick, so that its acceptance may be quick, and
nothing of life with its uncertain end may be wasted'. *Diuinae institutiones*, 3: 16; 8.

[130] In their class as represented by the *barba* and *pallium*. *Diuinae institutiones*, 3:
25; 6.

[131] *Diuinae institutiones*, 3: 25; 1–5.

[132] Garnsey, 'Lactantius and Augustine', p. 158; cited above, p. 183.

false religion or else fallen into atheism, and have no ability to teach the virtuous life:

> *Quanta itaque uoce possum, testificor proclamo denuntio: hic, hic est illud, quod philosophi omnes in tota sua uita quaesierunt nec umquam tamen inuestigare comprehendere tenere ualuerunt, quia religionem aut prauam retinuerunt aut totam penitus sustulerunt. Facessant igitur illi omnes, qui humanam uitam non instruunt, sed turbant. Quid enim docent aut quem instruunt qui se ipsos nondum instruxerunt? Quem sanare aegroti, quem regere caeci possunt?*[133]

However, it is not only a group of erroneous and self-serving philosophers who are responsible for misleading the ordinary people in their religious customs. The traditional characters of the gods themselves represent more than mere fabrications, and are traced to the influence of wandering demonic spirits. For Lactantius, it is demons who inspire oracular prophecy,[134] divinatory ritual,[135] human possession,[136] the everyday household *genii*,[137] and the ultimate instigation for anti-Christian persecution.[138] Although he does not go into any real theological detail, it is argued that the world exists under the control of the devil, and that the origin of demons are as corrupted former angels of God.[139] It is this demonic influence that has created the pantheon of Roman deities,[140] and they are equally culpable for the origin of the statues and images of religious worship.[141] Indeed, they even lie beneath the true characters of the gods themselves.[142] But nevertheless, they are subject to the power of pious Christians; an inference characteristically supported by the textual evidence of Hermes Trismegistus, rather

---

[133] 'And so as loud as I can, I testify, proclaim, and announce: this is what all the philosophers sought for throughout their whole lives and yet never could find, grasp, or hold, because they either upheld a crooked religion or else destroyed it all entirely. Away with all these, therefore, who do not teach human life, but disturb it. For what do they teach, or whom do they instruct, who have not yet instructed themselves? Who do the sick heal; who can the blind guide?'. *Diuinae institutiones*, 3: 30; 4–5.

[134] *Diuinae institutiones*, 2: 16; 13–15.

[135] *Diuinae institutiones*, 2: 16; 1–2.

[136] *Diuinae institutiones*, 2: 14; 14.

[137] *Diuinae institutiones*, 2: 14; 11–13.

[138] *Diuinae institutiones*, 5: 21; 3.

[139] *Diuinae institutiones*, 2: 14; 1–3.

[140] *Diuinae institutiones*, 2: 16; 5.

[141] *Diuinae institutiones*, 2: 16; 3.

[142] *Diuinae institutiones*, 4: 27; 9–18.

than by allusion to the Scriptures.[143] Lactantius is confident that this Christian power over demonic spirits has been recently manifested in the failure of the haruspex that provided the catalyst for the opening of the Diocletianic persecution.[144] On a more personal level, in fitting veneration of the gods, the populace naturally acts in like manner. As the gods are turbulent, violent and lustful characters, so too are their followers.[145] The people are not entirely excused for their behaviour, but the primary blame for human impiety is placed on the shoulders of the falsely-titled gods.[146] Within Lactantius' thesis of the theological purity of the 'Golden Age',[147] it is demons who are responsible for corrupting the once commonly-held true knowledge of the Creator God.[148] In response to the anticipated question of why God allows such misfortunes to take place, Lactantius answers with another theological duality; good and evil necessarily co-exist in balance.[149] This particular duality can be extended to include the metaphor of the alternate paths of human life; the earthly road leading to destruction, or the heavenly road leading to eternal salvation.[150] The devil is behind the pleasures of the earthly road, appealingly embossed with the glories of human munificence,[151] but servile to the corrupt nature of superstitious religion and the false learning of the philosophers.[152] Such is the picture of the religious situation into which Lactantius directs his apologetic presentation of true worship.

The *Diuinae institutiones* is characterised throughout by a recourse to dualities and distinctions in Lactantius' mode of expression, and this is nowhere more marked than in his outline of the difference between

[143] *Diuinae institutiones*, 2: 15; 6.

[144] *Diuinae institutiones*, 4: 27; 3–5. See also Lactantius' more specific description at *De mortibus persecutorum*, 10.

[145] *Diuinae institutiones*, 5: 10; 15–18.

[146] *Sic fit, ut uitam colentium deus pro qualitate numinis sui formet, quoniam religiosissimus est cultus imitari*. 'Thus it happens that a god fashions the life of his worshippers according to the character of his own will, since imitation is the most religious form of worship'. *Diuinae institutiones*, 5: 10; 18.

[147] For a discussion on this particular theme, see Louis J. Swift, 'Lactantius and the Golden Age'.

[148] *Diuinae institutiones*, 2: 16; 20.

[149] *Diuinae institutiones*, 2: 17; 1–3.

[150] *Diuinae institutiones*, 6: 3–4.

[151] *Diuinae institutiones*, 6: 4; 19–22.

[152] *Diuinae institutiones*, 6: 4; 23.

true and false religious worship (*religio* as opposed to *superstitio*).[153] Lactantius constructs a picture of an unbridgeable gulf between the divergent religious forms. The adherents of the gods are the corrupt and wandering impious,[154] practicing and enforcing their religion with no regard for either justice or virtue, and existing in a state of tragic and perpetual ignorance.[155] Although their religion has no foundation, yet it continues to be followed, and even imposed through the despicable usage of violence.[156] He is attacking the religious justification for persecution; condemning it as inescapably perverse within any moral framework:

> *Defendenda enim religio est non occidendo sed moriendo, non saeuitia sed patientia, non scelere sed fide. Illa enim malorum sunt, haec bonorum, et necesse est bonum in religione uersari, non malum. Nam si sanguine, si tormentis, si malo religionem defendere uelis, iam non defendetur illa, sed polluetur atque uiolabitur.[157]*

By way of a contrast, Christians require all to come to God entirely through their own volition; *at non est sacrificium quod exprimitur inuito.*[158] The Christian perception of God is one of complete transcendence of the human situation. True wisdom is enshrined in a correct awareness of the meaning of the person and work of Jesus, and true religion forms its naturally accompanying veneration. The *uera sapientia* and *uera religio* cannot be separated,[159] and co-exist in the proper recognition of God.[160] The two principles are united in the acceptance of the true character of God, represented by the Christian mode of spiritual worship. For Lactantius, this true knowledge of God is brought to a point in the passive Christian acceptance

---

[153] *Diuinae institutiones*, 6: 2; 11.

[154] *Diuinae institutiones*, 5: 19; 2.

[155] *Diuinae institutiones*, 5: 19; 4.

[156] *Diuinae institutiones*, 5: 19; 6.

[157] 'Religion should be defended not by killing but by dying, not by violence but by suffering, not by sin but by faith. For those belong to evil; and these to good, and it is necessary that good, not evil, dwells within religion. If you wish to defend religion by bloodshed, tortures, and evil, it will no longer be defended; but violated and polluted'. *Diuinae institutiones*, 5: 19; 22–23.

[158] 'That is not a sacrifice which is extorted unwillingly'. *Diuinae institutiones*, 5: 20; 7.

[159] *Diuinae institutiones*, 4: 3; 7.

[160] *Diuinae institutiones*, 4: 4; 2.

of temporal suffering. God's sovereignty precludes the need for his intervention in the matter of Christian persecution, and the Church rests secure in its eternal vindication, despite all earthly torments.[161] This explanation also covers the lack of forcible compulsion on the part of the Christians in promulgating their vision of God.[162] This true nature of God is as both Father and Son, united in a Godhead of spirit and substance, but one distinct entity.[163] Lactantius acknowledges the controversial background to this doctrine,[164] and it is no coincidence that heretical Christian groups form the subject matter of the immediately subsequent chapter.[165] The expression of the Godhead is the most fundamentally crucial piece of true Christian theology presented in the *Diuinae institutiones.*

The impiety and futility of Roman religion forms one of the essential parameters in the discussion,[166] but Christian practice is never detailed or explained in opposition. Lactantius argues from a standpoint of the nature of Christian worship as the only righteous way of living, unique in its proper veneration of the true God, and transcendent in its freedom from earthly ties of ritual and ceremony. His refusal to include any description of the ceremonial life of the Church is a product of this overriding principle; true religion before God is a just and pure life, lived under the guidance of the true wisdom that is bestowed by the Creator alone. Christianity is presented as a religion of theology and spiritual worship, observed in recognition of the true character of God. True religion, as the natural veneration performed by righteous humanity, is therefore above all material offerings and sacrifices. God has no use for gilded tokens, decaying flesh, or other corruptible items.[167] The only acceptable forms of sacrifice are praise

---

[161] *Diuinae institutiones,* 5: 20; 10.

[162] *Confidimus enim in maiestaem eius, qui tam contemptum sui possit ulcisci quam etiam seruorum suorum labores et iniurias.* 'For we trust in his sovereignty; he is able to avenge contempt of himself in the same way as the unjust sufferings of his servants'. *Diuinae institutiones,* 5: 20; 9.

[163] *Diuinae institutiones,* 4: 29.

[164] *Quae adseueratio plerosque in maximum impingit errorem.* 'An affirmation that has driven many people into the greatest error'. *Diuinae institutiones,* 4: 29; 1. Also of a further theologically controversial note due to Lactantius' clear omission of the Holy Spirit in this definition.

[165] Expressly identified as Phrygians, Novatians, Valentinians, Marcionites, and Anthropians. *Diuinae institutiones,* 4: 30; 10. Each group adhered to different understandings of the nature of the Godhead.

[166] *Diuinae institutiones,* 7: 6.

[167] *Diuinae institutiones,* 6: 25; 6–7.

and hymns, emanating from a just soul in the act of true piety.[168] This is the only picture of Christian worship given by Lactantius in the *Diuinae institutiones*, and it serves a clear theological purpose. It is the complete fulfilment of a transcendental theory of worship, in direct contrast to the propitiatory understanding of rendering sacrifice.[169] Prayers for mercy and the forgiveness of sins, added to the rendering of thanks, are encouraged as the only acceptable methods of conversing with God.[170] Lactantius would seemingly do away with all forms of ritual; *summus igitur colendi dei ritus est ex ore iusti hominis ad deum directa laudatio.*[171] Christian ceremony, even though it is not explicitly detailed in the *Diuinae institutiones*, would take a place under the broader definition of *laus et hymnus* as the acceptable mode of sacrifice.[172] Greater substance is absent, but it is in the service of a wider principle. Lactantius' own definition of the Eucharistic rite, for example, would serve little purpose within his argument of the Christian transcendence of all material aspects of religious worship.

The paragon of true religion and worship is epitomised in the *Diuinae institutiones* by the person of the Christian *uir iustus*.[173] Virtue, piety and justice are allied to the attainment of true wisdom, and inseparable from the mode of living of the man who truly recognises and follows God.[174] The supreme good, so often the subject of philosophical controversy,[175] is the eventual achievement of immortality at the hands of God.[176] For Lactantius, the definition of the just man is the incarnation of the true qualities of humanity, and the archetype of the most virtuous and devout human character.[177] The numerous duties and requirements of the just man may be arduous, but God's mercy is assured, and eternal recompense awaits.[178] Lactantius presents the Christian life as one of continual struggle to maintain

---

[168] *Diuinae institutiones*, 6: 25; 7.

[169] *Diuinae institutiones*, 6: 25; 4.

[170] *Diuinae institutiones*, 6: 25; 13–14.

[171] 'The supreme rite in the worship of God is praise directed to God from the mouth of a just man'. *Diuinae institutiones*, 6: 25; 12.

[172] *Diuinae institutiones*, 6: 25; 7.

[173] 'Just man'. *Diuinae institutiones*, 6: 12; 7.

[174] *Diuinae institutiones*, 6: 9.

[175] *Diuinae institutiones*, 3: 8.

[176] *Diuinae institutiones*, 7: 8.

[177] The image of the just man as the most religious believer is also present in Latin apologetics with Minucius Felix, at *Octauius*, 32: 3. See above, pp. 58–9.

[178] *Diuinae institutiones*, 6: 12; 32–41.

an existence of virtue and compassion in the service of a God who will reward the good deeds, but punish the bad.[179] Although eternal life can only be obtained through the salvific work of Jesus,[180] the life of the just man is one of perpetual exertion to continue in the practice of good. But acceptance of Christian wisdom does not bring gratuitous forgiveness of sins; penitence and generous good works form an important part of the Christian journey.[181] This is Lactantius' thinly-veiled address on the post-baptismal Christian life; salvation is not assured, and forgiveness is a state that must be continually worked towards.[182] Beneath human sin is the duality of body and soul; so long as man exists in the flesh, then sin remains impossible to completely avoid. Christians are not entirely purified in this life, but survive in an uninterrupted state of penitence in the search for eternal purification:

> *Itaque etiam iusti homines, qui frenare se possunt ab omni opere iniusto, nonnumquam tamen ipsa fragilitate uincuntur, ut uel in ira malum dicant uel in aspectu rerum delectabilium cogitatione tacita concupiscant. Quodsi mortalis condicio non patitur esse hominem ab omni macula purum, debent ergo largitione perpetua peccata carnis aboleri.*[183]

Penitence is offered freely to all – even to those compelled to sin by the forces of persecution.[184] The life of the just man may appear to be harsh and unrewarding in this world, but eternal benefits compensate for the temporary requirements of bodily self control.[185] Only such a man is a true follower of God, and his expression of religious worship lies solely in the purity of a virtuous life.[186] Lactantius also presents the just man as the very model of a good citizen;

---

[179] *Diuinae institutiones*, 6: 12; 41.

[180] *Diuinae institutiones*, 4: 19; 10–11.

[181] *Diuinae institutiones*, 6: 13; 1–2.

[182] *Diuinae institutiones*, 6: 13; 3–4.

[183] 'And so even just men, who are able to restrain themselves from all unjust things, are sometimes themselves overcome by weakness, and either say something evil in anger or are desirous with secret thoughts at the sight of something alluring. And if the mortal situation does not allow man to be free from every blemish, then the sins of the flesh ought to be effaced by continual giving'. *Diuinae institutiones*, 6: 13; 9–10.

[184] *Diuinae institutiones*, 6: 24; 1.

[185] *Diuinae institutiones*, 6: 23; 40.

[186] *Diuinae institutiones*, 6: 24; 26.

honest, compassionate and lawful in the eyes of both God and man.[187] This depiction reveals the core of Lactantius' apologetic principle beneath the outline of the *uir iustus*; although he may be ostracised by society for being considered naïve or ingenuous, he alone is found to be truly virtuous. This is Lactantius' apology for the Christian life, embodied in the archetype of human righteousness that is the just man.

Conclusion

Christianity is vindicated in the *Diuinae institutiones* not through a systematic correction of commonly-held prejudices, as with Minucius Felix's *Octauius* or Tertullian's *Apologeticum*, but instead through an appeal to the wider and more abstract concept of the just mode of religious worship. He evokes a sense of Christian transcendence of all earthly ritual, and continually reinforces the ideal of a completely pure form of worship existing in the hearts and minds of true believers. This method of approaching Christian belief, already present to a lesser degree in Minucius Felix,[188] comes to the fore with Lactantius. His allusions to Christian worship are intended throughout as the disparate alternative to the superstitious customs of Roman religion; as they are tied to their temples and altars, so the Christians carry themselves in a perpetual mode of living worship.[189] Further detail of Christian ceremony would only work against the argument, and is therefore omitted. The *Diuinae institutiones*, in spite of its lofty aim of becoming the most constructive and systematic work of Latin apologetics, is not a manual of Christian practice. It is primarily an apologetic justification of the validity of Christian belief, with particular focus on the establishment of Christianity as a deeply natural, and innately desirable, religious system. The apologetic setting is key to understanding many of Lactantius' concepts in the argument; the archetype of Christian belief, the *uir iustus*, as an example, is also the very paragon of virtue, morality and honesty. It is a fundamentally defensive mode of explanation, and one intended to exonerate the harassed believers from all accusations of immorality, impiety, and sedition. Christian belief is therefore described as distinctly transparent, and faithful only to the commands of its incorruptible Creator;

---

[187] *Diuinae institutiones*, 6: 24; 29.
[188] *Octauius*, 32: 1–3.
[189] *Diuinae institutiones*, 5: 19; 30.

in direct opposition to the dreary temples,[190] errant philosophy,[191] and ineffective ritual[192] of traditional Roman religion. The methodology used to achieve this end is also perhaps the most versatile in Latin apologetics before Augustine's *De ciuitate dei*. Lactantius is able to bring together textual sources from all locations whether Christian or philosophical, and deploy them with equal force in his wider arguments. He is not bound by Minucius Felix's or Arnobius' Scriptural reluctance, but neither is he as reliant on the Scriptures as Cyprian in the *Ad Demetrianum*. It is in the methodological sense above all that Lactantius remains Augustine's most prominent forbear in early Latin apologetics.

---

[190] *Quae aut mortuorum aut absentium monumenta sunt.* 'Which are monuments of men dead or absent'. *Diuinae institutiones*, 2: 2; 2.

[191] *Diuinae institutiones*, 3: 15; 4–5.

[192] *Diuinae institutiones*, 5: 19; 27–28.

CONCLUSION

The African Latin apologists represent an important location of the Church in some of its most formative centuries, and provide a significant contribution to early Christian literature. Their apologetic, as the literary outpouring of the defenders of the persecuted Church, speaks to the character of Christian belief in a desperate fight for survival and recognition, and forever enshrines some of the key issues in the controversies at hand. They are windows into the conflict between Christianity and Roman society in one of the most turbulent periods in the history of the Church. In spite of the fact that each piece of literature discussed in this study is marked by its own topics of individual concern, each writer has chosen to use the medium of the apology, and developed his own work out from the initial format of a defensive mode of expression. Apologetic is a highly fitting literary formulation of the perspective of harassed early Christianity, and perhaps most crucially, becomes something not too far removed from the textual articulation of Christianity on trial. As such, each apology bears inescapable relevance to its generative circumstances. If the Christians are being punished as criminals, then the legal aspects of Tertullian's *Apologeticum*, for example, carry something far more relative than a mere stylistic flourish. If Christianity is ridiculed as a religion of the credulous dregs of the populace, then Minucius Felix's attempt in the *Octauius* to establish a viable philosophical foundation for areas of Christian belief can be more fully appreciated. As the early history of Christianity is punctuated by the climactic events of the persecutions, so the Latin apologists' cries for fair judicial treatment can be read with deeply realistic meaning. Persecution, while providing the vehicle of martyrdom, has also allowed for the opportunity to defend the faith on trial. Cyprian's *Ad Demetrianum* and Lactantius' *Diuinae institutiones* speak to very present issues in the milieu of the Decian and Diocletianic persecutions respectively. But their works have survived the centuries due to a sense of continuing relevance to one Christian era after another, even in view of the intrinsically related nature of each text to its background. As the Church honours its martyrs from times of violent persecution, so it has maintained the texts compiled in defence of its historical belief, even after the widespread dominance of Christianity.

African Latin apologetics – a recap

Minucius Felix's *Octauius* is a genuine pearl of style and composition. It is by far the most polished of the early Latin apologies, and a strong example of the growing intelligentsia within the Christian Church of the late second/early third century. The *Octauius* unites its persuasive rhetorical argument and its confident use of the classical sources by a highly stylised literary medium, although never losing sight of its primary apologetic goal. It is likely that the particular apologetic concern of the *Octauius* is in response to the anti-Christian rhetoric of Marcus Cornelius Fronto, even if the exact degree is difficult to correlate. The *Octauius* is also not only relevant within its own background, but is one of the most eloquent apologies for Christian belief across all works in the apologetic genre. It is potentially the first Latin step in the presentation of Christianity as a viable philosophical school; in Minucius' eyes the most positive forward movement for the Church in its current circumstances. Lactantius' eventual depiction of the Christians as the sole true philosophers, in possession of both the *uera sapientia* and *uera religio*, is a more developed manifestation of the argument first advanced in Latin apologetics by Minucius' *Octauius*.

Minucius Felix and Tertullian will continue to be studied together by virtue of the numerous parallels between their apologetic works, but also for their likely close contextualisation in proximity to each other. They are the first steps of Latin apologetics, and the textual foundations utilised by those who followed. Tertullian's own apologetic work, though it perhaps lacks something of Minucius' literary fluidity, compensates by its passion, its candour, and its remarkable summation of the hugely significant character of its author. Tertullian remains the central figure in early Latin apologetics, regardless of the prospect of the earlier dating of Minucius. Whichever way the dating arguments slant, Tertullian's personality is deeply imprinted on the study of Latin apologetics like no other. His *Apologeticum* cannot be surpassed as the archetypal Latin apology due to its thorough address of one of the key hallmarks of any Christian apology at its very widest reach. Tertullian's forensic refutation of prevalent charges of criminality through the employment of legal structures and terminology, underlining the fundamentally germane and contemporary nature of the *Apologeticum*, combine in its undeniable definition as the quintessential work of Latin apologetics. Following the lead of Justin, and perhaps also Minucius Felix, Tertullian endows Latin Christian literature with one of its most powerful and iconic pieces of apologetic writing. But the *Apologeticum* is not Tertullian's sole apologetic text, and the *Ad Nationes*, *De testimonio animae* and *Ad Scapulam* all contribute in their own ways to a more rounded picture of Tertullian as the completely versatile Christian apologist. The varied points of polemical argument in the *Ad nationes* that make the work into something approaching a 'scrap-book' of polemical apologetic argument, added to the more philosophical character of the *De testimonio animae*, cement Tertullian's status as a truly unique Christian apologist. Even though the *Ad Scapulam* rehashes many of Tertullian's earlier apologetic arguments, the sense of direct focus gives them a new lease of life, and a further degree of meaning.

Cyprian's *Ad Demetrianum* marks a divergence from one of the most central characteristics of the apologetic work of Minucius and Tertullian. Although this would be once again reversed by Arnobius and Lactantius, Cyprian's own expression of the Latin apology serves a far more evangelical apologetic argument. That is to say, the *Ad Demetrianum* represents an explicit plea for conversion to the Christian faith, following from its defence of Christian practice, and grounded throughout by the evidence of Scripture. The Scriptures are fearlessly deployed as weapons in the refutation of accusations against the Christians, and in so doing, Cyprian has redefined one of the most pivotal aspects of Minucius and Tertullian's apologetic methodology. Their pre-eminent concern of expressly citing secular authorities in the justification of Christian principles has been firmly replaced by Cyprian with continual citation from the Scriptures. Cyprian employs these as his primary textual authorities, and interprets them with direct force against the exponents of anti-Christian slanders. The *Ad Demetrianum* is undoubtedly apologetic, but it also houses a corpus of prophetic Scriptural interpretation in response to the question of suffering in the world. The literary format of the apologetic defence provides Cyprian with the vehicle through which his plea for conversion to Christian belief, built upon the defence of his religious brethren, can be articulated. Whether the *Quod idola dii non sint* merits a place in the full Cyprianic corpus or not, will continue to be a favourite topic exciting scholars in the field. On the basis of the received text alone, this study has found no reason to conclusively dismiss the possibility of the work being authentic. The Cyprianic authorship of the *Quod idola dii non sint* would certainly add another level of depth to the Carthaginian bishop's apologetic concern, if still a comparatively minor contribution in itself due to its nature as a document of compilation.

Very much on similar lines as with Minucius and Tertullian, the similarities of context tend to ensure that the apologies of Arnobius of Sicca and Lactantius are studied alongside each other. Arnobius' *Aduersus nationes* is an extensive compendium of Christian polemic in the service of an apologetic argument, and by far the most offensive of all the early Latin apologies. It is also a highly insightful window into the religious dialogue of the early fourth century, particularly if its context is to be aligned with that of the Diocletianic persecution. Yet even conceding the difficult contextualisation of Minucius Felix, Arnobius is by far the most obscure figure in the group of the Latin apologists. The more than justifiable questions surrounding his own location within early Christian doctrine and theology precipitate further questions about both the essential character of the *Aduersus nationes*, and also the nature of the particular Christianity that Arnobius is defending. Although he shows likely evidence of a reading of Minucius Felix, Cyprian's *Ad Demetrianum* and perhaps also Tertullian's *Apologeticum*, he can rarely be shown to correspond with their theological positions outside of the more immediate textual borrowings. Arnobius may well have tutored Lactantius at some point,[1] but the *Aduersus nationes* and the *Diuinae institutiones* could scarcely be more different. Whatever the merits of the later definition of Arnobius as unorthodox, he does fit the bill as the exception in a developing tradition of African Latin apologetic writing, and remains something of an anomaly. But in spite of the many theological divergences of the *Aduersus nationes*, Arnobius

---

[1] See Jerome, *De uiris illustribus*, 80.

has produced a lengthy piece of Christian apologetics. If nothing else, Arnobius' *Aduersus nationes* is another valuable nuance in the definition of the early Christian apology.

The implications of a tradition of Latin apologetics, beginning with Minucius and Tertullian, and extending through Cyprian's *Ad Demetrianum*, come to a head in the express motivation behind Lactantius' *Diuinae institutiones*. By including an overview of the successes and shortcomings of his predecessors in the Latin production of apologetics, Lactantius consciously elevates his own work to a height superseding the forerunning works. The most enduring characteristic of the *Diuinae institutiones* lies in this identification; it is compiled to be the most sophisticated work of Latin apologetics, growing out from but eventually outstepping the foundations laid by Minucius Felix, Tertullian, and Cyprian. Although Lactantius is highly sympathetic with the methodology of Minucius and Tertullian in primarily dealing with non-Christian sources in the establishment of Christian points of argument, he also finds an important place for the interpretation of Scripture within the apologetic schema. A bridge with Cyprian's *Ad Demetrianum* could perhaps be constructed, even if Lactantius is scathing of Cyprian's unchecked deployment of the testimonies of Scripture. Lactantius finds a place for the Scriptures within his overall argument in the construction of peculiarly Christian beliefs;[2] a facet often restrained by the earlier apologists in favour of the more pressing need for the defence and exoneration of their fellow believers from persecution and harassment. But because Lactantius also focuses on constructive arguments in the support of Christian doctrine, the *Diuinae institutiones* becomes more than just a defence of Christian belief. Even if expressly nurtured in the surrounds of a more conventional apologetic text, Lactantius' work is not restricted to the sole refutation of anti-Christian arguments. This is the central aspect of Lactantius' contribution to Latin apologetics. He has redefined the concept of a Christian apology, and created an exceptionally rounded piece of Christian literature. Lactantius has produced a sophisticated defence of Christian belief and practice, which is intended to be of equal value to both its critics and its adherents. His answer to the opponents of the Church is a defence by explanation, but also a constructive justification of some of the core areas of Christian belief. The dual audience of apologetics, being both the Christian detractors and the Christians

[2] Lactantius' Christology is bound to Scriptural interpretation by necessity. See Lactantius' Scriptural engagement on the subject, at *Diuinae institutiones*, 4: 8–21.

themselves, receives its fullest Latin focus before Augustine's *De ciui-tate dei* in Lactantius' *Diuinae institutiones*.

A genre of Latin apologetics?

A case could be made for the classification of the African Latin apologists into one defined literary genre. One salient feature would be the observation that each apologist shows a particular awareness of his predecessors. The relationship between Minucius Felix and Tertullian emphasises their close dependence one way or the other, Cyprian can be located in a stream running from both the *Octauius* and the *Apologeticum*, and Lactantius goes even further by explicitly referring to his forerunners in the field. Even Arnobius, in spite of the problematic theological location of the *Aduersus nationes*, can be shown to display evidence of a reading of his Latin apologetic predecessors. With the exception of which of the two is the prime mover between Minucius and Tertullian, each apologist testifies to a conscious understanding of place within a shared mode of apologetic expression. By maintaining lines of influence behind a range of arguments and structures, and reproducing features common to other works, each apologist in succession is effectively nodding to one or more of those who came before him. These trails hint at a recognition on the part of the apologists that pre-existent works of Latin apologetics would continue to have great utility through the changing sets of circumstance. Whether as source-texts useful for particular approaches, or places of reference in further developing arguments grounded in the Latin apologetic propensity of moving away from the statements of Scripture, the forerunning works would continue to be used. With Lactantius, the more implicit lines of textual influence give way to a stronger emphasis on the establishment of the earlier works as preliminary landmarks in a developing Latin apologetic landscape.

Notwithstanding the more immediate differences in style and formation, there are underlying methodological principles that run through all the texts in question, and could be isolated to detail a shared apologetic ambition.[3] Firstly, there is the issue of the sources providing the key evidence in the apologetic argument. To one degree

---

[3] Against the organization of Minucius Felix, Tertullian and Cyprian into one genre of Latin apologetics, see Simon Price, 'Latin Christian Apologetics', in *Apologetics in the Roman Empire*, pp. 113–4. Although Price recognizes certain 'generic similarities' leading to the composition of the texts, he argues that 'the forms of communication were very varied, even on the part of one author, and did not constitute a formal genre of apologetic'.

or another, each text is concerned with establishing the inherent compatibility of Christianity with classical philosophy, and aims to depict their often-harassed minority religion as instead a viable philosophical school. Minucius' *Octauius*, Tertullian's *Apologeticum*, *Ad nationes* and *Ad Scapulam*, the pseudo-Cyprianic *Quod idola dii non sint*, and Arnobius' *Aduersus nationes*, all testify to the same purpose behind a common methodology. Lactantius' *Diuinae institutiones*, although showing a clear readiness to engage with the Scriptures, also bears witness to the same position. They represent an intellectual Christianity fully prepared to utilise the philosophers in the service of the Christian cause, and enthusiastic in repackaging Christian belief with the terminology of non-Christian authorities. But running parallel to the philosophical thread is another similar, if perhaps more tangible, apologetic theme. In each work of African Latin apologetics discussed in this study, the Church is presented as an innately desirable religious system for both humanity and society. For Tertullian, the Christians are the most steadfast and law-abiding members of society;[4] something further developed in Cyprian's *Ad Demetrianum*, where the Church suffers its mounting injustice in innocence and silence. Even in view of the dichotomy between the Church and the world, as long as the Christians live next to their non-Christian counterparts, so they will suffer everything together. The world may be afflicted by the gravest of misfortunes, but the Christians face each setback with untainted virtue. Lactantius will go on to cap the issue with his sweeping portrayal of the *uir iustus*; the archetype of the truly righteous follower of the divine, and also the very embodiment of the most complete human individual. Lactantius is fleshing out the presentation of Christianity as a legitimately positive movement across multiple fronts. The importance of the Church hinges around its faithfulness to God's *uera sapientia* and *uera religio*, and each individual believer plays a part in the overall validation of the purity of Christianity as the solitary manifestation of true worship. This mode of presenting the Church as both philosophically and socially desirable begins in Latin apologetics with Minucius Felix and Tertullian, extends through Cyprian, and reaches its apex with Lactantius' *Diuinae institutiones*. It is one key platform of argument held in common

---

[4] See also Minucius Felix, *Octauius*, 35: 6, on the Christians' unmatched personal morality, and 37: 3–5, on Roman heroes failing to match up to the basics of Christian virtue.

throughout these apologies, and contributes to the issue of generic identification.

The implications of a formal genre of African Latin apologetics would be built upon these incidences of textual influence, interpreted through displays of reference to earlier apologies, and brought together by the conscious awareness of tradition. It is clear that the African Latin apologists worked within the knowledge of those who came before them, but perhaps ascribing the observable lines of influence as facets of a uniform genre would be a step too far. All the writings discussed in this study are inescapably apologetic, and although they bear witness to the output of their predecessors, the individual concerns underpinning each separate text do begin to work against strict group classification. But if not a genre, it is still fair to say that a developing apologetic tradition can be noted from a study of the African Latin apologists, in spite of the immediate variances between the texts. Common recourse to some of the methods of apologetic in each work does count in favour of a positive genre identification, but as each work is produced, so it branches off from its predecessors. The apologetic core is present throughout, but subordinated to the particular nuances of each text. The differences spanning the works are paramount. Minucius Felix unfolds his *Octauius* along primarily philosophical and moral lines. Tertullian takes various approaches himself, but highlights the legal elements of anti-Christian harassment with the *Apologeticum*, goes on the offensive with the *Ad nationes*, and searches for a neutral philosophical source with the *De testimonio animae*. Cyprian's *Ad Demetrianum* is apologetics expressly subservient to evangelisation, and Arnobius' *Aduersus nationes* is a catalogue of polemical arguments against the religion of the persecutors, cited in defence of Christianity. Lactantius utilises the defensive standpoint in order to introduce an attempt at a far more sophisticated and multifaceted apology, bringing the full theological justification of particular areas of controversy above the deconstructive statements of more conventional apologetics. Although each African Latin writer analysed in this study has chosen to use some of the methods and templates of apologetics, the implications inherent in establishing a genre of African Latin apologetics cannot be grounded in the details of the texts themselves. Formal genre identification would suggest greater similarities throughout the works concerned that actually do not seem to exist upon further exploration. Each Latin apology may begin in the surroundings of a shared apologetic expression, but always maintains its own unique textual principles, and its own focus on the particular issues at hand. Conscious awareness of tradition does not necessitate the implied homogeneity of a genre, and the Latin apologists' continuing need to address a wide range of theological and doctrinal subjects conclusively pervades the structure of each work. In fine, retrospectively applying the label of a genre to a similar body of writings would be anachronistic in this case, and fails to do justice to the individual concerns of each author behind the compilation of the texts.

The particular differences of each African Latin apology contribute to the richness of their apologetic form of expression. They have united philosophy and theology, questions of morality and legality, and even direct evangelisation under the format of the Christian apology. From Minucius Felix and Tertullian, via Cyprian and Arnobius, down to Lactantius, and through a great variety of structures and methodologies, the field is aptly prepared for Augustine of Hippo's momentous *De ciuitate dei*. But although Augustine's influence within Christian theology is in many ways unsurpassed, his *De ciuitate dei* stepped into an already thriving tradition of Latin apologetic literature extending through some of the most critical years of early Christianity. The texts of the African Latin apologists are invaluable pieces of insight into one of the most significant confrontations in the entire history of the Church, by a reflection of crucial incidents in the religious and ideological conflict between Christianity and Rome.

BIBLIOGRAPHY

Primary Sources – Editions and Translations

Aland, Barbara, Kurt Aland, Johannes Karavidopoulos, Carlo M. Martini and Bruce M. Metzger, eds., (2001) *The Greek New Testament* [Fourth Revised Edition], Stuttgart: Deutsche Bibelgesellschaft.

Anonymous

Meecham, Henry G., ed., (1949) *The Epistle to Diognetus* [Textus Minores, 33], Manchester: Manchester University Press.
Thierry, J. J., ed., (1964) *The Epistle to Diognetus*, Leiden: E. J. Brill.
von Dobschütz, Ernst, ed., (1912) *Decretum Gelasianum*, in Adolf Harnack and Carl Schmidt (eds.) [TU, 38], Leipzig: J. C. Hinrichs.

Arnobius of Sicca

Bryce, Hamilton, and Hugh Campbell, trans., (1871) *The Seven Books of Arnobius Adversus Gentes* [ANCL, 19], Edinburgh: T. & T. Clark.
Marchesi, C., ed., (1953) *Arnobii Aduersus Nationes Libri VII* [Corpus Scriptorum Latinorum Paravianum], Turin.
McCracken, George E., trans., (1949) *Arnobius of Sicca: The Case Against the Pagans* [2 Vols., ACW, 7–8], New York: Newman Press.
Reifferscheid, A., ed., (1875) *Arnobii Aduersus Nationes Libri VII* [CSEL, 4], Vienna.

Athenagoras

Crehan, Joseph Hugh, trans., (1956) *Athenagoras: Embassy for the Christians, The Resurrection of the Dead* [ACW, 23], New York: Newman Press.

Schoedel, William R., ed., (1972) *Athenagoras: Legatio and De Resurrectione*, Oxford: Clarendon Press.

Augustine

Bogan, Mary Inez, trans., (1968) Augustine, *The Retractions* [FC, 60], Washington: Catholic University of America Press.

Dombart, Bernhard, ed., (1877–8) *Sancti Aurelii Augustini episcopi De ciuitate Dei libri XXII* [2 Vols.], Leipzig: Teubner.

Petschenig, M., ed., (1908) *Augustinus: Psalmus contra partem Donati, Contra epistulam Parmeniani, De baptismo* [CSEL, 51], Vienna.

Aulus Gellius

Rolfe, John C., ed., (1954–61) *The Attic Nights of Aulus Gellius* [3 Vols., LCL], London: William Heinemann.

Cassius Dio

Cary, Ernest, ed., (1954–5) Cassius Dio, *Roman History* [9 Vols., LCL], London: William Heinemann.

Cicero

Rackham, H., ed., (1933, repr. 1961) Cicero, *De Natura Deorum* [LCL], London: William Heinemann.

Clement of Alexandria

Butterworth, G. W., ed., (1968) *Clement of Alexandria* [LCL], London: William Heinemann.

Commodian

Dombart, Bernhard, ed., (1887) *Commodiani Carmina* [CSEL, 15], Vienna.

Ludwig, Ernst, ed., (1877) *Commodiani Carmina*, Leipzig: Teubner.

Martin, Joseph, ed., (1960) *Commodiani Carmina* [CCSL, 128], Turnhout: Brepols.

Cyprian

Bévenot, Maurice, ed., (1971) Cyprian, *De Lapsis and De Ecclesiae Catholicae Unitate*, Oxford: Clarendon Press.

Clarke, G. W., trans., (1984–9) *The Letters of St. Cyprian* [4 Vols., ACW, 43–4, 46–7], New York: Newman Press.

Fredouille, Jean-Claude, ed., (2003) Cyprian, *A Démétrien* [SC, 467], Paris: Les Éditions du Cerf.

Hartel, G., ed., (1868–71) Cyprian, *Opera Omnia* [3 Vols., CSEL, 3], Vienna.

Wallis, Robert Ernest, trans., (1868–73) *The Writings of Cyprian, Bishop of Carthage* [2 Vols., ANCL, 8, 13], Edinburgh: T. & T. Clark.

Eusebius

Lake, Kirsopp, ed., (1949) Eusebius, *The Ecclesiastical History* [2 Vols., LCL], London: William Heinemann.

Firmicus Maternus

Turcan, Robert, ed., (1982) Firmicus Maternus, *L'Erreur des religions Païennes*, Paris: Les Belles Lettres.

Fronto

Haines, C. R., ed., (1955–7) *The Correspondence of Marcus Cornelius Fronto with Marcus Aurelius Antoninus, Lucius Verus, Antoninus Pius and Various Friends* [2 Vols., LCL], London: William Heinemann.

Gaius

Gordon, W. M., and O. F. Robinson, eds., (1988) *The Institutes of Gaius*, London: Duckworth.

Gennadius

Bernoulli, Carl Albrecht, ed., (1895) *Hieronymus und Gennadius: De Viris Inlustribus*, Leipzig: J. C. B. Mohr.

Gregory of Nazianzus

Gallay, Paul, and Maurice Jourjon, eds., (1978) *Gregoire de Nazianze, Discours* 27–31 [SC, 250], Paris: Les Éditions du Cerf.

Herodian

Whittaker, C. R., ed., (1969–70) Herodian, *Historia* [2 Vols., LCL], London: William Heinemann.

Homer

Murray, A. T., ed., (1995) *Homer: The Odyssey*, [George E. Dimock (rev.)] [2 Vols., LCL], Cambridge, Mass.: Harvard University Press.

Jerome

Herding, Wilhelm, ed., (1879) *Hieronymi: De Viris Inlustribus Liber*, Leipzig: Teubner.

Hilberg, Isidore, ed., (1996) *Sancti Eusebii Hieronymi epistulae* [3 Vols., CSEL, 54–56/1], Vienna : Verlag der Österreichischen Akademie der Wissenschaften.

Migne, Jacques-Paul, ed., Jerome, *Chronicon*, in *PL*, 27. Digitised facsimile online at Documenta Catholica Omnia, <http://www.documenta-catholicaomnia.eu/02m/0347-0420,_Hieronymus,_Chronicun,_MLT.pdf> Date accessed: 29/11/2010

Josephus

Thackeray, H. St. J., ed., (1926, repr. 1961) Josephus, *Works* [9 Vols., LCL], London: William Heinemann.

Justin

Barnard, Leslie W., trans., (1997) *St. Justin Martyr: The First and Second Apologies* [ACW, 56], New York: Paulist Press.

Blunt, A. W. F., ed., (1911) *The Apologies of Justin Martyr* [Cambridge Patristic Texts], Cambridge: Cambridge University Press.

Dods, Marcus, George Reith and B. P. Pratten, trans., (1867) *The Writings of Justin Martyr and Athenagoras* [ANCL, 2], Edinburgh: T. & T. Clark.

Lactantius

Blakeney, E. H., ed., (1950) *Firmiani Lactantii Epitome Institutionum Divinarum*, London: SPCK.

Bowen, Anthony, and Peter Garnsey, trans., (2003, repr. 2007) *The Divine Institutes of Lactantius*, Liverpool: Liverpool University Press.

Creed, J. L., ed., (1984) *Lactantius: De Mortibus Persecutorum*, Oxford: Clarendon Press.

Heck, Eberhard, and Antonie Wlosok, eds., (2005–9) Lactantius, *Divinarum Institutionum Libri Septem* [3 Vols.], Leipzig: K. G Saur/ Berlin: Walter de Gruyter.

Ingremeau, Christiane, ed., (1982) *Lactance: La Colère de Dieu* [SC, 289], Paris: Les Éditions du Cerf.

Perrin, Michel, ed., (1974) *Lactance: L'Ouvrage du Dieu Créateur* [2 Vols., SC, 213–4], Paris: Les Éditions du Cerf.

Marcus Aurelius

Haines, C. R., ed., (1930, repr. 1961) Marcus Aurelius, *Mediations* [LCL], London: William Heinemann.

Minucius Felix

Beaujeu, J., ed., (1964) Minucius Felix, *Octavius*, Paris: Les Belles Lettres.

Clarke, G. W., trans., (1974) *The Octavius of Marcus Minucius Felix* [ACW, 39], New York: Newman Press.

Kytzler, B., ed., (1992) Minucius Felix, *Octavius*, Stuttgart and Leipzig: Teubner.

Rendall, Gerald H., ed., (1931, repr. 2003) Minucius Felix, *Octavius* [LCL], Cambridge, Mass. & London: Harvard University Press.

Waltzing, J. P., ed., (1909) *Octavius de M. Minucius Felix*, Bruges: Desclée, De Brouwer.

Origen

Chadwick, Henry, trans., (1953, repr. 1965) Origen, *Contra Celsum*, Cambridge: Cambridge University Press.

Ovid

Hill, D. E., ed., (1985) Ovid, *Metamorphoses I-IV*, Warminster: Aris & Phillips.

Plato

Archer-Hind, R. D., ed., (1888) *The Timaeus of Plato*, London and New York: Macmillan & Co.

Bluck, R. S., ed., (1961) *Plato's Meno*, Cambridge: Cambridge University Press.

Fowler, Harold North, ed., (1928) Plato, *Euthyphro, Apology, Crito, Phaedo, Phaedrus* [LCL], London: William Heinemann.

Pliny the Younger

Radice, Betty, ed., (1969) Pliny the Younger, *Letters, and Panegyricus* [2 Vols., LCL], London: William Heinemann.

Seneca

Basore, John W., ed., (1958) Seneca, *De Providentia* [LCL], London: William Heinemann.

Sextus

Chadwick, Henry, ed., (1959) *The Sentences of Sextus* [Texts and Studies, 5], Cambridge: Cambridge University Press.

Sidonius

Mohr, Paul, ed., (1895) *C. Sollius Apollinaris Sidonius*, Leipzig: Teubner.

Suetonius

Hurley, Donna W., ed., (2001) *Suetonius: Divus Claudius*, Cambridge: Cambridge University Press.

Symmachus

Barrow, R. H., ed., (1983) *Prefect and Emperor: The Relationes of Symmachus*, Oxford: Clarendon Press.

Tertullian

Bindley, T. Herbert, trans., (1890) *The Apology of Tertullian for the Christians*, London: Parker & Co.

Dekkers, E., ed., (1954) *Quinti Septimi Florentis Tertulliani Opera* [2 Vols., CCSL, 1–2], Turnhout: Brepols.

Glover, T. R., ed., (1931, repr. 2003) Tertullian, *Apology* [LCL], Cambridge, Mass. & London: Harvard University Press.

Zosimus

Paschoud, François, ed., (1971–89) *Zosime: Histoire Nouvelle*, [5 Vols.], Paris: Les Belles Lettres.

Secondary Sources

Allen, R. E., (1959) 'Anamnesis in Plato's "Meno and Phaedo"', *RMeta*, 13: 1, 165–174.

Andriessen, P., (1947) 'The Authorship of the Epistula Ad Diognetum', *VC*, 1: 2, 129–136.

Balfour, I. L. S., (1982) 'Tertullian's Description of the Heathen', in Elizabeth A. Livingstone (ed.), *SP*, 17: 2, 785–789, Oxford: Pergamon Press.

Bardy, Gustave, (1930) *The Christian Latin Literature of the First Six Centuries*, London: Sands and Co.

Barnard, Leslie W., (1972) *Athenagoras: A Study in Second Century Christian Apologetic*, Paris: Beauchesne.

Barnes, T. D., (1973a) 'Lactantius and Constantine', *JRS*, 63, 29–46.

— (1973b) 'Porphyry Against the Christians: Date and the Attribution of Fragments', *JTS*, 24, 424–442.

— (1976) 'Sossianus Hierocles and the Antecedents of the "Great Persecution"', *HSPh*, 80, 239–252.

— (1981) *Constantine and Eusebius*, Cambridge, MA: Harvard University Press.

— (1985) *Tertullian*, Oxford: Oxford University Press.

— (1994) 'Scholarship or Propaganda? Porphyry Against the Christians and its Historical Setting', *BICS*, 39, 53–65.

—(2010) *Early Christian Hagiography and Roman History*, Tübingen: Mohr Siebeck.

Baylis, H. J., (1928) *Minucius Felix and His Place Among the Early Fathers of the Latin Church*, London: SPCK.

Benson, Edward White, (1897) *Cyprian: His Life, His Times, His Work*, London: Macmillan & Co.

Berchman, Robert M., (2005) *Porphyry Against the Christians*, Leiden: Brill.

Bergjan, Silke-Petra, (2001) 'Celsus the Epicurean? The Interpretation of an Argument in Origen, Contra Celsum', *HTR*, 94: 2, 179–204.

Bowman, Alan K., Peter Garnsey and Dominic Rathbone, eds., (2000) *The Cambridge Ancient History* [Vol. 11], Cambridge: Cambridge University Press.

Bowman, Alan K., Peter Garnsey and Averil Cameron, eds., (2005) *The Cambridge Ancient History* [Vol. 12], Cambridge: Cambridge University Press.

Brakman, C., (1927) 'Commodianea', *Mnemosyne*, 55: 2, 121–140.

Brown, Peter, (1971, repr. 2004) *The World of Late Antiquity*, London: Thames & Hudson.

Burke, Gary T., (1986) 'Celsus and the Old Testament', *VT*, 36: 2, 241–245.

Burns, J. Patout Jr., (2002) *Cyprian the Bishop*, London: Routledge.

Burrows, Mark S., (1988) 'Christianity in the Roman Forum: Tertullian and the Apologetic Use of History', *VC*, 42: 3, 209–235.

Cameron, Euan, (2005) *Interpreting Christian History: The Challenge of the Churches' Past*, Oxford: Blackwell Publishing.

Canter, H. V., (1940) 'Roman Civilisation in North Africa', *CJ*, 35: 4, 197–208.

Carver, George L., (1974) 'Tacitus' Dialogus as a Source of Minucius Felix's Octavius', *CPh*, 69: 2, 100–106.

Chadwick, Henry, (1948) 'Origen, Celsus, and the Resurrection of the Body', *HTR*, 41: 2, 83–102.

— (1966) *Early Christian Thought and the Classical Tradition*, Oxford: Clarendon Press.

— (1993) *The Early Church*, London: Penguin.

— (2001) *The Church in Ancient Society*, Oxford: Oxford University Press.

Champlin, Edward, (1980) *Fronto and Antonine Rome*, Cambridge, Mass.: Harvard University Press.

Chapman, J., (1902) 'The Order of the Treatises and Letters in the MSS of St. Cyprian', *JTS*, 4, 103–123.

Christensen, Arne Søby, (1980) *Lactantius the Historian*, Copenhagen: Museum Tusculanum Press.

Clarke, G. W., (1965) 'The Literary Setting of the *Octavius* of Minucius Felix', *JRH*, 3, 195–211.

— (1967) 'The Historical Setting of the *Octavius* of Minucius Felix', *JRH*, 4, 267–286.

Cross, F. L., and E. A. Livingstone, eds., (2005) *The Oxford Dictionary of the Christian Church* [Third Revised Edition], Oxford: Oxford University Press.

Crouzel, Henri, (1989) *Origen* [A. S. Worrall (trans.)], Edinburgh: T. & T. Clark.

de Labriolle, Pierre, (2006) *History and Literature of Christianity* [Herbert Wilson (trans.)], London: Kegan Paul.

de Ste Croix, G. E. M., (1963) 'Why Were the Early Christians Persecuted?', *P&P*, 26, 6–38.

Dekkers, E., ed., (1995) *Clavis Patrum Latinorum*, Steenbrugis: in Abbatia Sancti Petri.

Digeser, Elizabeth DePalma, (1998) 'Lactantius, Porphyry, and the Debate over Religious Toleration', *JRS*, 88, 129–146.

— (2000) *The Making of a Christian Empire: Lactantius and Rome*, Ithaca and London: Cornell University Press.

Diller, H., (1935) 'In Sachen Tertullian-Minucius Felix', *Philologus*, 90, 98–114, 216–239.

Dunn, Geoffrey D., (2002) 'Rhetorical Structure in Tertullian's "Ad Scapulam"', *VC*, 56: 1, 47-55.

— (2004) *Tertullian*, London: Routledge.

Edwards, Mark, Martin Goodman and Simon Price, eds., (1999) *Apologetics in the Roman Empire*, Oxford: Oxford University Press.

Edwards, Mark, (2004) 'Dating Arnobius: Why Discount the Evidence of Jerome?', *Antiquité Tardive*, 12, 263–271.

Elyot, Thomas, (1970) *Dictionary* [Scolar Press Facsimile of original 1538 edn.], Menston, Yorkshire: The Scolar Press Limited.

Feldman, Louis H., (1990) 'Origen's "Contra Celsum" and Josephus' "Contra Apionem": The Issue of Jewish Origins', *VC*, 44: 2, 105–135.

Finney, P. C., (1982) 'Idols in Second and Third Century Apology', in Elizabeth A. Livingstone (ed.), *SP*, 17: 1, 684–687, Oxford: Pergamon Press.

Fisher, Arthur L., (1982) 'Lactantius' Ideas Relating Christian Truth and Christian Society', *JHI*, 43: 3, 355–377.

Fitzgerald, John T., et al., eds., (2003) *Early Christianity and Classical Culture*, Leiden: Brill.

Fredouille, Jean-Claude., (1995) 'L'apologétique Chrétienne Antique: Métamorphoses d'un Genre Polymorphe', *REAug*, 41, 201–216.

Frend, W. H. C., (1965) *Martyrdom and Persecution in the Early Church*, Oxford: Basil Blackwell.

— (1984) *The Rise of Christianity*, London: Darton, Longman and Todd.

— (2006) 'Some North African Turning Points in Christian Apologetics', *JEH*, 57: 1, 1–15.

Garnsey, Peter, (2002) 'Lactantius and Augustine', in Alan K. Bowman, Hannah M. Cotton, Martin Goodman and Simon Price (eds.), *Representations of Empire: Rome and the Mediterranean World*, Oxford: Oxford University Press.

Garvie, Alfred Ernest, (1913) *A Handbook of Christian Apologetics*, London: Duckworth & Co.

Goodspeed, Edgar J., (1946) 'The Date of Commodian', *CPh*, 41: 1, 46–47.

Grant, Robert M., (1955) 'The Chronology of the Greek Apologists', *VC*, 9: 1, 25–33.

— (1988) *Greek Apologists of the Second Century*, Philadelphia, Pennsylvania: The Westminster Press.

Hadas-Lebel, Mireille, (1993) *Flavius Josephus* [Richard Miller (trans.)], New York: Macmillan Publishing Company.

Hall, Stuart George, (2005) *Doctrine and Practice in the Early Church*, London: SPCK.

Hebblethwaite, Brian, (2005) *In Defence of Christianity*, Oxford: Oxford University Press.

Holford-Strevens, Leofranc, (2005) *Aulus Gellius: An Antonine Scholar and his Achievement*, Oxford: Oxford University Press.

Holmberg, Bengt, ed., (2008) *Exploring Early Christian Identity*, Tübingen: Mohr Siebeck.

Honoré, Tony, (1982) *Ulpian*, Oxford: Clarendon Press.

Hornblower, Simon, and Anthony Spawforth, eds., (2003) *The Oxford Classical Dictionary* [Third Revised Edition], Oxford: Oxford University Press.

Humphries, Mark, (2006) *Early Christianity*, London: Routledge.

Jones, A. H. M., J. R. Martindale and J. Morris, eds., (1971) *The Prosopography of the Later Roman Empire* [Vol. 1], Cambridge: Cambridge University Press.

Keresztes, Paul, (1979) 'The Imperial Roman Government and the Christian Church', in Wolfgang Haase (ed.), *ANRW*, II, 23. 1, 247-315, 375-386, Berlin: Walter de Gruyter.

Lane Fox, Robin, (1986) *Pagans and Christians*, London: Penguin.

Lössl, Josef, (2010) *The Early Church*, London: T. & T. Clark.

Mayor, J. E. B., (1910) 'Commodian's *Instructiones*. Days of the Week', *CR*, 24: 8, 240-241.

McCracken, George E., (1949) 'Review: Tertullian on the Soul', *CJ*, 44: 5, 348-351.

McGiffert, Arthur Cushman, (1950) *A History of Christian Thought* [2 Vols.], New York: Charles Scribner's Sons.

McGowan, Andrew, (1994) 'Eating People: Accusations of Cannibalism Against Christians in the Second Century', *JECS*, 2, 413-442.

McGuckin, Paul, (1982) 'The Non-Cyprianic Scripture Texts in Lactantius' Divine Institutes', *VC*, 36: 2, 145–163.

Milburn, R. L. P., (1954) *Early Christian Interpretations of History*, London: Adam and Charles Black.

Mitchell, Margaret M., and Frances M. Young, eds., (2006) *The Cambridge History of Christianity* [Vol. 1; *Origins to Constantine*], Cambridge: Cambridge University Press.

Momigliano, A., ed., (1963) *The Conflict Between Paganism and Christianity in the Fourth Century*, Oxford: Clarendon Press.

Mommsen, T., (1886) 'Zur Lateinischen Stichometrie', *Hermes*, 21: 1, 142–156.

Moreschini, Claudio, and Enrico Norelli, eds., (2005) *Early Christian Greek and Latin Literature: A Literary History* [2 Vols.], Peabody, Mass.: Hendrickson Publishers.

Musurillo, Herbert, ed., (1972) *The Acts of the Christian Martyrs*, Oxford: Clarendon Press.

Nautin, Pierre, (1977) *Origène: Sa Vie et Son Oeuvre*, Paris: Beauchesne.

Nicholson, Oliver, (2001) '*Caelum potius intuemini*: Lactantius and a Statue of Constantine', in M. F. Wiles and E. J. Arnold (eds.), *SP*, 34, 177–96, Leuven: Peeters.

Nock, A. D., (1933) *Conversion*, Oxford: Clarendon Press.

Norris, Richard A., (1966) *God and World in Early Christian Theology*, London: Adam and Charles Black.

Ogilvie, R. M., (1978) *The Library of Lactantius*, Oxford: Clarendon Press.

Osborn, Eric, (1973) *Justin Martyr* [Beiträge Zur Historischen Theologie, 47], Tübingen: J. C. B. Mohr [Paul Siebeck].

— (1997) *Tertullian, First Theologian of the West*, Cambridge: Cambridge University Press.

Parvis, Sara and Paul Foster, eds., (2007) *Justin Martyr and His Worlds*, Minneapolis: Fortress Press.

Quasten, Johannes, (1962–3) *Patrology* [3 Vols.], Utrecht – Antwerp: Spectrum Publishers.

Rankin, David, (1995) *Tertullian and the Church*, Cambridge: Cambridge University Press.

— (2006) *From Clement to Origen: The Social and Historical Context of the Church Fathers*, Aldershot, Hampshire: Ashgate.

Richardson, Alan, (1947) *Christian Apologetics*, London: SCM.

Roberts, Robert E., (1924) *The Theology of Tertullian*, London: The Epworth Press.

Rokeah, David, (1982) *Jews, Pagans and Christians in Conflict*, Leiden: E. J. Brill.

Sage, Michael M., (1975) *Cyprian*, Cambridge, Mass.: The Philadelphia Patristic Foundation.

Schaff, Philip, (1884) *Ante-Nicene Christianity* [2 Vols.], Edinburgh: T. & T. Clark.

Scott, Dominic, (1987) 'Platonic Anamnesis Revisited', *CQ*, New Series, 37: 2, 346–366.

Scourfield, J. H. D., (1996) 'The De Mortalitate of Cyprian: Consolation and Context', *VC*, 50: 1, 12–41.

Sider, Robert Dick, (1971) *Ancient Rhetoric and the Art of Tertullian*, Oxford: Oxford University Press.

Simmons, Michael Bland, (1995) *Arnobius of Sicca: Religious Conflict and Competition in the Age of Diocletian*, Oxford: Clarendon Press.

Simonetti, Manlio, (1950) 'Sulla Paternità del *Quod idola dii non sint*', *Maia*, 3, 265–288.

Snyder, Graydon F., (1985) *Ante Pacem: Archaeological Evidence of Church Life Before Constantine*, Mercer University Press.

Stevenson, J., ed., (1987) *A New Eusebius* [W. H. C. Frend (rev.)], London: SPCK.

Stevenson, J., ed., (1989) *Creeds, Councils and Controversies* [W. H. C. Frend (rev.)], London: SPCK.

Swift, Louis J., (1965) 'Arnobius and Lactantius : Two Views of the Pagan Poets', *TAPhA*, 96, 439–448.

— (1968) 'Lactantius and the Golden Age', *AJPh*, 89: 2, 144–156.

Thackeray, H. St. John, (1967) *Josephus: The Man and The Historian*, New York: Ktav Publishing House.

Timothy, H. B., (1973) *The Early Christian Apologists and Greek Philosophy*, Assen: Van Gorcum.

Tixeront, J., (1920) *A Handbook of Patrology*, St. Louis, MO.: B. Herder Book Co.

Trevett, Christine, (1996) *Montanism: Gender, Authority and the New Prophecy*, Cambridge: Cambridge University Press.

Trompf, G. W., (2000) *Early Christian Historiography: Narratives of Retribution*, London: Equinox.

von Campenhausen, Hans, (1964) *The Fathers of the Latin Church*, [Manfred Hoffman (trans.)], London: Adam & Charles Black.

Wacholder, Ben Zion, (1968) 'Biblical Chronology in the Hellenistic World Chronicles', *HTR*, 61: 3, 451–481.

Waszink, J. H., (1954) 'Minuciana', *VC*, 8: 3, 129–144.

Wilken, Robert L., (1984) *The Christians As the Romans Saw Them*, New Haven and London: Yale University Press.

Williams, Stephen, (1985) *Diocletian and the Roman Recovery*, London: B. T. Batsford.

Wurmbrand, Richard, (2004) *Tortured for Christ*, London: Hodder and Stoughton.

Young, Frances, et al., eds., (2004) *The Cambridge History of Early Christian Literature*, Cambridge: Cambridge University Press.

INDICES

Index of Sacred Scripture

Index of Ancient Authors

Index of Modern Authors